I0165391

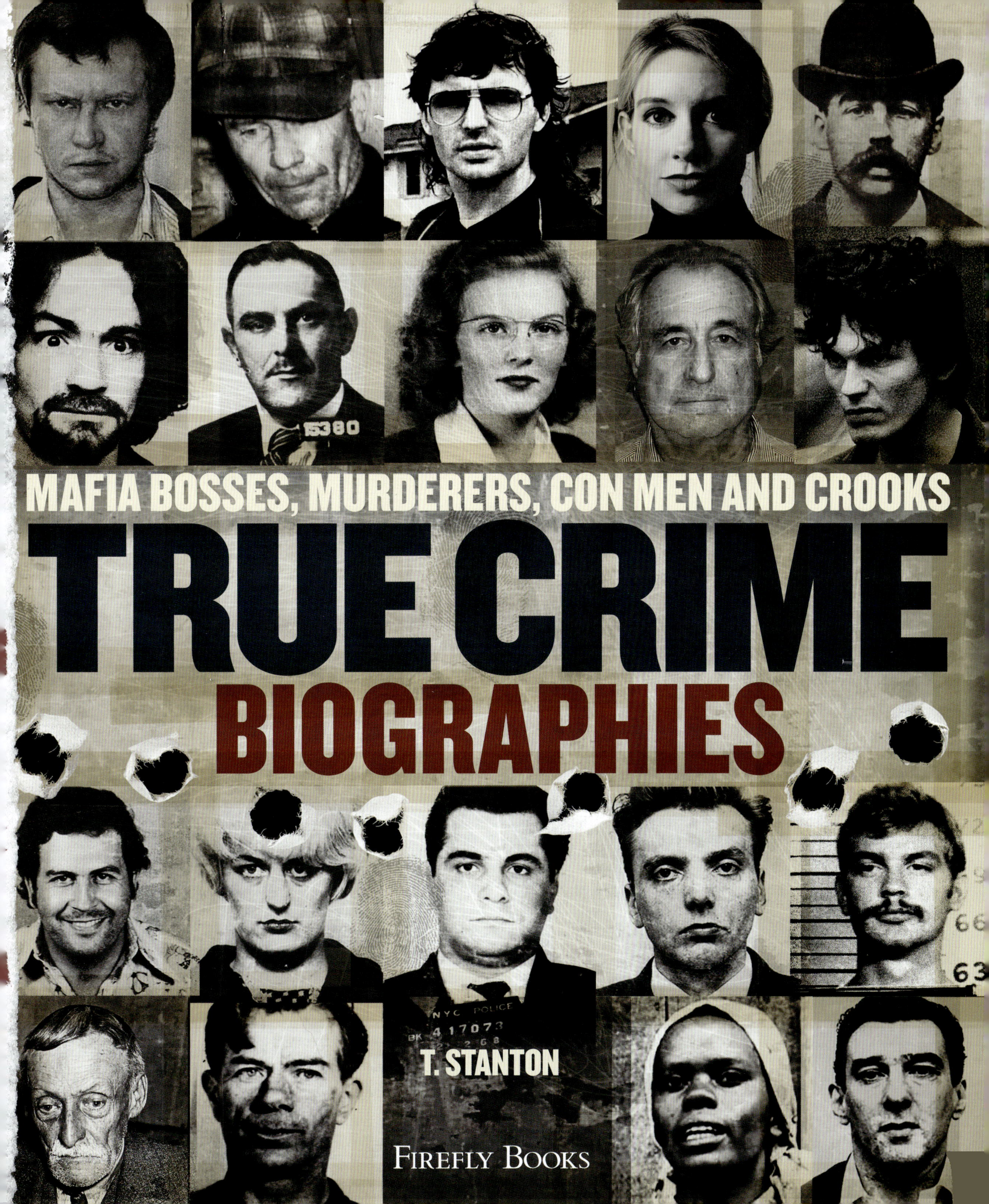
15380
MAFIA BOSSES, MURDERERS, CON MEN AND CROOKS
TRUE CRIME
BIOGRAPHIES
NYC POLICE
BK 417073
T. STANTON
FIREFLY BOOKS

Published by Firefly Books Ltd. 2024

First printing

Library of Congress Control Number: 2024939802

Library and Archives Canada Cataloguing in Publication
Title: True crime biographies : mafia bosses, murderers, con men and crooks / T. Stanton.
Names: Stanton, T., author.
Description: Includes index.
Identifiers: Canadiana 20240390768 | ISBN 9780228105084 (hardcover)
Subjects: LCSH: Criminals—Biography. | LCSH: Outlaws—Biography. | LCSH: Crime. | LCGFT: Biographies.
Classification: LCC HV6245 .S73 2024 | DDC 364.1092/2—dc23

Published by Canada by
Firefly Books Ltd.
50 Staples Avenue, Unit 1
Richmond Hill, Ontario L4B 0A7

Published in the United States by
Firefly Books (U.S.) Inc.
P.O. Box 1338, Ellicott Station
Buffalo, New York 14205

President: Sean Moore
International Rights: Karen Prince (kprince@moseleyroad.com)
Author: T. Stanton
Editing and project management: OilOften Graphic Design London
Proofreading: Karen Lawrence
Picture research, art direction and design: Duncan Youel at oiloften.co.uk

Printed in China | E

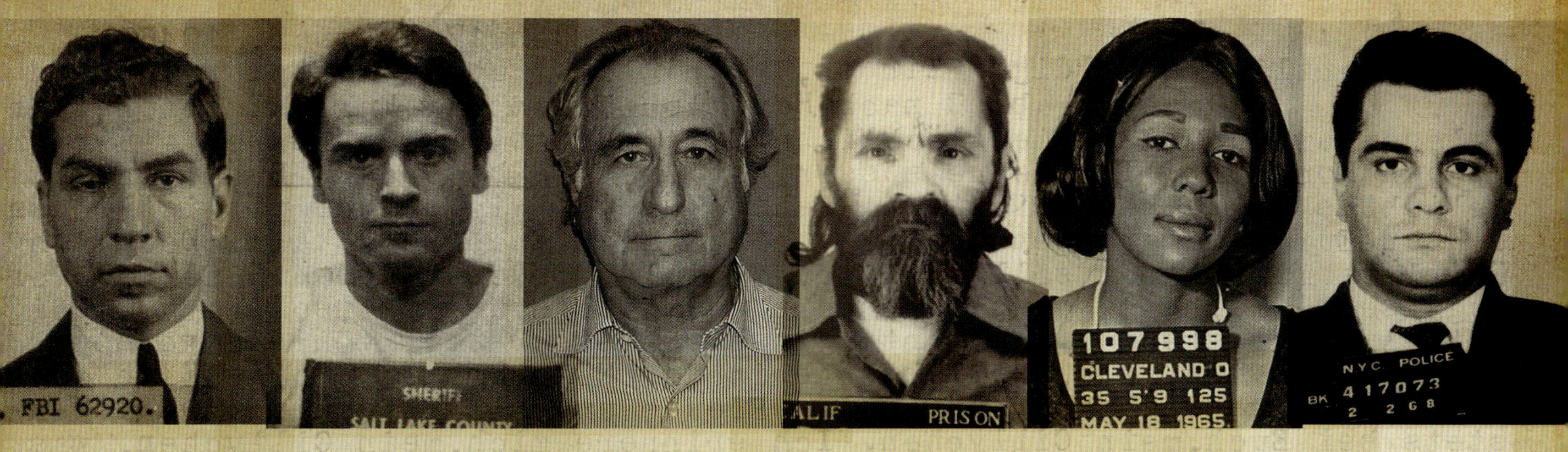

TRUE CRIME BIOGRAPHIES CONTENTS

CARCEL OTTO JUDICIAL
MEDELLIN
WAUKEE COUNTY

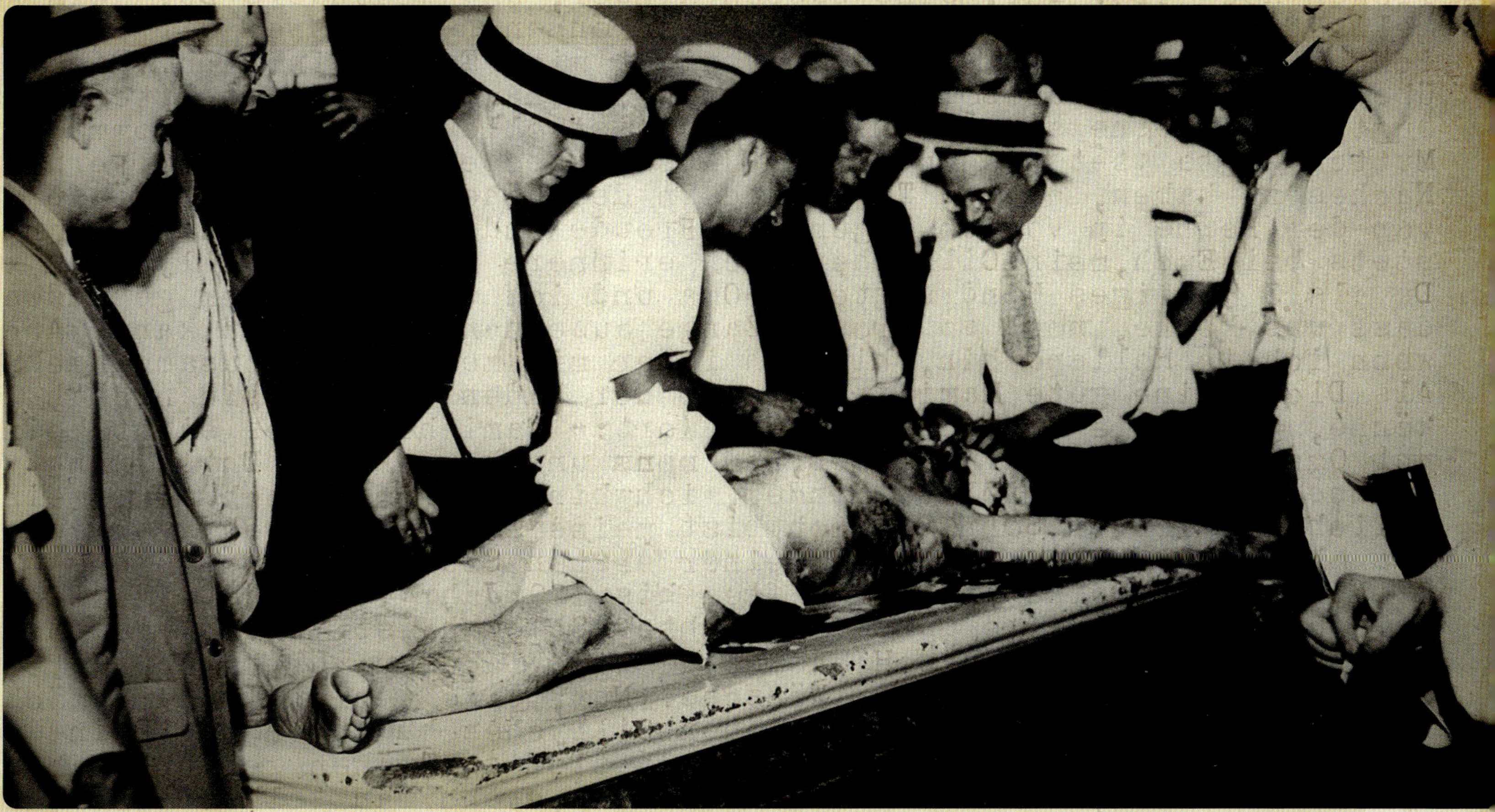

THE ALLURE OF TRUE CRIME

True crime has long captivated the public imagination, its stories offering a window into the darkest corners of human nature. The genre, which spans books, television, podcasts, and film, satisfies a complex array of psychological needs and curiosities. It confronts us with the extremes of human behavior, the intricacies of forensic science and detective work, the drama of courtroom battles, and the puzzle of criminal psychology. But what is it about true crime that compels so many to look so closely at such troubling subjects? One reason may be the desire to understand the unknown and make sense of the incomprehensible. True crime stories often involve acts that defy our moral compass and societal norms. By exploring these narratives, readers and viewers may seek to understand what drives individuals to commit such acts, perhaps as a way to reinforce their own moral boundaries or to feel a sense of control over the chaos of crime. Another draw is the adrenaline rush, the safe exploration of fear, and the relief of resolution when justice is served. True crime allows people to experience the thrill of the chase and the satisfaction of a mystery solved, all from a safe distance. It also provides a space to grapple with complex ethical questions and the failings of the justice system, offering a form of engagement with issues of societal importance.

The Impact of Sensationalism

While the fascination with true crime is understandable, it is not without its dangers. The sensationalizing of crime and criminals can have a profound impact

Top: The bloody, bullet-riddled corpse of celebrity criminal John Dillinger is brought into the Cook County Morgue in Chicago, July 22, 1934. It was on public display, and over 15,000 people queued up to get a sight of it. (*See* page 73); **Above:** The Russian serial killer Andrei Chikatilo, the "Butcher of Rostov." (*See* pages 130–131)

TABLOID Journalism

For more than a century the public's tendency to obsess over crime has been spurred, even encouraged, by sensationalized coverage in the press. It started in earnest in the late 1880s, during Jack the Ripper's London murder spree, when the penny press purposely ramped up levels of fear and pandered to reader fascination with bloody crimes—giving birth to tabloid journalism. At first, any entity posing a public threat became the new sensation: mummies, cannibals, ghosts, and other occult manifestations were reported on with little regard for research or facts. And soon real crimes were being treated with the same hyperbole as fabulous ones.

From that time to the present day, the press has created media circuses over certain high-profile police investigations. Recipients of this tabloid treatment include the Lindbergh baby kidnapping; the murder trials of Harry Thaw, Leopold and Loeb, Charles Manson, Robert Chambers, Ted Bundy, Jeffrey Dahmer, Casey Michaels, OJ Simpson, and Amanda Knox; and the abduction of toddler Madeleine McCann in Portugal. A sardonic newspaper slogan of the 20th century, "If it bleeds, it leads," has never gone out of style—and today it is estimated that 25 to 30 percent of most media news deals with violent predatory crime and murder.

on the public's perception of safety and justice. Sensationalism can distort the reality of crime, leading to a culture of fear and misunderstanding. It can glamorize criminals, turning them into celebrities and overshadowing the suffering of victims. This has been the case particularly with a number of serial killers throughout the years, many of whom have developed something of a cult following during their imprisonment and after their deaths. In the most extreme cases, copy-cat criminals are born—those who carry out heinous crimes in an attempt to imitate and connect with the killers they have come to idolize.

Classes of Criminals

This book is structured to provide a comprehensive look at the spectrum of criminality, featuring six distinct categories of criminals, each with its own motivations, methods, and impacts on society. **Swindlers** manipulate and deceive, their crimes often hidden behind a veneer of charm and sophistication. They remind us that not all criminals use brute force; some use their wits to exploit the trust of others. **Thieves** operate in the shadows, from pickpockets and burglars to the masterminds behind grand heists. Their stories often involve intricate planning and daring execution, challenging our notions of security and property. **Gangsters** build empires on the foundations of organized crime, their influence extending into legitimate and illicit spheres alike. They are a testament to the allure of power and the dangers of its unchecked pursuit. **Killers** commit the most final of crimes, taking the lives of others. Their acts stem from a variety of dark impulses, and their stories force us to confront the reality of mortality and the capacity for human cruelty. **Cult leaders** wield a dangerous charisma, leading their followers into collective delusion and, sometimes, collective doom. They challenge our understanding of leadership, belief, and the human need for belonging. **Hackers** represent a modern breed of criminal, operating in the digital realm. Their crimes, ranging from identity theft to cyberterrorism, highlight the vulnerabilities of our increasingly interconnected world.

High-Profile Cases

Throughout the last century, numerous true crime cases have captured the public's attention. The gruesome murders by Jack the Ripper in the late 1800s laid the groundwork for public interest in serial killers, a fascination

that continued with cases like those of Ted Bundy and Jeffrey Dahmer. The 20th century saw the rise of organized crime figures like Al Capone and the Kray twins, whose criminal activities became the stuff of legend. More recently, the digital age has given rise to cybercriminals like Kevin Mitnick, who hacked into dozens of networks and became a symbol of the era's new criminal capabilities. Cult leaders like Jim Jones and Charles Manson have shown the devastating impact of manipulative influence, leading to mass suicides and murders. Each of these cases, and others like them, will be explored in the following chapters, providing a detailed look at the individuals behind the crimes and the societal reactions they provoked. In this book, we aim to present these true crime biographies with the depth and nuance they deserve, offering insight into the complex tapestry of human behavior that leads to criminal acts. Join us as we explore the lives, crimes, and downfalls of some of the world's most notorious criminals.

Top: A drive-by assassination from the 1920s. The enforcing of the 18th Amendment in 1920—the prohibition of alcohol—rather than stabilizing society, as the temperance leagues had presumed, instead paved the way for the dramatic rise of 'organized crime' in the USA, ushering in a chaotic decade in American history; **Above left:** Al Capone in 1929 (*See* pages 66–69); **Above right:** From left to right, Johnnie Cochran, Robert Shapiro and OJ Simpson, during Simpson's trial for murder at the Los Angeles County Superior Court in 1994 (*See* pages 162–163); **Opposite:** The serial killer, necrophiliac, and cannibal Jeffrey Dahmer during his trial in 1992 (pages 134–135).

Swindlers, con artists, and master manipulators—these are the people who weave intricate webs of lies and deceit to ensnare their victims. Their tools are not guns or knives, but charm, persuasion, and the exploitation of trust. They are the architects of scams so elaborate that they often go undetected for years, leaving a trail of financial ruin and broken lives in their wake.

These criminals occupy a unique niche. They prey on the gullible and the greedy, the vulnerable and the unsuspecting. Their crimes require a blend of intelligence, psychological insight, and sheer audacity. From the charismatic charlatans who sold nonexistent land and fraudulent investments, to the smooth-talking tricksters who convinced the world of their invented identities, these accounts offer insights into the minds of those who view deception as a livelihood.

As we chronicle their elaborate schemes and the eventual unraveling of their lies, we will also reflect on the impact of their actions. The victims of swindlers are often left not only financially destitute but also emotionally scarred, their trust in others irrevocably shattered. The tales of these criminals serve as cautionary reminders of the potential cost of naivety and the importance of skepticism.

CHAPTER ONE
SWINDLERS

His story serves as a cautionary tale about the allure of "get-rich-quick" schemes and the dangers of financial systems built on illusion and deceit...

CHARLES PONZI
THE EPONYMOUS SWINDLER

Carlo Pietro Giovanni Guglielmo Tebaldo Ponzi, better known as Charles Ponzi, was born on March 3, 1882, in Lugo, Italy. Growing up in Parma, Ponzi was well-educated, attending the University of Rome La Sapienza. However, financial hardships drove him to seek opportunities in North America. He arrived in Boston in 1903 and after years of low-paying jobs, he moved to Montreal in 1907. Soon after he was imprisoned for check forgery. After his sentence, he moved back to the United States.

Initial Endeavors

Ponzi's early years in the United States were marked by a series of odd jobs and brushes with the law. His pursuits ranged from working in restaurants to short changing customers and thefts from the restaurant.

The Securities Exchange Company

In 1920, Ponzi founded the Securities Exchange Company in Boston. Here, he introduced the idea

BABE RUTH'S LIFE STORY By BABE RUTH On Page 13 of Today's Post

The Boston Post

18 Pages Today

FRIDAY, AUGUST 13, 1920

PONZI ARRESTED; ADMITS NOW HE CANNOT PAY--$3,000,000 SHORT

Auditor Smashes Greatest Financial Bubble in Years—Finds Ponzi Owes at Least $7,000,000 and Has Assets of Less Than $4,000,000, Most of Which Is Tied Up—Took in $15,000,000 in Eight Months—Has No Great Financial Secret—Did Not Clean Up on Postal Orders—Held in $25,000 Bail in Federal Court, Also $10,000 Bail in State Court—Hanover Trust Company Wrecked—Arrests Expected to Follow

COX SAYS WAR SHOULD CEASE

Reason Rather Than Force Should Dominate World Affairs, He Tells Ohio Guardsmen

$125,000 STATE CASH IN BANK

Governor Gets the Facts From Burrell, Who Attacks the Bank Commissioner in Statement

M'GRAW MUST TELL OF FIGHT

State Had $125,000 in Hanover Trust—Depositors Not Expected to Lose

Bank Crash May Have Far Reaching Effect—Great Sensation Promised

that profits could be made quickly by buying international reply coupons (IRCs) in countries with devalued currencies and redeeming them in the U.S. at a higher rate. He promised investors a 50% return on their investment in 45 days or a 100% return in 90 days.

Ponzi Scheme

While his IRC idea had some theoretical validity, the profits he promised were unrealistically high. To meet the returns he had promised, Ponzi began using the money from new investors to pay previous investors, essentially creating a robbing-Peter-to-pay-Paul system. This structure, now widely referred to as a "Ponzi scheme," was destined to collapse, as the funds owed to earlier investors far exceeded the company's actual earnings.

Collapse and Conviction

By August 1920, the unsustainable nature of Ponzi's operation became evident. As doubts spread, there was a rush to withdraw funds. With liabilities mounting up to $7 million and an investigation by the Boston Post exposing the scheme's flaws, Ponzi's empire crumbled. On August 12, 1920, he was arrested. Ponzi was tried and convicted, serving three and a half years of a five-year sentence. Upon his release, he faced additional charges in Massachusetts and then in Florida. By 1934, after additional legal troubles, Ponzi was deported to Italy.

Legacy

In Italy, Ponzi tried various ventures, including a stint in Brazil. He died in a charity hospital in Rio de Janeiro on January 18, 1949. Charles Ponzi's name became synonymous with financial schemes where returns to earlier investors are paid using the capital of newer investors. His story serves as a cautionary tale about the allure of "get-rich-quick" schemes and the dangers of financial systems built on illusion and deceit. To this day, Ponzi schemes continue to ensnare victims around the world, making Ponzi's legacy a lasting and infamous one in the annals of financial crime.

Above: Ponzi's mugshot; **Top left:** Ponzi poses for the press; **Top right:** *The Boston Post* Friday 13th August, 1920—a black day for the swindler's investors; **Opposite, below:** Boston in the early 20th century; **Opposite, top:** A colorized shot of the flamboyant Ponzi.

VICTOR LUSTIG
THE TEN COMMANDMENTS FOR CON MEN

Victor Lustig was born on January 4, 1890, in Hostinné, a small town in what is now the Czech Republic. Little is known about his early years, but by his twenties, Lustig had already embarked on a life of crime, operating mainly in Europe.

Monumental Deception

One of Lustig's most audacious cons involved the Eiffel Tower. In 1925, taking advantage of public sentiment that the tower was becoming a costly and dilapidated eyesore, Lustig posed as a government official and convinced a group of scrap metal dealers that the French government intended to sell the tower for scrap. He created fake government stationery and even took one dealer, André Poisson, to the tower for an "inspection." Poisson, convinced of the scheme's legitimacy, handed over a substantial bribe to secure the winning bid. By the time he realized he had been duped, Lustig had already fled to Austria.

Lustig posed as a government official and convinced a group of scrap metal dealers that the French government intended to sell the tower for scrap. He created fake government stationery and even took one dealer, André Poisson to the tower for an 'inspection.' Poisson, convinced of the scheme's legitimacy, handed over a substantial bribe to secure the winning bid...

The Counterfeit Kingdom

Teaming up with a skilled chemist named William Watts, Lustig embarked on another significant venture: counterfeiting. The duo produced over $100,000 in counterfeit bills monthly, distributing them throughout the U.S. Their operation was meticulous, with Watts perfecting a process that mimicked the feel of real currency, while Lustig focused on distribution, ensuring their fakes entered circulation without detection.

Capture and Incarceration

However, even the most careful plans are prone to failure. In 1935, Lustig's lover, disillusioned by his unfaithfulness, reported him to the authorities. Following his arrest, the U.S. Secret Service found a set of meticulously crafted tools in his possession. In 1935, he was tried, convicted, and sentenced to 20 years in Alcatraz.

Death and Legacy

Victor Lustig's life came to an end on March 11, 1947, when he died from complications related to pneumonia. Throughout his criminal career, Lustig operated using 47 aliases, was arrested over 40 times across various countries but served only one significant prison sentence. He left behind a legacy encapsulated in a document titled "The Ten Commandments for Con Men," which provided a satirical insight into the mind of one of history's most notorious swindlers. Victor Lustig's life story remains a testament to the audacity of human deception and the lengths individuals will go to for personal gain. His exploits, especially the Eiffel Tower scam, are often cited in discussions about the psychology of deception and the gullibility of victims.

Above: The iconic technological achievement of the Eiffel Tower was built using the latest construction techniques of the Victorian era, in 1889; **Opposite, top left:** Lustig's police mug shot; **Opposite, top right:** A closer view of the extraordinary Parisian structure; **Opposite, below:** Money! Lustig and his collaborator, the chemist William Watts, came up with a massive counterfeiting scheme to produce $100,000 in dollar bills. However, "loose lips sink ships" as the old saying goes, and Lustig's amorous infidelities caused his lover to sell him out...

NATWARLAL THE TALE OF INDIA'S ROBIN HOOD

Mithilesh Kumar Srivastava, better known by his alias Natwarlal, was born in 1912 in the small town of Bangra, in the Siwan district of Bihar, India. Raised in a middle-class family, he showed a penchant for deceit and cunning from a young age, traits that would define his criminal career.

Beginning of Criminal Activities

Natwarlal initially studied law, aspiring to become a lawyer. However, he abandoned this path in favor of a life of crime. He was a con artist who specialized in forging documents and carrying out complex financial frauds. Notably, he was an expert in imitating signatures, a skill that allowed him to forge the signatures of prominent individuals.

High-Profile Cons

One of the most sensational episodes in Natwarlal's life was his audacious attempt to "sell" the Taj Mahal, one of India's most iconic monuments, not just once but multiple times. Posing as a government official, he fooled foreign tourists and wealthy investors into buying the monument, only to disappear with their money. He also tried to sell the Indian Parliament building (along with its sitting members!), again relying on forged documents and a convincing demeanor.

Arrests and Escapes

Natwarlal was arrested numerous times but managed to escape from police custody on several occasions. He executed these escapes with theatrical flair, often leaving the authorities baffled and humiliated. Once, he even escaped from a moving train while being transported from prison to hospital.

Multiple Identities

Adding to his enigmatic persona, Natwarlal used more than 50 aliases during his criminal career. This made it incredibly difficult for authorities to keep track of his activities or to locate him after he went into hiding. He was known for altering his appearance, sometimes disguising himself as a government official or a high-ranking businessman to evade capture.

Later Years and Legal Troubles

Natwarlal was finally caught and faced a myriad of charges, including cheating, forgery, and fraud. He was sentenced to 113 years in prison by various Indian courts but never served the complete term due to his numerous escapes.

Disappearance and Speculations

Natwarlal vanished under mysterious circumstances in the late 1990s. He was last seen by authorities in 1996 when he was in his 80s, and his subsequent whereabouts remain unknown. Some reports suggest that he died in 2009, but his death was never confirmed. His younger brother, Ganga Kumar Srivastava, took up the legal battles for him. Though he admitted to Natwarlal's wrongdoings, he also expressed admiration for his audacious exploits, describing him as a "Robin Hood" figure who took from the rich. Natwarlal remains one of India's most enigmatic and elusive criminals, his life a tale of audacity, deceit, and unparalleled cunning.

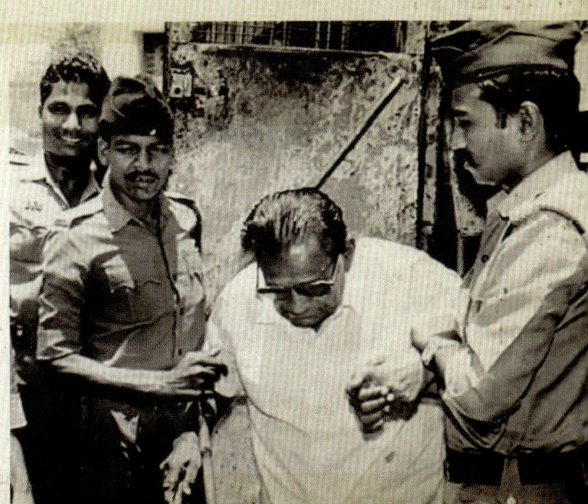

Opposite, top left: The old Indian Parliament building, 1926, by Sir Edwin Lutyens. Using his forged documents Natwarlal attempted to sell it; **Opposite, top right:** Natwarlal; **Opposite, bottom left:** A rare photo of Natwarlal in very old age; **Main image:** Natwarlal "sold" the iconic Taj Mahal several times; **Above:** Natwarlal captured.

His ability to deceive was rooted in his impressive memory and a skill for quickly absorbing vast amounts of information. He also had a knack for forging documents and manipulating bureaucratic systems to his advantage...

FERDINAND WALDO DEMARA THE GREAT IMPOSTOR

Top: The Great Impostor, Ferdinand Waldo Demara; **Above:** HMCS Cayuga, on which Demara impersonated Dr. Joseph Cyr and carried out surgeries on wounded men during the Korean War. The ship was a Tribal-class destroyer that served in the Royal Canadian Navy from 1946 until 1964, seeing action in the Korean War. She was named after the Cayuga nation, a First Nations people of Canada.

Born on December 21, 1921, in Lawrence, Massachusetts, Ferdinand Waldo Demara —"Fred"—was an individual whose early life gave little indication of the colorful and varied life he would later lead. Coming from a moderately affluent family, Demara's educational pursuits were inconsistent, marked by several dropouts and expulsions.

The Great Impostor

Demara's knack for impersonation earned him the title "The Great Impostor." Throughout his life, without the benefit of formal training or proper credentials, he successfully assumed numerous identities. His impersonations ranged from a Trappist monk and prison warden to a college dean. However, among his most audacious impersonations was that of a naval surgeon during the Korean War. Posing as Dr. Joseph Cyr, Demara successfully performed surgeries on wounded soldiers aboard the Royal Canadian Navy destroyer, HMCS Cayuga.

Astonishingly, despite his lack of medical training, there were no reported complications or fatalities from his surgeries.

Exposure and Later Ventures

Demara's true identity as the impostor surgeon was eventually discovered when the real Dr. Cyr's mother read a magazine article lauding her son's achievements on the Cayuga. The subsequent exposure brought Demara infamy. Post this incident, he continued his impersonations, albeit with a lower profile. His ability to deceive was rooted in his impressive memory and a skill for quickly absorbing vast amounts of information. He also had a knack for forging documents and manipulating bureaucratic systems to his advantage.

Public Perception and Media

The audacity of Demara's deceptions, combined with the non-malicious nature of most of his impersonations, made him a figure of public fascination. Rather than seeking financial gain, Demara often seemed to be in search of respect, challenge, and validation, making his motives a topic of intrigue. His life story was adapted into a 1961 movie, *The Great Impostor*, starring Tony Curtis.

Final Years

In the latter part of his life, Demara settled in Anaheim, California. He took on a more consistent identity, working in various roles, including a hospital chaplain and a teacher. Demara died on June 7, 1982. The tale of Ferdinand Waldo Demara stands out in the annals of impersonation. His ability to step into and competently perform complex roles without formal training is unparalleled. His life raises questions about identity, the nature of expertise, and the lengths to which one man can go in search of purpose and validation.

Top left: Demara's exploits brought him exposure to a fascinated American public; **Top right:** In 1956, Fred arrives on North Haven Island, Maine and poses as a new teacher at the local school. After a suspicious mom contacts the FBI, Demara is arrested and questioned; **Above:** Tony Curtis plays Demara in *The Great Impostor* movie of 1961.

FRANK ABAGNALE, JR. LEGENDARY DARING

Top left: Frank Abagnale, Jr. (left), with movie star Leonardo DiCaprio at the premiere of *Catch Me If You Can* in 2002; **Above, and top right:** Abagnale photographed in a pilot uniform, circa 1963–4; **Opposite, top left:** DiCaprio and director Steven Spielberg on the set of *Catch Me If You Can*; **Opposite, top right:** *Catch Me If You Can* movie poster; **Opposite, below right:** A production still from *Catch Me If You Can*.

Frank William Abagnale, Jr. is one of the most famous impostors in history. Before he turned 22, he had successfully assumed no fewer than eight identities, defrauded banks out of millions of dollars, and evaded law enforcement across multiple countries. His exploits, characterized by audacity, intelligence, and an unparalleled knack for deception, have made him a legend.

A Troubled Youth

Born on April 27, 1948, in Bronxville, New York, Abagnale's early life was marred by his parents' divorce. This event profoundly affected him, leading him to embark on his life of crime. By the age of 15, he had begun his foray into the world of fraud, starting with altered checks from his father's credit card account.

Impersonations and Exploits

Abagnale's crimes were not limited to check fraud. His ability to forge documents and assume false identities led him to impersonate an airline pilot for Pan American World Airways. Under this guise, he flew over 250 flights across 26 countries, hitching rides by "deadheading" on scheduled flights. His other impersonations were equally audacious. He posed as a chief resident pediatrician in a Georgia hospital for almost a year. He took on the role of a sociology professor at a college, despite having no credentials. His other identities included a lawyer, a U.S. federal agent, and more.

Capture and Turnaround

Abagnale's globe-trotting exploits and continuous fraud eventually caught up with

him. At the age of 21, he was arrested in France and subsequently extradited to the U.S. After serving five years of his 12-year sentence, he was released on the condition that he would help U.S. federal law enforcement agencies by teaching and advising on fraud prevention. This marked a significant turnaround in Abagnale's life. He went on to become a consultant and lecturer for the FBI, specializing in anti-fraud measures and secure document creation. His transformation from a master of deception to a protector against fraud is nothing short of remarkable.

Legacy and Pop Culture

Frank Abagnale, Jr.'s life story was immortalized in the 2002 film *Catch Me If You Can*, starring Leonardo DiCaprio as Abagnale and Tom Hanks as his pursuer. His autobiography, also titled *Catch Me If You Can*, offers a detailed account of his exploits and insights into his motivations. Today, Abagnale is recognized not only for his early life of crime but also for his significant contributions to fraud prevention and secure documentation. His journey, from one of the world's most wanted fugitives to a respected authority on anti-fraud measures, serves as a testament to the possibility of redemption and change.

DAVID HAMPTON

CONFIDENCE TRICKSTER. FRAUDSTER. IMPOSTOR.

Above: David Hampton's mugshot in 1985.

David Hampton was born on April 28, 1964, in Buffalo, New York. He grew up in a middle-class family and was well-educated, attending private schools throughout his youth. However, the seemingly stable background masked underlying issues that would later play a role in Hampton's criminal activities.

Move to New York City

Hampton moved to New York City in the early 1980s, ostensibly to study at Juilliard, although there is no record of him actually enrolling there. It was in New York City that Hampton commenced the series of deceptions that would make him infamous.

Impersonation of a Celebrity Offspring

Hampton gained notoriety for impersonating David Poitier, the supposed son of famous actor Sidney Poitier. His modus operandi was to befriend wealthy socialites, claiming that he had been mugged and needed a place to stay temporarily. Once welcomed into their

Left, main image: David Hampton the Impostor, who frequently claimed to be the son of Sidney Poitier **(Left, inset)**. He used this lie to gain entry to Studio 54, and to ingratiate himself with the wealthy elite of Manhattan; **Above:** Hampton's arrest in 1983, on various charges of fraud; **Below:** After playwright John Guare's friends gave him the lowdown on Hampton, he wrote *Six Degrees of Separation*, which premiered at Lincoln Center in 1990. Stockard Channing won an Obie Award for Best Actress. Thereafter it transferred to Broadway, running for 485 performances; **Bottom:** A movie based on the play, also called *Six Degrees of Separation*, was released in 1993, with Will Smith, Stockard Channing, and Donald Sutherland starring.

homes, Hampton would live off the generosity of his hosts for as long as he could.

Methods and Techniques

Hampton was a master manipulator and extremely charming. His deception was aided by his detailed stories and apparent cultural literacy, which lent credibility to his impersonation. He also had an uncanny ability to read people and situations, knowing when to push further and when to retreat.

Capture and Legal Repercussions

Hampton's criminal enterprise unraveled when several of his victims compared notes and discovered the deception. He was arrested in 1983 and convicted of multiple counts of fraud. Although he served 21 months in prison, this legal outcome didn't deter him from continuing similar fraudulent activities after his release.

Inspiration for Media

While Hampton's criminal activities were damaging and deceitful, they also caught the public imagination. His life story inspired the play and subsequent film, *Six Degrees of Separation*, which explored themes of trust, social status, and human connections.

Legal Troubles Continued

Even after serving time, Hampton couldn't shake off his criminal tendencies. He was arrested again in 1991. Legal woes followed him for the rest of his life, including a defamation lawsuit he filed against the creators of *Six Degrees of Separation*, which he eventually lost.

Death

David Hampton died on July 18, 2003, from complications related to AIDS. His death marked the end of a life that was as much about manipulation as it was about the exploration of social boundaries and human gullibility. In the final analysis, Hampton was a paradoxical figure—both a predator exploiting the trust of others and a complex individual whose actions compelled society to examine the assumptions underpinning social interactions and status. His life serves as an uncomfortable yet fascinating mirror to societal values and vulnerabilities.

JOHN DREWE & JOHN MYATT
THE ART FORGERS

Above: A rare photograph of John Drewe, in his study, circa late 1980s; **Top left:** John Myatt at work in his studio, circa 1990s; **Top right:** Detail of one of Myatt's works, copying Impressionist Claude Monet's *Water Lilies* series.

John Drewe was born in 1948 in Sussex, England. Not much is known about his early life, but what is clear is that Drewe was a man of considerable intellect and charisma, traits that would later serve him well in his criminal endeavors.

Art Forgery Ring

Drewe gained notoriety as the mastermind behind one of the most sophisticated art forgery rings in history. In the late 1980s and throughout the 1990s, Drewe collaborated with artist John Myatt, who produced exceptionally convincing forgeries of famous artworks. Drewe sold these as authentic pieces to art galleries, auction houses, and private collectors.

Methods

What set Drewe's operation apart from other art forgers was firstly, the great talent and skilled artistry of his collaborator, John Myatt, and the extent to which Drewe himself went to authenticate the forgeries. He would meticulously research the artists whose work was being copied, obtaining materials from the same time period to create the artworks. Drewe even went so far as to insert fake records into art archives and libraries to verify the provenance of the paintings. He created false ownership histories, complete with counterfeit documents, photographs, and claims that the artworks had been part of esteemed collections. Myatt did the same with his paint brushes and canvases—as he himself described his approach—to inhabit as far as possible the heart, soul, and life of the artist.

The Unraveling

For years, Drewe's operation went undetected. However, suspicion arose when experts noticed tiny inconsistencies in some of the artworks. Drewe's associate, Myatt, was eventually arrested in 1995, and cooperation from him led to Drewe's own arrest in 1996. John Drewe was tried and found guilty of multiple charges, including conspiracy to defraud and forgery. He was sentenced to six years in prison in 1999 but was released after two years.

Life After Prison

Following his release from prison, Drewe was sentenced again in 2012 to eight years for defrauding a senior of her life savings. John Myatt, on the other hand, leveraged his notoriety into a legitimate art career, even starring in a television series where he educated the public about art forgeries. John Drewe's operation raised questions about the effectiveness of provenance research in the art world. His ability to manipulate esteemed institutions revealed significant vulnerabilities in the methods used to authenticate artworks, forcing galleries and auction houses to revisit and strengthen their verification processes. As of January 2024, there was no public record of his death, and information about his activities post-prison remain scarce. The tale of "the two Johns" is a compelling narrative in the annals of art forgery. His operation was not just a testament to the vulnerabilities and pretences of the art world and its dealers, but also to the lengths people will go in the pursuit of sophistication and social standing.

Above: Copy of a Vincent van Gogh self-portrait by John Myatt; **Top, main image:** John Myatt after his release from prison.

BARRY MINKOW CON MAN

Above, and top: Minkow, the master self-publicist. Portraits from two of his various photoshoots. (Top photo courtesy of Zuma Press Inc.)

Barry Jay Minkow was born on March 22, 1966, in Inglewood, California. From a young age, Minkow exhibited a keen sense of ambition and a proclivity for entrepreneurship.

ZZZZ Best

At the mere age of 16, Minkow started a carpet cleaning company called ZZZZ Best from his parents' garage. Through a combination of genuine services, aggressive marketing, and fabricated restoration contracts, ZZZZ Best experienced rapid growth. By 1987, the company went public and was valued at over $280 million. Minkow, not even 21, was celebrated as a business prodigy.

The Scam Unravels

However, beneath the facade of a booming business, Minkow had been orchestrating an elaborate Ponzi scheme. The purported restoration contracts, which made up a significant portion of ZZZZ Best's revenue, were fictitious. Minkow created fake sites, staged phone calls, and crafted bogus documents to deceive auditors and investors. The scheme began to unravel when discrepancies in the company's insurance restoration contracts were discovered. As investigations deepened, the enormity of Minkow's fraud came to light, leading to the collapse of ZZZZ Best's stock and causing investors to lose millions.

Conviction and Redemption

In 1988, Minkow was arrested and, in 1989, was convicted on 57 federal counts of fraud. He was sentenced to 25 years in prison but served only seven. On his release, Minkow reinvented himself, becoming a pastor and a fraud investigator. He spoke openly about his past, offering his insights into the psychology of fraud. He wrote a book about his experiences, *Cleaning Up*, and even worked with the FBI to uncover financial fraud.

Relapse

However, Minkow's propensity for deceit resurfaced. In 2011, he was implicated in a

scheme that manipulated the stock price of Lennar Corporation, a home construction company. Minkow spread false information about Lennar, causing a significant drop in the company's stock. He profited from this manipulation through short sales. In 2011, Minkow pleaded guilty to insider trading related to Lennar and was sentenced to five years in prison. In 2014 he pleaded guilty to several charges and was sentenced to five years.

Legacy

Barry Minkow remains a perplexing figure in the annals of financial fraud. His transition from a teenage business sensation to a convicted fraudster, followed by a seemingly genuine attempt at redemption, and then a relapse into criminal activity, makes his story both unique and cautionary. Minkow's life serves as a reminder of the seductive allure of easy money and the complexities of human behavior.

Left, center and above: Minkow's redemption began after his release from prison in 1996, after serving only seven years of his 25-year sentence for 57 counts of fraud. (Courtesy of Zuma Press Inc.); **Top:** Minkow holds forth yet again, circa 2009.

Reed Slatkin was the ordained Scientology minister behind one of the biggest Ponzi schemes in U.S. history. From 1986 to 2001 he raised $593 million from 800 investors, many of them from his own Scientology community...

REED SLATKIN
ANOTHER PONZI SCHEMER

Above: Reed Slatkin photographed in the late 1990s, around the time the U.S. Securities and Exchange Commission began looking at him.

Reed Eliot Slatkin was born on January 22, 1949, in Detroit, Michigan. He was raised in a comfortable, middle-class Jewish household. Slatkin exhibited entrepreneurial instincts from an early age, starting various small ventures during his school days. Later, he moved to California, where he would ultimately involve himself in one of the largest Ponzi schemes in U.S. history.

Involvement in Scientology

Slatkin was a committed member of the Church of Scientology, an affiliation that would later prove significant in his fraudulent activities. He was ordained as a minister in the church and held various roles within the organization.

Financial Operations

In the early 1980s, Slatkin started an investment club. His initial clientele primarily consisted of fellow Scientologists, who readily invested large sums of money with him. Over

Left, main image: "Big Blue," the West Coast headquarters of The Church of Scientology. The organization has been variously described over the years as a religious movement, a cult...and a business; **Above:** Slatkin in the 1980s; **Below:** Amongst those high-profile people who suffered losses were, according to Wikipedia, actors Anne Archer **(below)**, and Joe Pantoliano **(bottom)**.

the years, he expanded his reach, attracting high-net-worth individuals, including Hollywood celebrities and business executives.

Ponzi Scheme

Slatkin's investment operation was, in reality, a Ponzi scheme. He promised high returns, claiming to invest in stock options and other securities. However, the returns paid to earlier investors were funded by the capital of new investors. Slatkin continued this deception for nearly 15 years.

Regulatory Scrutiny and Downfall

Slatkin managed to avoid regulatory scrutiny for a considerable period, partly due to his well-crafted facade of legitimacy. However, in the late 1990s, the U.S. Securities and Exchange Commission (SEC) began investigating him for operating without a license. Facing increased pressure, Slatkin filed for bankruptcy in May 2001, revealing the insolvency of his so-called investment operation.

Arrest and Legal Proceedings

Subsequent investigations led to his arrest in 2002. Charged with multiple counts of fraud, conspiracy, and money laundering, Slatkin pleaded guilty. During the trial, it was revealed that he had defrauded investors of approximately $593 million.

Imprisonment

In 2003, Reed Slatkin was sentenced to 14 years in federal prison. He was also ordered to pay restitution to his victims, although the amount was only a fraction of what had been stolen. Slatkin was released from prison in 2013 and he died on June 23, 2015, at the age of 66. The cause of death was reported as natural causes, but specific details were not publicly disclosed.

Post-Conviction Impact

The fallout from Slatkin's Ponzi scheme was immense. Numerous individuals and organizations found themselves in financial ruin, and the case prompted calls for tighter financial regulations. Notably, the Slatkin case also impacted the Church of Scientology, drawing attention to the church's connections with fraudulent financial operations.

Reed Slatkin's life is a complex tapestry of entrepreneurial flair, religious engagement, and criminal deceit, ending in one of the most significant financial collapses of its time.

LOU PEARLMAN THE SHYSTER

Above: Lou Pearlman. He was first cousin to Art Garfunkel; **Top:** Pearlman and members of the boy band O-Town, assembled for the first season of the ABC reality television series *Making the Band*. From left to right: Trevor Penick, Dan Miller, Jacob Underwood, Erik-Michael Estrada, and Ashley Angel. Lou Pearlman, right, gives his advice.

Born on June 19, 1954, in Flushing, New York, Louis Jay Pearlman showed early entrepreneurial tendencies. From running a newspaper delivery route to operating a blimp advertising business, Pearlman's ventures were varied, leading him to a pivotal foray into the music industry.

Boy Band Mogul

In the mid-1990s, Pearlman became a central figure in the U.S. pop music scene by creating and managing boy bands. He was the driving force behind the formation of the Backstreet Boys in 1993, followed by *NSYNC in 1995. Both bands achieved massive success, turning Pearlman into a music industry powerhouse. This success led to the creation of other bands like O-Town, LFO, and Take 5.

Financial Deception

While Pearlman's bands were generating millions, he was orchestrating a vast Ponzi and investment fraud scheme. He founded Trans Continental Airlines Travel Services Inc. and Trans Continental Airlines Inc., yet neither company operated any flights. Through these entities, Pearlman convinced individuals to invest in his ventures, showing them fake financial statements and touting significant returns. Estimates suggest he defrauded investors out of at least $300 million. Additionally, many of the bands he managed began to discover financial discrepancies. Lawsuits emerged, revealing that while the artists were achieving platinum-level sales, they were not receiving equitable financial payment. *NSYNC and the Backstreet Boys, among others, entered into legal battles against Pearlman, seeking to regain their rightful earnings.

Downfall and Conviction

By the early 2000s, the weight of numerous lawsuits and growing suspicions about his investment ventures began to catch up with Pearlman. In 2007, after being on the run, he was apprehended in Bali, Indonesia, and was extradited to the U.S. In 2008, Pearlman

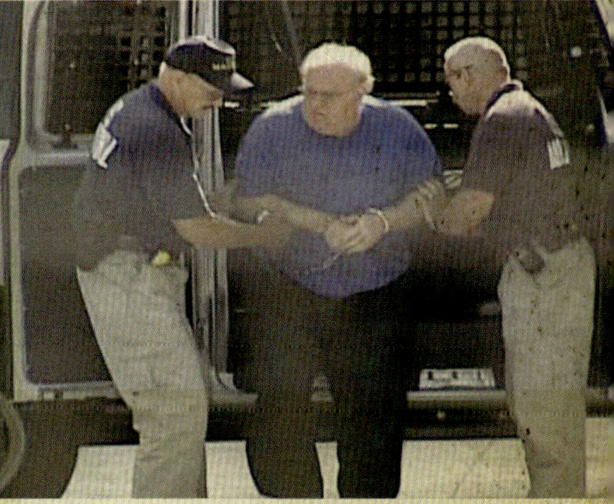

was convicted for his role in the Ponzi and investment fraud scheme. He was found guilty on multiple counts, including conspiracy, money laundering, and making false statements during a bankruptcy proceeding. He was sentenced to 25 years in federal prison.

Conclusion

On August 19, 2016, Pearlman died in federal custody from cardiac arrest. His life was a dichotomy of brilliance and deception. On one hand, he possessed an undeniable knack for identifying and nurturing musical talent, giving rise to some of the most iconic pop acts of the 1990s and early 2000s. On the other, his legacy is marred by one of the largest and most elaborate Ponzi schemes in U.S. history. His story underscores the volatility of the entertainment industry and the cynical and unprincipled lengths some will go to maintain wealth and influence.

Left: Pearlman in 2002; **Top and center:** Backstreet Boys in 1997 (top); *NSYNC in 2001 (center). Both Backstreet Boys and *NSYNC took out lawsuits against Pearlman to be paid their rightful earnings. Other bands in Pearlman's stable did the same; **Above:** Pearlman, in chains, after his arrest and extradition to the United States in 2007.

CHRISTOPHE ROCANCOURT A CAREER OF DECEPTION

Above: Portrait of Rocancourt; **Top:** Rocancourt in the company of the model Naomi Campbell.

Born on July 16, 1967, in Honfleur, France, Christophe Rocancourt was raised in a disadvantaged environment. His mother was a prostitute, and his father, absent for most of his life, was an alcoholic. This challenging upbringing became the backdrop against which Rocancourt would develop a life of deceit and exploitation.

Initial Ventures into Fraud

Rocancourt moved to Paris as a young man, where he began his career in deception. He posed as a French aristocrat and persuaded people to invest in nonexistent business ventures. Realizing the potential for greater rewards, he eventually took his act to the United States.

Life in the U.S.

Upon arrival in the U.S. in the late 1980s, Rocancourt continued his charades with renewed vigor. He assumed various identities, including posing as a member of the Rockefeller family. His schemes were elaborate, often involving convincing stories of business ventures, inheritance, or investment opportunities. Rocancourt exploited the human propensity to trust, as well as the allure of mingling with "high society," to defraud wealthy individuals out of substantial sums.

Methods and Tactics

His tactics involved not just name-dropping but also presenting fake documents, staging elaborate scenes with accomplices, and, in some cases, offering small payouts to investors from subsequent investments, akin to a Ponzi scheme. He lived a lavish lifestyle, staying in luxurious hotels and dining at expensive restaurants, thereby providing a veneer of legitimacy to his claims.

Legal Troubles

Rocancourt's web of deceit began to unravel in the late 1990s. After a series of arrests for various offenses, including possession of false identification, he became the subject of multiple investigations. The FBI and other law enforcement agencies became

involved, compiling a litany of charges against him, including fraud, perjury, and passport falsification.

Capture and Conviction

Rocancourt was arrested in 2001 in the town of Oak Bay, British Columbia, Canada, and was extradited to the United States. In 2003, he pleaded guilty to charges of wire fraud and passport falsification. Rocancourt was sentenced to five years in prison and was ordered to pay restitution to his victims. While in prison in Canada, he wrote an autobiography, *I, Christophe Rocancourt: Orphan, Playboy, and Convict*, in which he seemed unapologetically reflective of his life choices.

Deportation and Further Convictions

After serving his sentence in the U.S., Rocancourt was deported to France in 2006, where he faced additional charges of fraud. He was again convicted and served another prison term.

Post-Prison Life

As of the latest available information, Rocancourt was released from prison. Rocancourt's life is a study in audacity and deceit, demonstrating the fragility of trust and the potency of well-crafted lies. His story adds a complex layer to the landscape of criminal fraud.

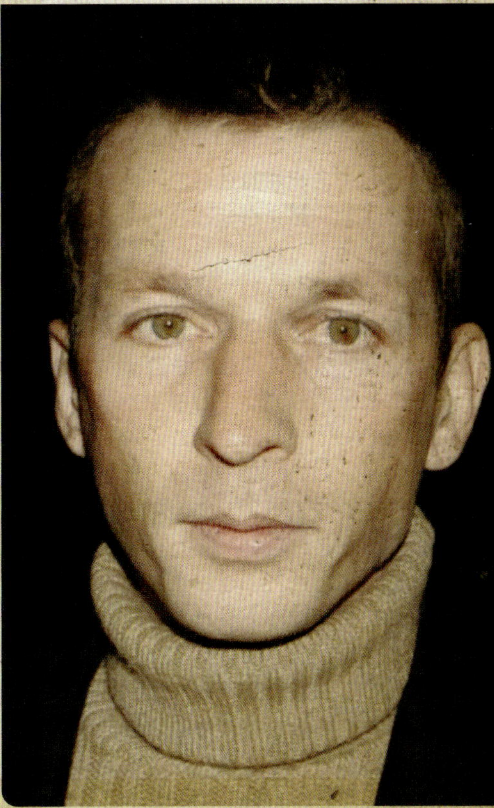

Above left: Whilst dining, Rocancourt adopts a "clinking glasses" pose for the photographer; **Top and above:** Rocancourt across the years.

CALISTO TANZI
EUROPE'S BIGGEST CORPORATE SCANDAL

Above: A solemn Calisto Tanzi after his arrest in December 2003; **Top:** Italian police take away a Claude Monet canvas, one of 19 works of art belonging to Tanzi that had been concealed elsewhere. Worth more than a projected €100 million, they included works by Picasso, Monet, and van Gogh. Tanzi had always denied owning any art, but prosecutor Gerardo Laguardia said that his people had raided the houses of Tanzi's friends after discovering that they had been offered for sale.

Calisto Tanzi was born on November 17, 1938, in Collecchio, a small town in province of Parma, Italy. He hailed from a modest background, and his family owned a small meat-trading business. Tanzi attended the University of Parma, but he dropped out to join the family enterprise.

Business Ventures

In 1961, Tanzi expanded the family business into the dairy sector and founded Parmalat, a name that would eventually become synonymous with one of Europe's biggest corporate scandals. The company initially produced pasteurized milk, and its introduction of shelf-stable, UHT milk in the late 1960s was a revolutionary move in the Italian dairy industry.

Global Expansion

Throughout the 1970s and 1980s, Parmalat expanded rapidly. The company became the first Italian organization to venture into the American market, followed by entries into Asia and other parts of Europe. Under Tanzi's

leadership, Parmalat diversified into various sectors, including baked goods, tourism, and even football sponsorship.

Financial Irregularities

However, the massive global expansion masked a network of fraudulent activities. Tanzi and his associates had created a complex web of offshore companies to siphon off Parmalat's revenue. By the late 1990s, there were warning signs, such as the sale of core assets, but these were overlooked by investors and regulators.

The Scandal is Revealed

The house of cards came tumbling down in 2003 when Parmalat defaulted on a €150 million bond payment. A subsequent investigation revealed that the company's account held a €3.95 billion hole, contrary to the €4 billion surplus that was reported. This marked the beginning of Europe's largest bankruptcy at the time, with about €14 billion in debt disclosed.

Arrest and Trial

Tanzi was arrested in December 2003 and faced multiple charges, including market rigging, obstructing regulators, and fraudulent bankruptcy. The trial, one of the largest in Italian legal history, involved several high-profile executives and financial institutions.

Conviction and Sentence

In 2008, Calisto Tanzi was convicted and sentenced to 10 years in prison. Another trial in 2010 sentenced him to 18 years. He was found guilty of fraudulent bankruptcy and criminal association. A separate market-rigging charge in 2011 added another 10 years to his sentence, although Italian law capped the maximum effective imprisonment time at 20 years for people over the age of 70.

Imprisonment and Release

Tanzi served part of his prison sentence before being granted house arrest in 2012 due to health reasons. He was officially released in 2017, having served a fraction of his total sentence due to his age and health conditions. Calisto Tanzi died on New Year's Day 2022. His life serves as a cautionary tale of how unchecked ambition and lack of corporate governance can lead to unprecedented financial disasters.

Top left, top right, and center: Tanzi was the driving force of Parmalat and was often seen in the Italian media. He was always the face of the company; **Above:** Tanzi, with his health failing, 2011.

The 2008 financial crisis proved to be Madoff's undoing. As clients requested a total of $7 billion in returns, his scheme began to unravel. Unable to meet these demands, he confessed to his sons, who subsequently reported him to the authorities. On December 11, 2008, Madoff was arrested...

BERNIE MADOFF THE 64 BILLION

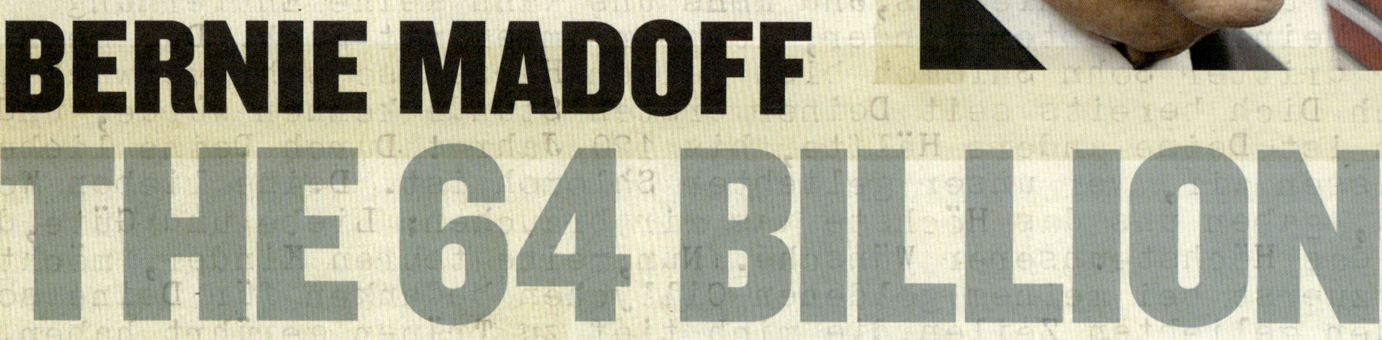

Bernard Lawrence Madoff, commonly known as Bernie Madoff, was born on April 29, 1938, in Queens, New York. Hailing from a middle-class Jewish family, Madoff exhibited an early interest in finance. He attended the University of Alabama for a year before transferring to and graduating from Hofstra University with a degree in political science.

Career Ascension

In 1960, with an initial investment of $5,000 from his lifeguarding job, Madoff founded Bernard L. Madoff Investment Securities LLC. His firm quickly ascended the ranks, becoming one of the top market-maker businesses on Wall Street. By the 1980s, it was one of the leading trading venues for S&P 500 stocks.

Ponzi Scheme

While his business was recognized for its market-making and trading successes, Madoff ran an entirely separate and covert operation. He managed an investment advisory division which, unbeknownst to the world, was a massive Ponzi scheme. Claiming to provide

DOLLAR STEAL

consistent returns to his investors through a strategy he called the "split-strike conversion," Madoff attracted a plethora of clients, ranging from individual investors to celebrities and charities. However, instead of genuine investments, incoming funds were used to pay returns to earlier investors, creating the illusion of legitimate profits. Over the years, this scheme swelled into billions of dollars.

Exposure and Arrest

The 2008 financial crisis proved to be Madoff's undoing. As clients requested a total of $7 billion in returns, his scheme began to unravel. Unable to meet these demands, he confessed to his sons, who subsequently reported him to the authorities. On December 11, 2008, Bernie Madoff was arrested.

Trial and Imprisonment

In March 2009, Madoff pleaded guilty to 11 federal felonies, admitting to turning his wealth management business into the world's largest Ponzi scheme, valued at an estimated $64.8 billion. In June 2009, he received a 150-year prison sentence, effectively a life term for the then 71-year-old. Madoff died in prison on April 14, 2021, from chronic kidney disease.

Impact and Legacy

Madoff's deceit had far-reaching consequences. His investors, many of whom lost their life savings, included individuals, charities, and universities. The scale of his deception led to calls for tighter financial regulations and oversight, but incredibly, this has not happened, and the financial trading landscape and wealth management world are as susceptible to fraud as they were before the 2008 crash. The Securities Investor Protection Corporation (SIPC) has since worked to return funds to Madoff's victims, but the financial and emotional damage remains incalculable for many. His story serves as a glaring example of the perils of unchecked greed and the vulnerabilities inherent in financial systems. It stands as a testament to the need for transparency, oversight, and—more than ever—ethical conduct in the world of finance.

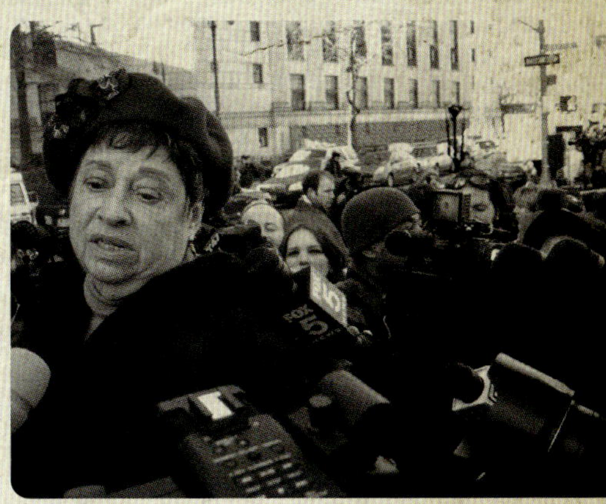

Above: Judith Welling, one of thousands of individual investors defrauded by Madoff, demonstrates outside the U.S. District Court New York City, as Madoff arrives for his arraignment; **Top left:** Madoff's mug shot; **Top right:** Wall Street and Manhattan's financial district; **Opposite, below:** Moving money. Traders in Wall Street; **Opposite, top:** Madoff leaving court in March 2009 after pleading guilty to 11 federal felonies.

ELIZABETH HOLMES A METEORIC RISE AND FALL

Top left: The building that was the headquarters for Theranos; **Top right, above and opposite center right:** The several faces of Elizabeth Holmes, from young female billionaire TV talk show guest, to careworn stress during her trials and tribulations.

Elizabeth Anne Holmes was born on February 3, 1984, in Washington, D.C. Displaying an early zeal for business, Holmes declared her intent to become a billionaire entrepreneur as a child. She pursued her undergraduate studies in chemical engineering at Stanford University but dropped out in 2003 to follow her entrepreneurial aspirations.

Theranos and Its Vision

In 2003, Holmes founded Theranos, a health technology company with the goal of revolutionizing blood testing. Her vision was a device that could quickly and inexpensively conduct comprehensive tests using only a few drops of blood. With her charisma and compelling narrative, Holmes garnered significant attention and managed to draw hefty investments from notable figures, valuing Theranos at its peak at over $9 billion.

The Fall

However, beneath the veneer of innovation, there were significant issues. The technology Holmes championed did not deliver on its promises. Inside the company, concerns grew about the accuracy and reliability of Theranos' blood tests. Yet, Holmes and former company president Ramesh "Sunny" Balwani allegedly engaged in deceptive practices, misleading investors—and patients—about the device's capabilities. By 2015, *The Wall Street Journal* published an investigation into Theranos, revealing the company's inconsistencies and failures. Regulatory and legal actions soon

followed. The Centers for Medicare and Medicaid Services sanctioned Theranos in 2016, barring Holmes from owning or operating a laboratory for two years.

Legal Repercussions

In 2018, the U.S. Securities and Exchange Commission charged Holmes with massive fraud, alleging that she had engaged in an elaborate, years-long scheme to deceive investors. Holmes settled with the SEC, relinquishing her voting control of Theranos, returning a substantial amount of her stock, and paying a half-million-dollar penalty. She was also barred from serving as an officer or director of a public company for ten years. Separately, in June 2018, a federal grand jury indicted Holmes and Balwani on wire fraud and conspiracy charges. The trial ended in January 2022 when Holmes was found guilty of defrauding investors, but acquitted of defrauding patients. Balwani's 12-year prison sentence began in April 2023, whilst Holmes' 11-year prison term began in May the same year. She and Balwani were also jointly fined $452 million to be paid to the victims of the fraud.

Public Perception and Impact

Elizabeth Holmes' rise and fall were meteoric. Once lauded as the world's youngest self-made female billionaire and compared to tech giants like Steve Jobs, her downfall was a cautionary tale in Silicon Valley. Holmes' story underscored the dangers of hyperbolic tech narratives, especially in the sensitive arena of healthcare.

Legacy

The Theranos saga has had a profound impact on startups and investors. It stressed the importance of due diligence, transparency, and the ethical responsibilities companies bear, especially in the healthcare domain. Elizabeth Holmes, from a wunderkind of the tech world, became a symbol of deception and overreach in the startup ecosystem.

Top left: Theranos meeting space on the set of *The Dropout*, designed by Kimberly Leonard; **Top right:** *The Wall Street Journal* noted that: "Craving growth, Walgreens dismissed its doubts about Theranos"; **Above, center left:** At the height of her fame, Holmes was a magnet for Health and Beauty magazines; **Above:** Ramesh "Sunny" Balwani, convicted of two counts of conspiring with Holmes, six counts of defrauding investors and four counts of patient fraud. He began his 12-year prison sentence, plus probation, in April 2023.

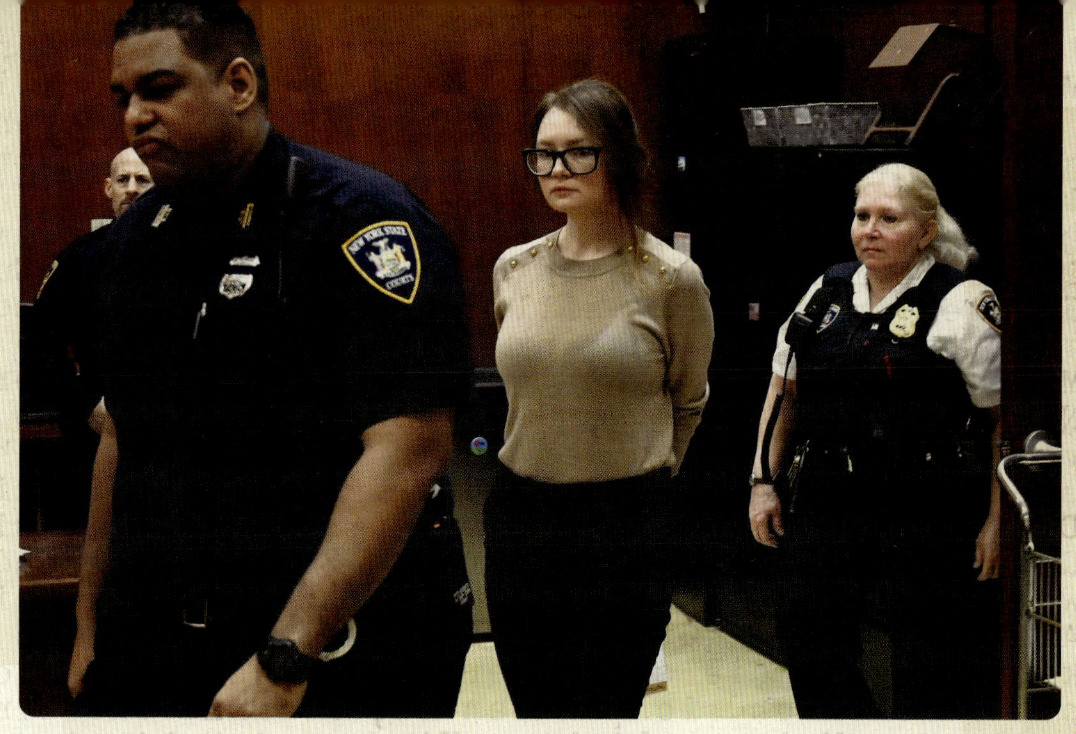

ANNA SOROKIN
WEALTH, STATUS... AND ILLUSION

Top: Sorokin is led into court, March 2019; **Above:** Actress Julia Garner, who played Sorokin in *Inventing Anna*, is taking a photograph of herself.

Born on January 23, 1991, in Domodedovo, a satellite town in Moscow, Russia, Anna Sorokin experienced a far from glamorous upbringing. The daughter of a truck driver and a housewife, she moved to Germany with her family when she was 16 years old.

Reinvention in New York

After moving to New York City in 2013, Sorokin began her transformation into Anna Delvey. She crafted a persona as a wealthy German heiress with a trust fund worth 60 million euros. With her new identity, she entered elite circles, staying in upscale hotels, dining at exclusive restaurants, and joining the city's vibrant arts and fashion scenes.

Scams and Luxurious Lifestyle

Portraying herself as a wealthy socialite, Sorokin convinced friends and businesses to cover her extravagant expenses, always promising to pay them back. She floated between boutique hotels, leaving behind unpaid bills, and even sought multimillion-dollar loans for a purported arts club project. Her ability to manipulate and charm those around her allowed her to maintain this facade for several years.

Downfall

However, as debts piled up, suspicions arose. When she failed to pay for a lavish trip to Morocco, a close friend was stuck with a bill of $62,000. This event set off alarms and gradually

led to her exposure. Sorokin was arrested in 2017 and charged with multiple counts of theft and grand larceny.

The Trial

The trial, which began in March 2019, was widely covered by the media. Sorokin's defense argued that she had not committed any crime and had only been trying to make a life for herself. The prosecution, on the other hand, painted her as a career con artist. After a month-long trial, Sorokin was convicted of multiple felonies, including second-degree larceny and theft of services.

Incarceration and Later Developments

Anna Sorokin was sentenced to 4 to 12 years in prison, ordered to pay nearly $200,000 in restitution, and fined $24,000. In February 2021, after serving nearly four years, she was released on parole. The story of Anna Sorokin, or Anna Delvey as she's more famously known, captivated the public. Her audacity, combined with the New York City backdrop and the world of glitz and glamour she navigated, made her tale both shocking and enthralling. This fascination led to various media adaptations, most notably the Netflix series *Inventing Anna*, which delved into her life and the personas she adopted.

Legacy

Anna Sorokin's story serves as a modern cautionary tale about deceit, social climbing, and the lengths to which individuals might go to maintain a facade. It also highlights society's fascination with wealth and status and how these obsessions can blind people to the realities right in front of them.

Top left: Keeping up the facade—Sorokin poses for another seductive photograph, complete with electronic tagging device; **Top right:** Yet another provocative selfie for her followers; **Above, center:** Reality bites...Sorokin in court; **Above:** Sorokin poses with an acquaintance.

CHAPTER TWO

THIEVES

Thievery, in its many forms, is as old as property itself. The individuals featured here have elevated it to a high-stakes game, often planning their operations with precision and care. Their stories provide insight into the motivations that drive people to commit theft, whether it be poverty, greed, or the thrill of the challenge.

This chapter delves into the lives of the most cunning and notorious thieves who have ever slipped through the cracks of law enforcement, leaving behind legends that are sometimes admired, often reviled, but always compelling. These are the individuals who turned theft into an art form, whose audacity and skill in the act of stealing have etched their names into the annals of true crime history.

Thieves come in many guises, from the pickpockets and burglars who operate on the fringes of society to the sophisticated heist masters who plan and execute grand-scale larcenies. Their targets may vary—jewels, art, money, or even identities—but their defining characteristic is the same: an insatiable appetite for what is not rightfully theirs.

It's widely believed that Sir Arthur Conan Doyle used Worth as an inspiration for Sherlock Holmes' arch-nemesis, Professor Moriarty...

ADAM WORTH GENTLEMAN THIEF

Adam Worth, often dubbed the "Napoleon of Crime," was a master criminal who operated during the latter half of the 19th century. Born in 1844, in Germany, Worth eventually emerged as one of the most notorious and enigmatic figures in the underworld, respected and feared by both law enforcement and fellow criminals.

Journey to America and Early Crimes

Worth's family emigrated to the United States when he was young. By the age of 17, he had enlisted to fight in the American Civil War. He served with distinction but, after being mistakenly reported as dead in a hospital mix-up, decided to use this erroneous status to start afresh. Worth began his life of crime with small thefts and swindles but quickly graduated to more significant heists.

Ascension to Notoriety

Moving to New York, Worth became involved with pickpockets and shoplifters, often

orchestrating elaborate heists and burglaries. His operations were meticulous, always ensuring no harm came to civilians during his crimes. This earned him a reputation as a "gentleman thief." In the late 1860s, facing increasing heat from the Pinkerton Detective Agency in the U.S., Worth relocated to England. Here, under the pseudonym Henry J. Raymond, he expanded his criminal enterprise, which now included a network of fences, informants, and other criminals.

The Theft of the Duchess

Perhaps Worth's most audacious crime was the theft of Thomas Gainsborough's portrait, "Georgiana, Duchess of Devonshire," in 1876. The painting was stolen from London's Thomas Agnew & Sons Gallery. Worth, enamored by the artwork, kept it with him for over two decades, even using it as collateral for loans.

Capture, Prison, and Later Years

Worth's reign came to an end in 1892 when he was arrested in Belgium after attempting a train heist. He was extradited to England and sentenced to seven years in prison. While incarcerated, Worth's reputation led to numerous interviews with journalists and authors, increasing his notoriety. On his release, Worth decided to right some of his wrongs. With the help of an American Pinkerton detective, he returned the stolen Gainsborough portrait in exchange for immunity. He then moved back to the U.S., living out his days in relative obscurity.

Legacy and Influence

Adam Worth passed away on January 8, 1902. In the annals of crime, he stands out not only for his audacity but also for his code of ethics. He never harmed anyone during his heists and often went out of his way to ensure the safety of bystanders. It's widely believed that Sir Arthur Conan Doyle used Worth as an inspiration for Sherlock Holmes' arch-nemesis, Professor Moriarty. The parallels between Worth's real-life escapades and Moriarty's fictional endeavors are undeniable, adding another layer of intrigue to the legacy of the "Napoleon of Crime."

Opposite, main image: A rare photograph of Adam Worth; **Opposite, center:** A unit of Union soldiers poses for the new medium of photography; **Main image, above:** Gainsborough's portrait of Georgiana, Duchess of Devonshire, which Worth stole from Agnew's Gallery in London; **Above:** Sir Arthur Conan Doyle, author of the inimitable Sherlock Holmes stories, and **Top:** A Sidney Paget illustration of Holmes' arch-nemesis, Professor Moriarty.

WILLIE SUTTON

Willie Sutton, often referred to as "Slick Willie" or "The Actor," was one of the most prolific bank robbers in American history. Over his four-decade criminal career, Sutton stole an estimated $2 million (equivalent to over $20 million today) and became famous not just for his heists but also for his multiple prison escapes and his ability to elude the authorities.

The Early Life of a Future Criminal

Born on June 30, 1901, in Brooklyn, New York, Sutton's criminal career began in his late teens. Driven by circumstances and personal choices, he eventually graduated from petty crimes to full-blown bank robberies.

The Art of Robbery

Sutton's bank heists were meticulously planned. He would spend days, if not weeks, studying his target, noting the routines of bank employees, the layout of the bank, and the patterns of local law enforcement. What set Sutton apart from other criminals was his flair for disguise. He assumed various identities during his heists, ranging from a postal telegraph messenger to a police officer, and even a maintenance man. These disguises allowed him to gain entry into banks without arousing suspicion.

Captures and Escapes

Despite his careful planning, Sutton was arrested multiple times. However, he proved

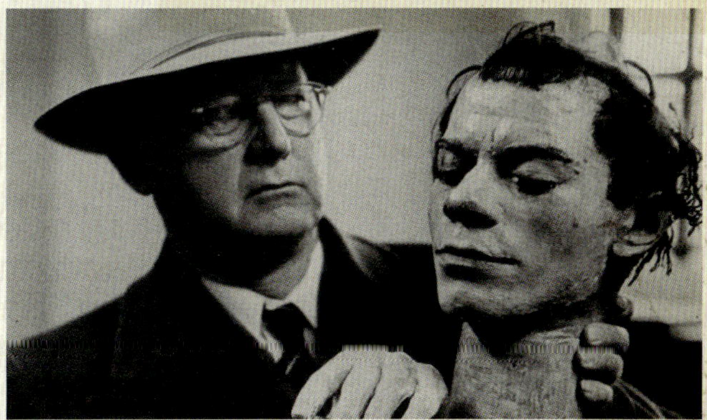

to be as adept at escaping from prison as he was at robbing banks. He broke out of jail three times during his criminal career, each escape more audacious than the last.

The Reason for His Crimes

When asked why he robbed banks, Sutton reportedly replied, "Because that's where the money is." This quote became legendary and is often cited in discussions about criminal motivation, though Sutton later denied ever making such a statement.

Final Years and Legacy

Sutton's life of crime came to an end in 1952 when he was arrested for the final time. He was paroled in 1969, having served 17 years of his latest sentence, and spent his remaining years living quietly. He passed away in 1980. In his later years, Sutton wrote two books and even consulted with banks on improving their security measures. He expressed regret over his life choices, wishing he had pursued a different path. Willie Sutton's legacy is a complex one. On the one hand, he was a criminal responsible for causing fear and harm to many. On the other, he was a master of disguise, a clever strategist, and, by most accounts, a "gentleman robber" who avoided violence.

Opposite, bottom left: Willie Sutton's mugshot taken at Eastern State Penitentiary, April 3, 1945. This was the same day that Sutton and 11 other inmates had tunneled to freedom. Unfortunately for the escapees, they were all recaptured almost immediately, and Sutton's mugshot appears to have been shot on his recapture—he looks like he's been underground; **Opposite, top left:** Willie Sutton's burglar toolkit, on display at New York City Police Museum; **Opposite, top right:** The dapper Sutton in handcuffs; **This page, top left:** Sutton, again in 'cuffs and custody, is led into the New York City Hall by officers; **Top right:** Eastern State Penitentiary, closed in 1971 and now a National Monument; **Above, center right:** Erle Stanley Gardner, the best-selling mystery author and creator of the Perry Mason character, examines the fake head and hand that Sutton made, using clippings of his own hair, in order to facilitate his escape from the Eastern State prison; **Above:** Erle Stanley Gardner looks over the cell at Eastern State, from where Sutton escaped.

RONNIE BIGGS
GREAT TRAIN ROBBER

Top left: Bridego Bridge, Buckinghamshire, where the Great Train Robbers took sacks of cash from the train to the waiting getaway vehicles; **Top right:** Biggs, circa 1963; **Above:** An aerial view of Leatherslade Farm, where the robbers holed up after the heist; **Opposite, top left:** Biggs in his England soccer shirt, on Copacabana Beach, Rio de Janeiro; **Opposite, top right:** Biggs poses for the British tabloids, flanked by Sex Pistols' drummer Paul Cook (left), and guitarist Steve Jones, 1978.

Ronnie Biggs, born in London in 1929, is best remembered for his role in the "Great Train Robbery" of 1963, a crime that shocked Britain and earned him notoriety as one of the country's most wanted men. His subsequent life on the run and eventual return to Britain solidified his place in the annals of British criminal history.

Early Life and Crime

Ronnie Biggs' criminal activities started with petty crimes during his youth. However, it was his association with Bruce Reynolds, the mastermind behind the Great Train Robbery, that would thrust him into the limelight. Biggs was responsible for providing the driver for the train, a task he failed at, but the robbery proceeded nonetheless.

The Great Train Robbery

On August 8, 1963, Bruce Reynolds, along with Biggs, who were part of a 15-man gang, intercepted a Royal Mail train carrying banknotes worth £2.6 million (equivalent to around £50 million today). Using a fake signal light, they stopped the train, attacked the train staff, and made off with the money. The audacity and scale of the robbery captured the nation's attention and led to a nationwide manhunt.

Capture, Escape, and Life Abroad

Biggs was arrested in 1963 and was sentenced to 30 years in prison. However, after serving just 15 months, he made a dramatic escape from Wandsworth Prison in London by scaling the wall with a homemade rope ladder and fleeing in a waiting furniture van. Following his escape, Biggs underwent plastic surgery to alter his

appearance and embarked on a life of exile. He traveled to Paris, then to Australia, and finally settled in Brazil, a country that didn't have an extradition treaty with the UK.

Return to the UK and Later Life

Despite living freely in Brazil and fathering a son there, Biggs' health began to deteriorate. In 2001, at the age of 71, and in need of medical care, Biggs voluntarily returned to the UK. Upon his return, he was immediately arrested and sent back to prison. His health continued to decline, and in 2009, on compassionate grounds, he was granted release from prison. Ronnie Biggs passed away in 2013 at the age of 84.

Legacy

Ronnie Biggs' life was marked by audacity, cunning, and a flair for the dramatic. The Great Train Robbery and his subsequent life on the run captured the public's imagination, making him one of the most infamous figures in British criminal history. His story, with its twists and turns, remains a fascinating chapter in the annals of crime, shedding light on the lengths an individual can go to evade justice and the eventual consequences of their actions.

Above, center right: Biggs takes lead vocals on the Sex Pistols' single "No One is Innocent," recorded in 1978. Steve Jones helps him out; **Right:** Biggs photographed in Brazil, prior to his return to the UK.

She would enter luxury jewelry stores, posing as a well-to-do woman...with her charm, she'd engage the staff, asking to see multiple high-end pieces, particularly diamond rings...

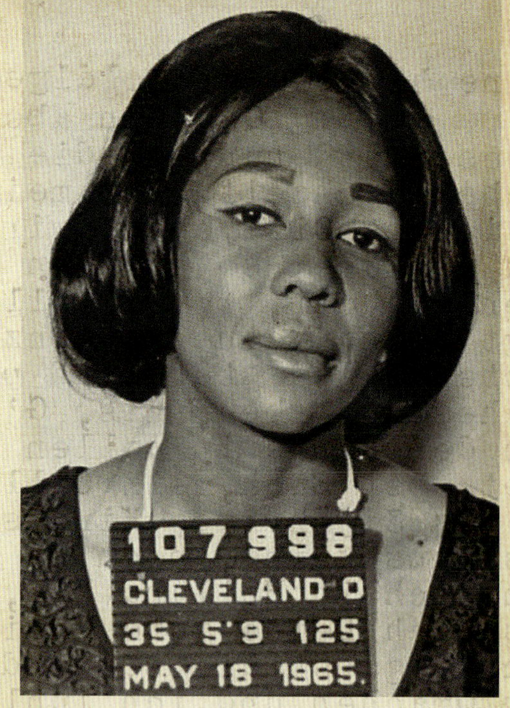

DORIS PAYNE

GLAMOUR, GEMS AND DECEPTION

Doris Payne, whose criminal career spans over six decades, is perhaps one of the most intriguing figures in the world of high-stakes theft. With her charm, wit, and audacity, Payne became a legendary figure in the world of jewel heists, managing to elude capture multiple times and continuing her illicit activities well into her eighties.

The Early Years

Born in Slab Fork, West Virginia, in 1930, Payne's foray into the world of theft began in her early twenties. She quickly realized that her beauty, combined with her intelligence and ability to spin convincing tales, made her perfectly suited for the world of jewel theft.

Modus Operandi

Payne's method was consistent yet effective. She would enter luxury jewelry stores, posing as a well-to-do woman and often adopting false identities, including that of a wealthy international buyer. With her charm, she'd

WANTED

LARCENY

AGE	36 years
RACE	Negro
HEIGHT	5'9"
WEIGHT	125 lbs.
HAIR	Black
COMPL.	Light
BUILD	Slender
OTHER	Wore expensive jewelry

DORIS MARIE PAYNE
PHILA. NO. C13608

Wednesday, November 30, 1966, about 11:45 A.M., inside room 942, Fidelity Philadelphia Trust Building, 123 S. Broad Street, Harold Brondfield and Doris Payne examined several trays of diamond rings and requested to see more expensive rings, when the jeweler returned the couple left and two rings were missing.

[redacted] represented himself as the widowed Payne's attorney. She was interested in investing a large sum of money, that she had inherited, in the purchase of valuable rings.

I M P O R T A N T . . . . Immediately report any information including name, address, physical description and license number. Information will be confidential.

(See reverse side.)

PHILADELPHIA POLICE DEPARTMENT

NOTIFY: DETECTIVE BUREAU
MUnicipal 6-3330 or 3093

December 12, 1966 No. 39

EDWARD J. BELL
POLICE COMMISSIONER

engage the staff, asking to see multiple high-end pieces, particularly diamond rings. Amidst the confusion of viewing numerous pieces, she would pocket one or two items, leaving the store before the theft was discovered.

International Heists

While Payne committed many of her thefts in the U.S., she wasn't limited by borders. Her criminal activities took her to places like Monaco, Paris, and Tokyo. In Monte Carlo in the 1970s, one of her most audacious thefts involved a diamond ring valued at over half a million dollars.

Arrests and Releases

Over the years, Payne was arrested multiple times. However, she always managed to serve relatively short sentences, often due to the non-violent nature of her crimes. Her ability to charm, became a hallmark of her career. Even in her later years, Payne's penchant for theft didn't wane. In her seventies and eighties, she was still reported to be involved in thefts, proving that age had not diminished her skills or her audacity.

In Popular Culture

Doris Payne's life and crimes captured the public's imagination. Her story was the subject of a 2013 documentary titled *The Life and Crimes of Doris Payne*, where she candidly discussed her adventures, motivations, and the world of theft.

Legacy

Doris Payne's legacy is a complex one. While her crimes were undeniably illegal and caused significant distress to her victims, her story is also one of resilience, audacity, and charm. In an industry dominated by men, Payne carved a niche for herself, becoming one of the most notorious and enduring figures in the world of jewel theft.

Above, and opposite, top right: Two separate mugshots for two separate arrests in 1965; **Opposite, below:** Monte Carlo, Monaco, the playground of the international rich, in a 1970s postcard. One of Doris Payne's hunting grounds; **Top left:** Doris poses for publicity pictures, circa 2006; **Top right:** "Wanted for Larceny," Doris at it again in December 1966.

DB COOPER THE SKYJACKING

Somewhere over the rugged wilderness of southwestern Washington state, Cooper opened the rear door of the Boeing 727 and parachuted into the night with the ransom money. Despite extensive manhunts and investigations, he was never found, and his true identity remains unknown...

DB Cooper, a pseudonym adopted by an unidentified individual, remains one of the most enigmatic figures in the annals of American crime. In 1971, he executed a daring airplane hijacking and parachuted to an uncertain fate with $200,000 in ransom, leaving behind a trail of mysteries that continue to perplex investigators and captivate the public.

The Skyjacking

On November 24, 1971, a man using the alias "Dan Cooper" boarded Northwest Orient Airlines Flight 305 from Portland to Seattle. He was described as middle-aged, wearing a dark suit, and appeared as any ordinary business traveler. However, shortly after takeoff, he handed a note to a flight attendant, revealing that he had a bomb and was hijacking the plane. Cooper demanded $200,000 in cash, four parachutes, and a fuel truck standing by in Seattle to refuel the plane for a getaway. The airline and authorities complied with his demands. Upon

receiving the ransom and releasing the 36 passengers at the Seattle-Tacoma International Airport, Cooper instructed the remaining crew to fly the plane to Mexico City.

The Mysterious Escape

Somewhere over the rugged wilderness of southwestern Washington state, Cooper opened the rear door of the Boeing 727 and parachuted into the night with the ransom money. Despite extensive manhunts and investigations, he was never found, and his true identity remains unknown.

Investigation and Theories

The FBI launched one of its most extensive manhunts in history, combing the suspected landing zone, interviewing thousands of individuals, and following countless leads. In 1980, a young boy camping in the Columbia River area found a decaying package containing $5,800, which was confirmed to be a part of the ransom money. However, this discovery only deepened the mystery, as it provided no conclusive evidence about Cooper's fate. Over the years, multiple theories about Cooper's identity and fate have been proposed. Some believe he was an experienced skydiver who planned the heist meticulously, while others speculate that he might have been an inexperienced thrill-seeker who did not survive the jump.

Legacy

In 2016, the FBI officially closed the DB Cooper case, citing a lack of new information. The hijacking remains one of the greatest unsolved mysteries in the history of American crime, and DB Cooper's audacious act has left an indelible mark on American pop culture. He has been the subject of numerous books, documentaries, songs, and films. His story, filled with intrigue, speculation, and mystery, continues to fascinate and mystify, serving as a testament to the enduring allure of unsolved crimes.

Above, left and right: Two FBI composite drawings, which were the closest the authorities got to a physical likeness of "DB Cooper."

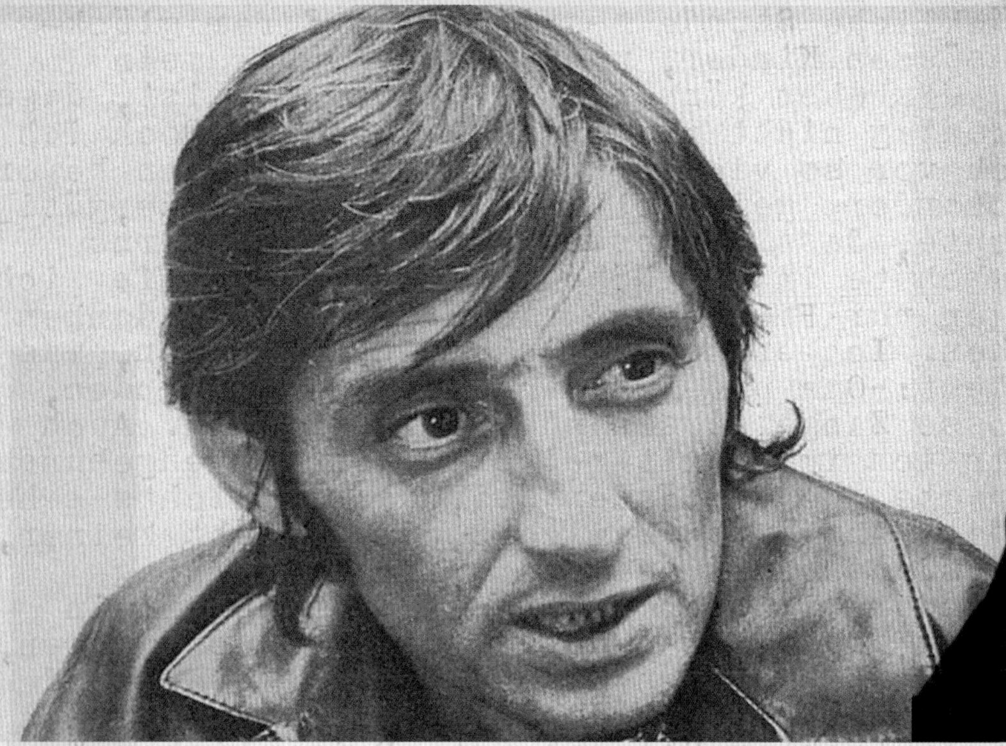

ALBERT SPAGGIARI THE SEWER HEIST

Above: Spaggiari sporting shades and cigar; **Top left:** A portrait of Spaggiari taken whilst on the run; **Top right:** Spaggiari in 1977.

Albert Spaggiari, born on December 14, 1932, in Laragne-Montéglin, France, was a criminal mastermind best known for orchestrating the 1976 Nice bank heist, often referred to as the "crime of the century." This audacious robbery, which saw Spaggiari and his gang break into a bank vault via the city's sewers, became legendary and solidified Spaggiari's reputation as one of the most cunning criminals of his time.

A Varied Past

Before embarking on his life of crime, Spaggiari wore many hats. He served in the French paratroopers during the First Indochina War and later ran a photography shop. However, beneath this veneer of respectability, Spaggiari harbored a penchant for crime and rebellion.

The Sewer Heist

In 1976, Spaggiari set his sights on the Société Générale bank in Nice. With a meticulously chosen crew, he spent months planning the heist. The group decided to access the bank vault from beneath, using Nice's sewer system. Over the Bastille Day weekend, while the city celebrated above, Spaggiari and his team tunneled into the bank's vault. For two days, they emptied safety deposit boxes, making off with an estimated 60 million francs (equivalent to tens of millions of dollars today) in cash, jewelry, and other valuables. The true genius of the heist was in its execution. The gang took their time, even pausing to enjoy meals and wine inside the vault. Before making their escape, Spaggiari left a message on the vault wall: "Sans armes, ni haine, ni violence" –

"Without weapons, hate, or violence."

Capture and Escape

Though the heist was masterfully executed, Spaggiari's involvement eventually came to light after a member of his crew was arrested on an unrelated charge and began to talk. Spaggiari was arrested and brought to trial. However, true to his audacious nature, Spaggiari wasn't done surprising the world. During a court hearing, he handed a note to the judge, then leaped out of a window and landed on a car and then on the back of a waiting motorcycle. He managed to evade capture and disappeared.

Later Life and Legacy

For years, Spaggiari lived in hiding, popping up now and then to taunt authorities. Rumors of his whereabouts and activities were rife, but he remained a step ahead of the law. He eventually passed away in 1989, leaving behind a legacy of one of the most daring bank heists in history. In the world of crime, Albert Spaggiari stands out not for the scale of his theft, but for the style, audacity, and panache with which he carried it out. His story, particularly the Nice heist, has been retold in numerous books, documentaries, and films, cementing his place in the annals of criminal legend.

Top left: A crowd gathers outside the Société Générale bank in Nice, July 1976, as news of the robbery spreads; **Top right:** Francis Huster, the French filmmaker and actor plays Albert Spaggiari in Jose Giovanni's 1979 movie, *Les Égouts du paradis* (*The Sewers of Paradise*), which retraces "the crime of the century" robbery of the Société Générale bank; **Above:** Spaggiari, apprehended by French police.

ALAN GOLDER
THE DINNERTIME BANDIT

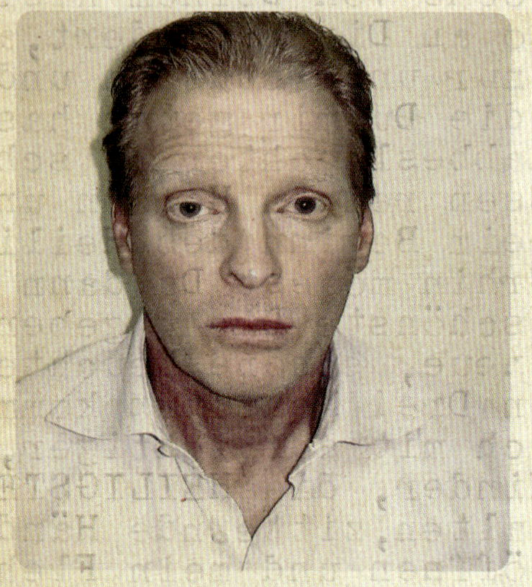

Above: Golder's mugshot, November 2007.

Alan Golder, more commonly known as the "Dinnertime Bandit," was a sophisticated burglar who specialized in robbing the opulent homes of America's elite during the 1970s and 1980s. His modus operandi, striking homes during the dinner hour while homeowners were still present but distracted, earned him his infamous nickname and set him apart from other criminals of his era.

Background and Beginnings

Born on August 9, 1955, in New York, Golder grew up in an environment surrounded by crime. He quickly learned the art of burglary and started his criminal career with smaller thefts. However, his ambition and keen observation skills soon led him to target wealthier neighborhoods.

The Dinnertime Heists

Golder's operations were methodical and well-planned. He would meticulously study his targets, noting their routines, security measures, and potential escape routes. Opting to strike during the evening, often while families were dining, Golder believed that the noise from the dinner gatherings would mask his movements. This audacious approach, combined with his knack for evading security systems, made him incredibly successful. His targets were not just any homes; they were the mansions and estates of high society, including celebrities and business tycoons. Over time, Golder amassed a fortune in stolen jewelry, artwork, and cash.

Partnerships and Downfall

Golder's success wasn't entirely a solo act. He frequently collaborated with other criminals, fencing stolen goods and occasionally partnering for bigger heists—he was an associate of the Genovese mafia family and its boss, Vincent "The Chin" Gigante. However, as with many in the criminal world, these partnerships proved to be his undoing. In the late 1980s, Golder's luck began to wane.

After a series of failed heists and close calls with law enforcement, the pressure began to mount. The final blow came when one of his associates, facing legal troubles of his own, turned informant and provided information leading to Golder's arrest.

Incarceration and Later Life

In 1988, Alan Golder was sentenced to prison for his numerous burglaries. He served a significant portion of his sentence and was released on parole in 1996. The Connecticut burglaries started up again three months later, with estimates ranging up to $1 million in jewels taken from homes in Greenwich and Darien. An arrest warrant was filed on Golder in 1998, but he had already fled the country, flying to Amsterdam on Thanksgiving Day 1997 on a fake passport. He says he was forced to flee after being assaulted by one of his associates. Golder attempted to live a life out of the spotlight post-incarceration. However, his past occasionally came back to haunt him, both in the form of legal troubles and the enduring legacy of the "Dinnertime Bandit."

A Legend in Crime

Alan Golder's exploits have become legendary in the annals of American crime. His audacity, combined with his ability to elude capture for so long, has made him a subject of fascination. The tales of the "Dinnertime Bandit" serve as a reminder that sometimes, the boldest criminals operate right under our noses, striking when we least expect it.

Above, and opposite, top: Detectives escort 52-year-old Golder (center), from Greenwich Police Department, *en route* to court in Stamford, Connecticut in November 2007, to face 40 felony counts in connection with the Darien and Greenwich heists. After almost a decade on the run—mainly living the good life in France and Belgium—Golder was extradited back to the U.S. (Photo: Associated Press, The Greenwich Time, Keelin Daly)

His transition from a successful businessman to the oldest bank robber in America serves as a stark reminder of the unpredictable paths life can take...

RED ROUNTREE
THE USA'S OLDEST BANK ROBBER

JL Hunter Rountree, commonly known as "Red" Rountree, holds the dubious distinction of being one of the oldest known bank robbers in the United States. Starting his life of crime in his late 80s, Rountree's story is as surprising as it is unconventional, reflecting personal tragedies and a late-life turn to the wrong side of the law.

Prosperous Early Life

Born on December 16, 1911, in Brownsville, Texas, Rountree enjoyed early success in the business world. He established a prosperous business selling heavy equipment and led a comfortable life with his family. For most of his life, Rountree was the very definition of a law-abiding citizen.

A Series of Misfortunes

However, as the years passed, Rountree faced significant financial hardships. His business faced bankruptcy, and personal tragedies, including the deaths of his wife and stepson, took a toll on him. The culmination of these events led to a radical shift in Rountree's behavior.

A Late Start in Crime

In 1998, at the age of 86, Rountree robbed his first bank in Mississippi. He did not use any disguises and was quickly apprehended but received a lenient sentence due to his age. Undeterred, he continued his criminal activities, robbing two more banks in Florida and Texas. His final heist in 2003, at the age of 91, ended in his capture. His modus operandi was straightforward: he would hand a teller a note demanding money, intimating he had a weapon. Given his age and demeanor, few would have pegged him as a bank robber, allowing him to carry out his crimes with little suspicion.

Final Years

After his last robbery, Rountree was sentenced to 12 years in prison. Reflecting on his actions, he cited his late-life financial troubles and a sense of anger and frustration at banks as the driving forces behind his crimes. He expressed regret, not necessarily for the crimes themselves, but for getting caught. JL Hunter "Red" Rountree passed away in prison in 2004, at the age of 92.

A Unique Legacy

Rountree's story challenges conventional perceptions about criminals. His transition from a successful businessman to the oldest bank robber in America serves as a stark reminder of the unpredictable paths life can take. While his actions in his later years were undoubtedly illegal, they also highlight the complexities of human behavior and the factors that can drive individuals to unexpected extremes.

Above: Rountree is helped out of the police vehicle and into the courthouse; **Opposite:** Rountree in his prison cell in 2004, shortly before he died. (Copyright and courtesy GQ magazine)

Gugasian would study his target banks meticulously, often observing them for months. He chose banks near wooded areas to facilitate a quick escape. Using police scanners, disguises, and a variety of weapons, he would execute his heists swiftly, often leaving before authorities were even alerted...

CARL GUGASIAN
THE FRIDAY NIGHT METHOD

Top: Gugasian's mugshot, February 2002; **Above left:** Gugasian snapped during the time he cooperated with the FBI on cases; **Above right:** As well as an interest in model trains and ballroom dancing, Gugasian was a Karate black belt third dan. It was one of the routes by which the FBI finally traced him—he would vault the counter in a standing jump, then stuff his bag with money and leave quickly, usually after less than two minutes in all.

Carl Gugasian, known in criminal circles and the media as the "Friday Night Bank Robber," stands out as one of the most prolific bank robbers in U.S. history. Over a span of 30 years, from the 1970s to the early 2000s, Gugasian is believed to have committed more than 50 bank robberies, amassing millions. His meticulously planned heists, combined with a disciplined approach and almost military precision, earned him both infamy and grudging respect.

An Unusual Background

Born in 1947, Gugasian's early life showed promise of a bright future. He had an IQ over 140, placing him in the genius category. By the age of 16, he was already attending Villanova University, studying statistics. However, a turn to crime, including an explosive mishap, landed him in juvenile detention, altering his path.

The Friday Night Method

Gugasian's nickname wasn't just a catchy moniker; it described his modus operandi. He preferred robbing banks on Friday evenings, especially during bad weather or other conditions that would ensure a slower police response. This strategy also gave him a head start on the weekend, making immediate pursuit more challenging. Each robbery was a result of careful planning. Gugasian would study his target banks meticulously, often observing them for months. He chose banks near wooded areas to facilitate a quick escape. Using police scanners, disguises, and a variety of weapons, he would execute his heists swiftly, often leaving before authorities were even alerted.

Life Outside Crime

Remarkably, Gugasian maintained a relatively low profile outside his criminal activities. He lived in a modest home and pursued hobbies like model trains. Those who knew him described him as quiet and introverted. This double life, combined with his careful planning, kept him free from law enforcement's grasp for decades.

Capture and Aftermath

Gugasian's downfall came in the early 2000s. Two boys, while playing in the woods, stumbled upon a stash of his robbery gear. This discovery led to a comprehensive investigation, and through a mix of forensic evidence and surveillance, the authorities closed in on the elusive robber. In 2002, Carl Gugasian was arrested and subsequently sentenced to 17 years in prison. Following his conviction, he cooperated with the FBI, offering insights into his methods and assisting in security consulting.

Legacy of The Friday Night Bank Robber

Gugasian's story is both a tale of criminal cunning and a cautionary account about wasted potential. His intelligence and methodical nature could have been assets in countless legitimate fields. However, his choice to utilize these gifts in the world of crime made him a legend among bank robbers and a case study for criminologists.

Top: Gugasian carried out the robberies on Friday evenings, just before closing time, with few customers present. He wore a Freddie Krueger mask whilst waving his revolver around. Wearing a scent block to disguise his trail, he would escape into nearby woods and stash the evidence in his cache; **Above:** Supposedly the entrance to one of Gugasian's hidden stashes, discovered by kids playing in the woods. Aficionados of Stephen King's *Finders Keepers* might recognize the similarity of this aspect of Gugasian's modus operandi...

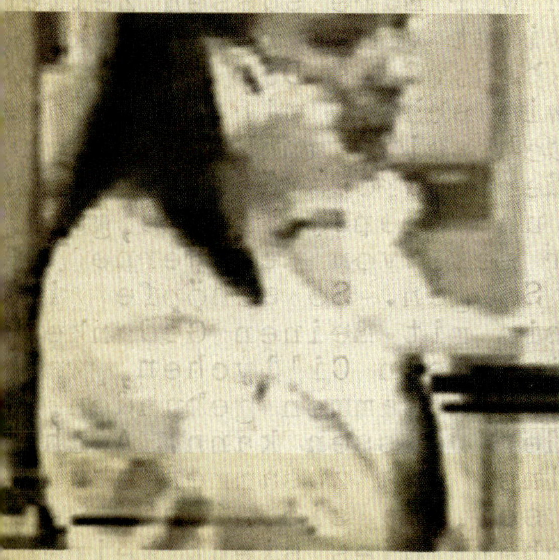

CANDICE ROSE MARTINEZ
THE CELL PHONE BANDIT

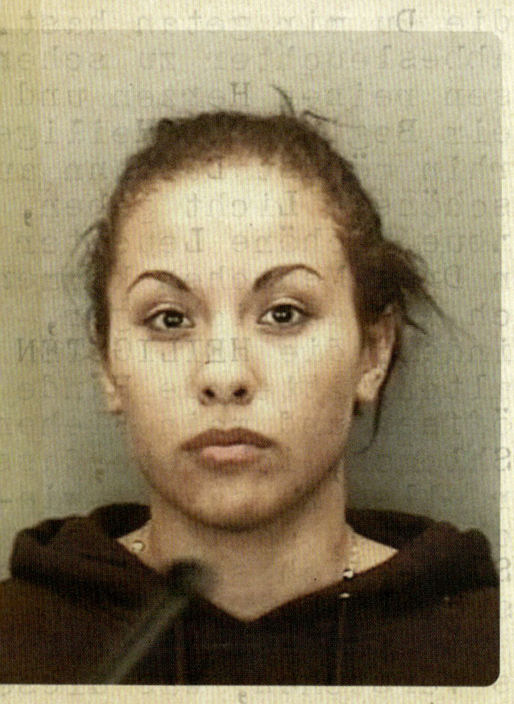

Candice Rose Martinez, often referred to as the "Cell Phone Bandit," emerged in the early 2000s as one of the most unexpected and widely publicized bank robbers in the United States. Her youthful appearance, coupled with her audacious modus operandi, made her a media sensation and added a unique chapter to the annals of American crime.

Unexpected Criminal Beginnings

Born in 1986, Martinez was a college student when she embarked on her criminal path. There was nothing in her early life to suggest a proclivity for crime, making her later actions all the more surprising.

The Cell Phone Heists

In late 2005, Martinez, along with her then-boyfriend Dave Chatram Williams, perpetrated a series of bank robberies in Northern Virginia. What stood out in these robberies was her demeanor: during the heists, she would calmly talk on her cell phone while handing notes to bank tellers demanding cash. This nonchalant attitude, along with her use of the phone, earned her the nickname "Cell Phone Bandit." Over a span of a few weeks, Martinez and Williams successfully robbed four banks, garnering significant media attention and baffling law enforcement.

Capture and Prosecution

The end for Martinez came when a tip led to her identification. Video footage from the banks, widely circulated in the media, played a crucial role in her capture. Martinez was arrested in November 2005, and her involvement in the heists was soon uncovered. During her trial, it was revealed that while Martinez was the face of the robberies,

In late 2005, Martinez, along with her then-boyfriend Dave Chatram Williams, perpetrated a series of bank robberies in Northern Virginia…during the heists, she would calmly talk on her cell phone while handing notes to bank tellers demanding cash…Over the span of a few weeks, Martinez and Williams successfully robbed four banks, garnering significant media attention and baffling law enforcement…

Williams was the mastermind behind them. He would be on the other end of the phone during the heists, guiding and instructing Martinez. Both were found guilty of their crimes.

Aftermath and Reflection

Candice Rose Martinez's story is a cautionary tale about the consequences of poor choices and the influence of negative peer pressure. Her descent into crime was rapid, taking many by surprise, including those who knew her. Martinez was sentenced to 12 years in prison, while Williams received a slightly longer sentence. Following her conviction, Martinez expressed remorse for her actions, acknowledging the pain and fear she had caused her victims.

Legacy

The case of the "Cell Phone Bandit" remains a unique episode in modern crime history. Martinez's youthful appearance, the audacity of the robberies, and the widespread media coverage combined to make this a notable and unusual criminal case. It serves as a reminder that appearances can be deceiving, and that life-altering decisions can sometimes be made in the blink of an eye.

Opposite, top left and top center: CCTV stills of one of Martinez's robberies; **Opposite, top right:** Dave C. Williams, then-boyfriend of Martinez, and on the other end of the line as she carried out each crime; **Opposite, bottom left:** Candice Rose Martinez's mugshot in 2005; **Top:** A candid Candice in a post-release interview; **Above:** Another CCTV still of Martinez.

In 2003 they robbed the Graff store in London and stole $30 million worth of diamonds. In 2007, in Tokyo, they made off with a tiara and necklace also valued at $284 million yens—Japan's biggest-ever jewel robbery and with the entire operation taking about three minutes...

THE PINK PANTHERS AUDACIOUS

Above: The Graff in London was one of the targets of The Pink Panthers; **Top right:** Tokyo at night.

The Pink Panthers, a moniker inspired by the famous Pink Panther comedy films, refers to an international network of jewel thieves primarily from the Balkans. With a reputation for executing some of the most audacious heists in criminal history, their exploits span continents and have resulted in the theft of hundreds of millions of dollars worth of gems.

Origins and Network

Emerging in the early 2000s, The Pink Panthers are believed to have their roots in the Balkans, specifically Serbia and Montenegro. This network, comprising of former soldiers and individuals with military expertise, quickly expanded, recruiting members with a variety of skills essential to their operations.

Modus Operandi

The Pink Panthers are known for their meticulous planning, speed, and the sheer audacity of their heists. Often, they would enter the targeted store posing as customers, surveying the environment and noting any vulnerabilities. Their actual robberies were swift, typically completed within minutes, if not seconds. They often used disguises, luxury cars, and even bikes for quick getaways. One of their hallmark tactics was the use of vehicles to smash into stores, allowing quick access and escape, now infamously termed as "smash-and-grab" robberies.

Notable Heists

Several high-profile heists can be attributed to this group. In 2003 they robbed the Graff store in London and stole $30 million worth of diamonds. In 2007, in Tokyo, they made off with a tiara and necklace also valued at more than $284 million yens—Japan's biggest-ever jewel robbery and with the entire operation about three minutes. Their series of heists in Dubai, Switzerland, Monaco, and many other countries have added to their lore, making them one of the most sought-after criminal syndicates globally.

Capture and Ongoing Pursuits

Given their international operations, the Pink Panthers have been pursued by law enforcement agencies from various countries, often collaborating in their efforts. Over the years, several members have been captured, leading to substantial insights into their operations. However, many still remain at large, with reports of their activities continuing to emerge. Interpol set up a dedicated task force named "Pink Panthers Project" to coordinate international efforts to apprehend members of this elusive group.

A Legacy of Glamour and Crime

The Pink Panthers have left an indelible mark on the world of crime. Their operations, often characterized by precision, audacity, and a flair for drama, have both frustrated and fascinated law enforcement and the public alike. While their actions have been widely condemned, their reputation as some of the most skillful and daring thieves in recent history is undoubted.

Top: Casino hotels in Dubai are also prime targets for the Pink Panthers organization; **Above:** Diamonds are precious and are often stolen by criminals.

CHAPTER THREE

GANGSTERS

The term "gangster" conjures images of ruthless outlaws, shadowy figures who command both fear and fascination. This chapter delves into the lives of some of the most notorious gangsters who have ever orchestrated crime on the streets. These are the individuals and groups who built criminal empires, defying the law with a mix of charisma, brutality, and cunning. Their stories are woven into the fabric of the societies they operated within, often becoming larger-than-life legends.

Gangsters have played a significant role in the underworld, their influence extending beyond mere criminal activities to impact the economic and political spheres of their times. They are the godfathers and kingpins, the mob bosses and cartel leaders who have turned organized crime into a global phenomenon. From the Prohibition-era bootleggers to the modern-day drug lords, each biography in this chapter will explore the ascent of these criminal masterminds, the power structures they created, and the violence that often accompanied their rise to infamy.

The capture or downfall of these gangsters often comes with a heavy price, marked by bloody power struggles, relentless law enforcement efforts, and sometimes, their own hubris. Their stories are cautionary tales of what happens when the pursuit of power goes unchecked, and the law's long arm finally reaches those who once seemed untouchable.

A Mafia hit, 1990. Details and exact date unknown.

Capone himself became a high-profile figure in Chicago society...but despite his notoriety he was well-liked by many Chicagoans for his charitable activities, such as opening soup kitchens during the Great Depression...

AL CAPONE THE ENIGMATIC BOOTLEGGER

Alphonse Gabriel Capone, commonly known as Al Capone, was born on January 17, 1899, in Brooklyn, New York, to Italian immigrants Gabriele and Teresina Capone. Raised in a rough neighborhood, he was expelled from school at 14 for hitting a teacher, effectively ending his formal education.

Rise to Infamy

Al Capone moved to Chicago in his early twenties and quickly climbed the ranks of Johnny Torrio's crime syndicate. After Torrio retired following an assassination attempt, Capone took over as the de facto leader of the organization. His bootlegging operations flourished during the Prohibition era, a period from 1920 to 1933 when the sale, production, and transportation of alcohol were illegal in the United States. Capone's empire included speakeasies, gambling houses, brothels, and a network of breweries and distilleries. Under Capone, the Chicago Outfit's profits soared into the millions, and Capone himself became a high-profile figure in Chicago society,

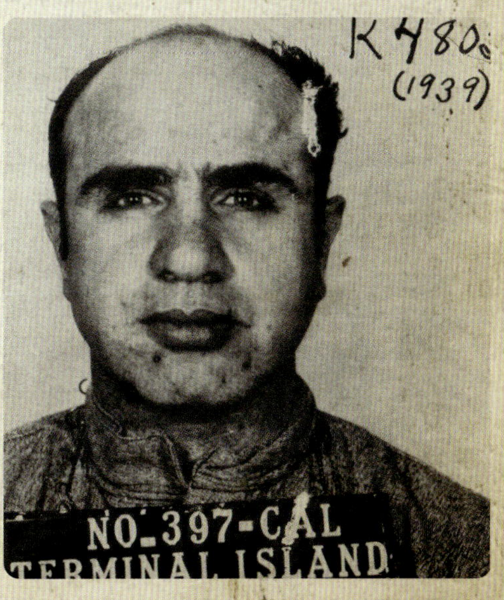

frequently appearing in newspaper articles and attending major events. Despite his notoriety, he was well-liked by many Chicagoans for his charitable activities, such as opening soup kitchens during the Great Depression.

Notable Crimes and Activities

Al Capone was involved in a myriad of criminal activities, but his name is most often associated with the St. Valentine's Day Massacre in 1929. Though never officially linked to the crime, it was widely assumed that Capone orchestrated the killing of seven members of Chicago's North Side Gang during a gunfight. This event significantly diminished public favor towards Capone and led to increased federal scrutiny.

Capture and Imprisonment

Ironically, it was not murder or racketeering that led to Capone's downfall, but tax evasion. Unable to pin any violent crimes on him, the federal government charged him with income tax evasion in 1931. He was found guilty and sentenced to 11 years in federal prison. He spent some time in Atlanta U.S. Penitentiary before being transferred to Alcatraz, the notorious island prison, where he would serve most of his sentence.

Later Life and Death

While in prison, Capone's health rapidly deteriorated due to complications from syphilis, which he had contracted in his youth. Released on parole in 1939 for good behavior and because of his failing health, Capone lived the remainder of his life in seclusion at his estate in Palm Island, Florida. He died on January 25, 1947, of cardiac arrest after suffering a stroke. Al Capone remains one of the most infamous and enigmatic figures in American criminal history. His life has been the subject of countless books, documentaries, and films, each attempting to unravel the complex man behind the enduring legend.

Opposite, above left: Al Capone, the enigmatic bootlegger; **Opposite, right:** Capone's bomb- and bullet-proof Cadillac in 1933; **Opposite, bottom left:** Capone's 1931 mugshot; **This page, top left:** "Free Soup, Coffee and Doughnuts"—opened by Capone to help ameliorate the dire consequences of the Depression; **Right, top to bottom:** Capone—an exuberant personality; Young people drink Old Log Cabin bootleg whiskey during Prohibition in Chicago in 1927. The label "Old Log Cabin" was actually Canadian Club Whiskey, imported by Capone and Bugs Moran then rebottled and distributed in the Chicago area; Capone's 1939 Alcatraz mugshot.

THE ST. VALENTINE'S DAY MASSACRE

This image spread: The St. Valentine's Day Massacre was the murder of seven members of Chicago's North Side Gang on the morning of February 14, 1929. The men were lured into a meeting at a Chicago auto garage, then lined up against a wall and shot by four gunmen—two of whom were disguised as police officers. The Massacre arose from the competition for control of organized crime in the city during Prohibition, between the Irish North Siders, headed by George "Bugs" Moran, and their Italian Chicago Outfit rivals—run by Al Capone. The killers have never been conclusively identified...

MA BARKER MYTH OR REALITY?

Arizona Donnie Clark, commonly known as "Ma" Barker, was born on October 8, 1873, in Ash Grove, Missouri. Little is known about her early life, but by the early 20th century, she had married George Barker and was raising four sons: Herman, Lloyd, Arthur (also known as "Doc"), and Fred. The Barker family, particularly the sons, would go on to gain notoriety as criminals involved in a string of robberies, kidnappings, and other illicit activities.

The Barker-Karpis Gang

During the 1930s, at the height of the Public Enemy era, the Barker sons joined forces with Alvin Karpis, forming the infamous Barker-Karpis Gang. They embarked on a series of high-profile crimes across the Midwest, making headlines and drawing the attention of law enforcement, including the FBI.

Myth and Reality

While the Barker sons and Karpis were undoubtedly deeply involved in criminal activities, the extent of Ma Barker's involvement remains a subject of debate. Popular media and the FBI portrayed her as the mastermind behind the gang's operations, controlling and directing her sons in their criminal pursuits. This portrayal earned her the reputation of "the most vicious, dangerous, and resourceful criminal brain of the last

decade." However, later accounts, including statements by Karpis, suggested that while Ma Barker was aware of her sons' activities and was fiercely loyal to them, she might not have been the criminal genius she was portrayed to be. Instead, she may have been more of a motherly figure, providing care and support without directly orchestrating the crimes.

Downfall and Death

The law caught up with the Barkers on January 16, 1935. Acting on a tip, the FBI located Ma and her son Fred in a rented house in Ocklawaha, Florida. A fierce gun battle ensued, lasting several hours. When the shooting ceased and agents entered the house, they found the bodies of Ma and Fred Barker; both had been killed in the firefight.

Legacy and Cultural Impact

Ma Barker's image as a ruthless matriarch leading her sons in a life of crime captured the public's imagination. Over the years, her story has been the subject of numerous books, films, and songs, often blurring the lines between fact and fiction. In popular culture, Ma Barker stands as a symbol of the lawless era of the 1930s, challenging traditional gender roles and societal expectations. Her tale is a testament to the power of myth-making and the allure of the criminal underworld in the American psyche.

Opposite, above left: Arizona Clark—"Ma" Barker, circa 1930; **Opposite, top right:** Ma Barker (right), and her son Fred (second right) with neighbors, during the time they spent in Ocklawaha, Florida; **Opposite, center right:** The Barkers' rented house in Ocklawaha, by Lake Weir; **Opposite, below left:** Fred Barker; **Left, above and top:** Press photos of the rented house after the extensive shootout with the FBI; **Right, top:** J. Edgar Hoover, Director of the FBI, effectively from 1924–1972; **Above:** Shelley Winters in the 1970 movie *Bloody Mama*. Directed by Roger Corman, it's based largely on the myths of Ma Barker's life.

Dillinger's criminal activities were extensively covered by the media, making him one of America's first "celebrity criminals"...

JOHN DILLINGER
THE BANK ROBBER CELEBRITY

Born on June 22, 1903, in Indianapolis, Indiana, John Herbert Dillinger lived in a middle-class household marred by an unstable family environment. His mother passed away when he was just four years old, and the absence of maternal guidance left a lasting impression on him. His early life was largely nondescript, though young Dillinger exhibited a proclivity for petty mischief and rebellion.

Entry into Criminal Life

Dillinger's foray into crime began with a failed mugging at the age of 21, which landed him in prison for nearly a decade. The experience was transformative, acting as a criminal finishing school where he met seasoned bank robbers and other felons. Upon his parole in 1933, the United States was deep in the throes of the Great Depression, offering few legitimate prospects for men like Dillinger.

A Wave of Crime

Choosing instead a life of outlawry, he became involved in a series of increasingly audacious bank robberies across the Midwest. Flanked by his gang—comprised of seasoned criminals like Baby Face Nelson and Homer Van Meter—

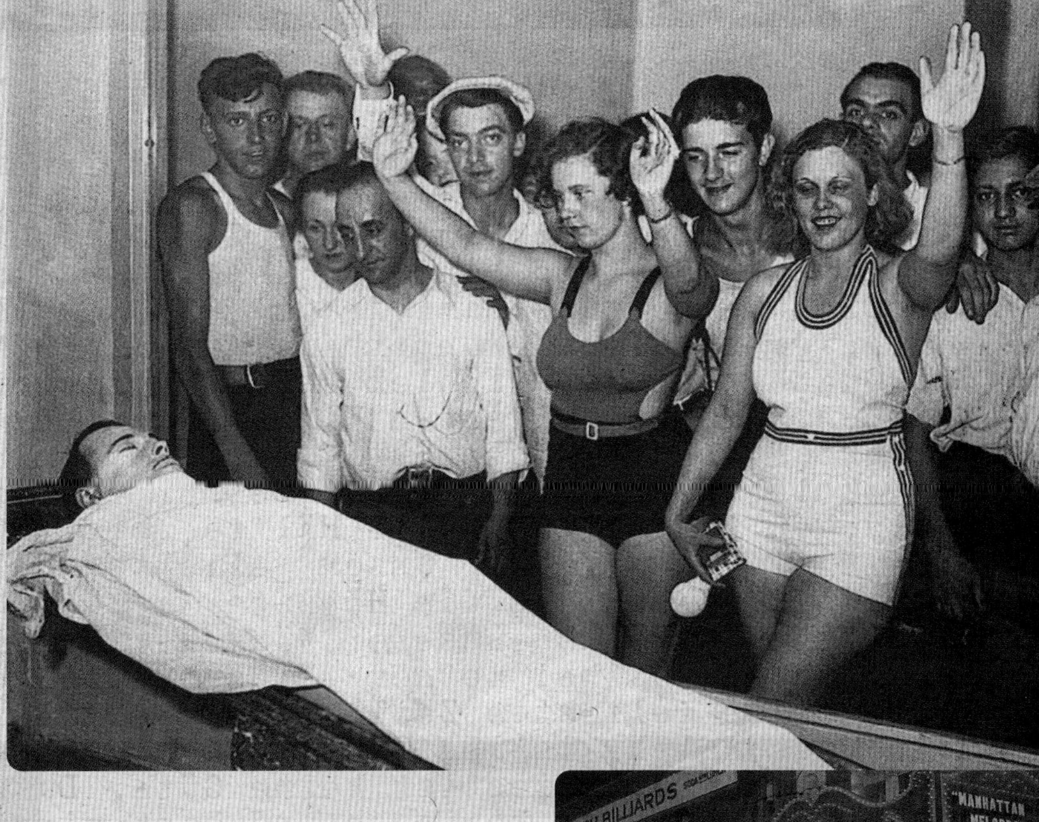

Dillinger became a folk hero of sorts. He was able to elude capture multiple times, even breaking out of prison twice, further enhancing his legendary status. The gang's exploits were violent, often involving shootouts with law enforcement, but they also displayed tactical sophistication; Dillinger's gang used bulletproof vests, mapped out escape routes for getaway cars in advance, and established specific roles for each member of the gang.

Media Sensation and Public Perception

Dillinger's criminal activities were extensively covered by the media, making him one of America's first "celebrity criminals." The public was oddly captivated by his daring escapades, partly because banks, often seen as culprits of the financial collapse, were his primary targets. However, the FBI labeled him as Public Enemy No. 1, intensifying the manhunt for his capture.

Capture and Death

The end for Dillinger came on the night of July 22, 1934, outside Chicago's Biograph Theater. Betrayed by a companion, Anna Sage, Dillinger was ambushed by federal agents as he left the movie theater. Despite his attempts to flee, he was shot and killed. His death was as sensational as his life, witnessed by a crowd and widely publicized, solidifying his place in the annals of American criminal history.

Lasting Impact and Cultural Legacy

Dillinger's life and crimes have been the subject of numerous films, books, and articles. From documentaries that attempt to demystify the man to Hollywood adaptations that romanticize his exploits, Dillinger remains an enduring symbol of 1930s American outlaw culture. Though his criminal career was short-lived, lasting barely more than a year, the mythology surrounding John Dillinger is outsized. He is often depicted as a symbol of defiance against a system perceived as corrupt, even if his actions caused pain and loss for many. Dillinger stands as an enigmatic figure, reflecting America's complex relationship with crime and celebrity.

Opposite, center: A young Dillinger's police mugshot; **Opposite, below:** Dillinger gets pally with Prosecuting Attorney, Robert Estill (center), and Sheriff Lillian Holley (left), his jailer, as the three pose for the press, at Crown Point Jail, Indiana; **Main image, above:** The corpse of John Dillinger in Chicago's Cook County Morgue, with press photographers and onlookers allowed open access. It's estimated over 15,000 visited the body in 24 hours; **Above, left:** Dillinger poses with submachine gun in one hand and homemade imitation handgun with which he escaped jail in the other; **Above:** A large crowd has gathered outside the Biograph Theater, in the aftermath of Dillinger's ambush and shooting by federal agents on the night of July 22, 1934.

BONNIE & CLYDE ROBBERIES, CAR CHASES AND SHOOTOUTS

Bonnie Elizabeth Parker was born on October 1, 1910, in Rowena, Texas, while Clyde Chestnut Barrow came into the world on March 24, 1909, in Ellis County, Texas. Both endured economic hardship in their early lives, particularly during the Great Depression. Bonnie aspired to be a singer and poet but worked as a waitress, and Clyde, initially an amateur musician, quickly turned to a life of crime, including petty thefts and burglaries.

The Fateful Meeting

The two met in 1930 in West Dallas, Texas, and the chemistry was instantaneous. Bonnie was married at the time but estranged from her husband, and Clyde was a small-time criminal with grand ambitions. Their relationship was not only passionate but also mutually reinforcing in their criminal endeavors.

The Crime Spree Begins

Shortly after they met, Clyde was imprisoned for robbery. Bonnie smuggled a gun into the prison to aid his escape, although he was quickly recaptured. After his release, they reunited and embarked on a series of bank robberies and heists that spanned multiple states, from Texas to Iowa and even as far north as Minnesota. Their exploits included armed robberies, car thefts, and kidnappings, often executed with a brazenness that shocked and captivated the public.

The Barrow Gang

Joined by various accomplices, including Clyde's older brother, Buck, and his wife, Blanche, the duo became part of the notorious "Barrow Gang." The group was infamous for their violent methods, including shootouts with law enforcement. While they were viewed as

dangerous criminals, some also saw them as modern-day Robin Hoods, rebelling against a system that seemed stacked against the common man.

Eluding the Law

Bonnie and Clyde seemed almost invincible, evading capture via high-speed car chases and dramatic shootouts with the police. Their audacity and Bonnie's penned poems sent to newspapers only added to their mystique. They weren't just criminals; they were folk legends, albeit ones who left a trail of destruction in their wake.

The Bloody End

Their criminal odyssey came to an abrupt end on May 23, 1934, in Bienville Parish, Louisiana. Law enforcement, having caught wind of their whereabouts, set up an ambush. As Bonnie and Clyde drove down a rural road, they were met with a hail of bullets that took their lives. Their deaths were as sensational as their lives, with crowds gathering to see their bullet-ridden car and lifeless bodies.

Cultural Afterlife and Legacy

The story of Bonnie and Clyde has been immortalized in numerous forms of media. Their life and dramatic demise were the subject of the 1967 film *Bonnie and Clyde*, which was both a commercial and critical success. More recently, documentaries, books, and television shows continue to dissect their relationship, their crimes, and their enduring impact on American folklore.

In Retrospect

Despite the romanticism that often surrounds their story, it's important to remember the reality: Bonnie and Clyde were responsible for multiple murders and a swath of crimes that spread terror across the Central United States. Yet, their story remains embedded in the American psyche—a complex tale of love, ambition, and lawlessness during one of the most challenging periods in American history.

Opposite page: The iconic series of photos that the gang took of themselves, and which did much to plant their legend into the minds of the United States public; **This page, top left:** Frank Hamer, the former Texas Ranger who masterminded the successful ambush of Bonnie & Clyde; **Top right and center right:** The bullet-riddled car with the two dead outlaws. There were 112 bullet holes, over 40 had struck the couple. The gunfire was so loud that the posse was temporarily deafened that afternoon; **Above:** Still from the set of *Bonnie and Clyde*, 1967. From left: Gene Hackman as Buck Barrow, Estelle Parsons as Blanche Barrow, Warren Beatty as Clyde Barrow, Faye Dunaway as Bonnie Parker, and Michael J. Pollard as C.W. Moss.

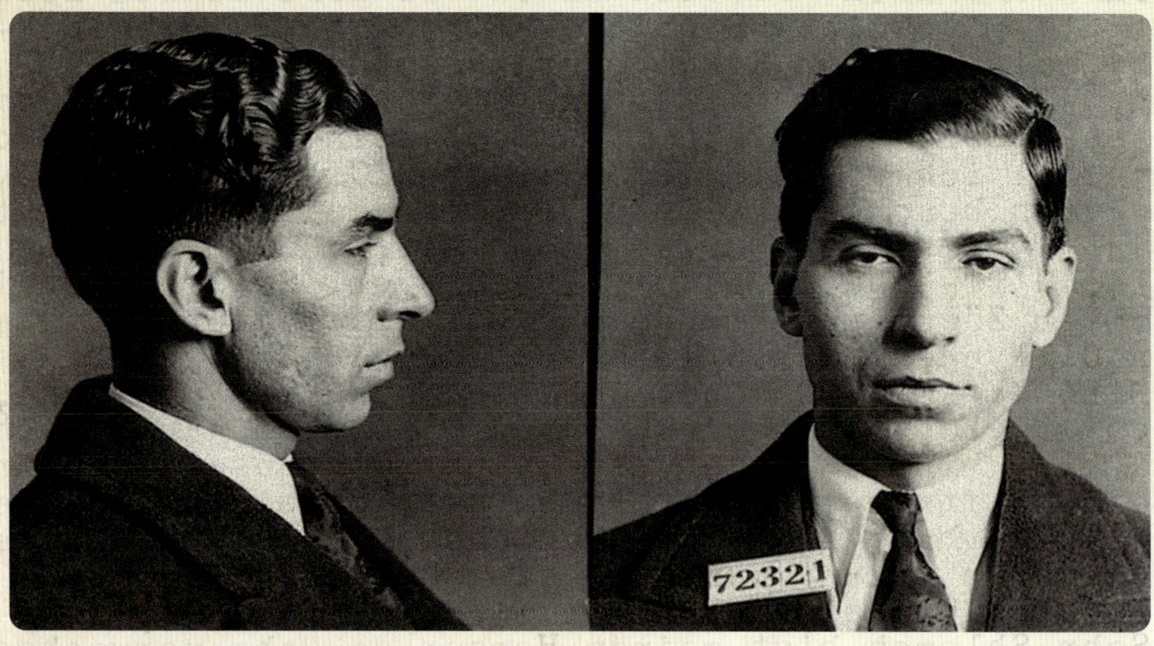

CHARLES "LUCKY" LUCIANO
MASTERMINDING THE MAFIA

Salvatore Lucania, known to the world as Charles "Lucky" Luciano, was born on November 24, 1897, in Lercara Friddi, Sicily. In search of better opportunities, his family immigrated to the United States in 1906, making their new home in New York's Lower East Side. Life in America was far from idyllic, however, as young Salvatore quickly became accustomed to the hardships and violence that pervaded his immigrant neighborhood.

Pathway to Criminal Ascendancy

Luciano didn't waste much time falling into petty crime. As a teenager, he was involved in a variety of schemes, including extortion and drug trafficking. His criminal endeavors led him to cross paths with other rising figures in the underworld, such as Meyer Lansky and Benjamin "Bugsy" Siegel. Their alliances would prove to be long-lasting and highly influential.

Criminal Exploits and The Syndicate

Luciano earned his nickname "Lucky" not just through happenstance but through a brutal mix of cunning, ambition, and occasional violence. In the early 1930s, he orchestrated the assassination of two leading mob bosses, Joe Masseria and Salvatore Maranzano, effectively consolidating power and giving birth to what would become the modern American Mafia. Luciano's real innovation came with the formation of The Commission, a governing body for organized crime families across the United States. This framework brought a degree of order and efficiency to the underworld, proving highly lucrative for those involved. Luciano's empire branched into various forms of illegal

activities—gambling, loan-sharking, and of course, bootlegging during the Prohibition era.

Legal Troubles and Imprisonment

In 1936, Luciano's world came tumbling down when he was convicted on compulsory prostitution charges. He was sentenced to 30 to 50 years in prison, where he continued to run his empire by appointing his consigliere as acting boss in his absence. However, in 1942, World War II offered him a chance at redemption. Luciano allegedly assisted U.S. naval intelligence in safeguarding New York Harbor in exchange for a more lenient prison sentence. True to the deal, his sentence was commuted in 1946, after which he was deported to Italy.

Final Years and Legacy

Although banished from American soil, Luciano still managed to exert considerable influence in criminal activities across the Atlantic. He continued to operate in the drug trade and other illegal enterprises until his death in Naples on January 26, 1962, from a heart attack. Luciano's impact on organized crime in America is nothing short of transformative. By institutionalizing the Mafia and setting up frameworks for criminal activities, he imparted a legacy of organized crime that endures to this day.

Cultural Resonance

The life and myth of Lucky Luciano have inspired a multitude of films, books, and television series. His tale captures the essence of a self-made man, albeit one who chose a life steeped in crime and corruption. As such, he remains a complex figure—both reviled and romanticized—in the annals of American history.

Opposite, top: Luciano's mugshot, circa 1936; **Opposite, bottom left:** Luciano's NYPD mugshot from April 1936. By the time of this picture, Luciano had already organized the assassination of gang bosses Joe Masseria and Salvatore Maranzano; **Above:** Four gangsters in the line-up for the police photographer, 1920s. Left to right: Ed Diamond, his older brother Jack "Legs" Diamond (the ace bootlegger), Fatty Walsh, and Lucky Luciano.

MEYER LANSKY THE MOB'S FINANCIAL GENIUS

Meyer Lansky was born Maier Suchowlansky on July 4, 1902, in Grodno, then part of the Russian Empire and now in Belarus. Lansky immigrated to the United States with his family in 1911, settling in New York City's Lower East Side. Living in a tough neighborhood and facing anti-Semitic prejudices, Lansky quickly became street-smart, which served as his introduction to a life of crime.

Rise to Infamy

Lansky's entry into organized crime came through his friendship with Benjamin "Bugsy" Siegel, whom he met as a teenager. Together, they formed a small gang involved in theft and illegal gambling. Lansky gained a reputation for his intelligence and business acumen, which led him to form alliances with other influential mob figures, such as Charles "Lucky" Luciano and Frank Costello. In the 1930s, Lansky was instrumental in the formation of the National Crime Syndicate, an alliance of Italian-American and Jewish mobsters. He primarily focused on gambling operations and soon expanded his interests to include casinos in Las Vegas, Cuba, and other parts of the Caribbean.

Notable Crimes and Activities

Meyer Lansky is often considered the "Mob's Accountant," credited with creating a financial network for organized crime that was both sophisticated and impenetrable to law enforcement. He was involved in various illegal ventures, including gambling, loan-sharking, and even narcotics, though he always publicly denied any involvement in drug trafficking. During World War II, Lansky and other mob figures cooperated

with the U.S. government in a partnership dubbed "Operation Underworld," aimed at protecting the East Coast's ports from Axis spies and saboteurs.

Capture and Imprisonment

Unlike many of his contemporaries, Lansky managed to avoid long stints in prison. He was indicted several times but was either acquitted or the charges were dropped. In the early 1970s, he fled to Israel to escape tax evasion charges but was eventually deported back to the U.S. In 1973, he was acquitted of federal income tax evasion, a significant legal victory for him.

Later Life and Death

After the acquittal, Lansky lived a relatively quiet life in Miami Beach, Florida. Though he had amassed significant wealth, various legal battles and seizures had dwindled his fortune. He died of lung cancer on January 15, 1983.

Legacy

Meyer Lansky remains one of the most enigmatic figures in American organized crime history. His influence stretched beyond the underworld into business and even politics, both domestically and internationally. His life inspired several characters in films and literature, most notably Hyman Roth in "The Godfather Part II." Lansky's ability to elude significant jail time, coupled with his financial genius in organizing criminal enterprises, has made him a subject of fascination and study. His story serves as a window into the complex interplay between organized crime, business, and politics in the 20th century.

Opposite, top left: Lansky in 1958; **Opposite, top right:** Lansky photographed arriving for his trial in 1973; **Opposite, bottom left:** Lansky's mugshot from 1949; **Above:** The diminutive Lansky, typically in the center of things with his close associate Lucky Luciano. From left to right: Paul Ricca, Salvatore Agoglia, Lucky Luciano, Meyer Lansky, John Senna, and Harry Brown, in a police shot from 1932.

STEPHANIE ST. CLAIR HARLEM'S QUEEN OF NUMBERS

Above: A young Stephanie St. Clair, photographed during her early twenties, circa 1920, when she was at the outset of her criminal career.

Stephanie St. Clair was born on December 24, 1897, in Martinique, the French-speaking Caribbean island. After her mother died in 1910 she immigrated to Canada. By 1912 she had made her way to the United States and learned English along the way. Like many immigrants of her era, sought the promise of a better life in Harlem, New York. The district she encountered was rife with racial tensions and economic struggles—but also opportunities for those willing to seize them.

Rise to Prominence

Amidst the backdrop of the Harlem Renaissance, St. Clair carved a niche for herself in the world of organized crime. Recognizing the profitability of the illegal numbers game, or policy banking, she established her own operation, quickly earning the moniker "Queen of Numbers." Under her leadership, the operation flourished, demonstrating both her business acumen and her fearlessness.

Clashes and Challenges

Stephanie St. Clair's ascent was not without challenges. The more established male-dominated criminal syndicates, particularly Dutch Schultz's outfit, sought to push her out of the lucrative numbers game. However, with determination and tactical alliances, including hiring the notorious Bumpy Johnson as her chief enforcer, St. Clair managed to hold her ground against her rivals. In addition to her skirmishes with other crime figures, St. Clair was a vocal

critic of police corruption. She openly challenged and exposed police officers on her payroll, making her both an adversary and an asset to law enforcement.

Advocate for Justice and Later Life

Beyond her life in crime, St. Clair was deeply committed to the well-being of Harlem's African American community. She became an advocate for justice, using her wealth to support civil rights causes and local community endeavors. After the numbers game was eventually legalized and transformed into the state lottery, St. Clair retired from crime but remained an influential figure in her community. In her later years, St. Clair continued her advocacy, penning essays and speaking out against police brutality, racism, and other social injustices faced by African Americans.

Legacy and Impact

Stephanie St. Clair passed away in 1969, but her legacy as one of the few women, and even fewer Black women, to achieve prominence in the male-dominated world of early 20th-century organized crime endures. Beyond her criminal exploits, her dedication to racial and social justice has cemented her status as an iconic figure in Harlem's storied history.

Cultural Resonance

St. Clair's life has been the subject of numerous articles, books, and films, with her story being featured in the movie "Hoodlum." Her journey—from a young immigrant with dreams of a better life to a powerful crime boss and advocate for justice—reflects the complexities of the American experience and challenges the traditional narratives of organized crime.

Opposite, top left: In 1936 St. Clair met and married Sufi Abdul Hamid, (pictured right), an eccentric Black activist and anti-semite who was also in charge of his own mosque. Their marriage was stormy—and short. In 1938 St. Clair shot, but did not kill him; **Opposite, top right:** St. Clair is photographed after her arrest for shooting Hamid. Found guilty by an all-white jury, she was released in the early 1940s; **Above, main image:** St. Clair after her release in the early 1940s. Steering clear of criminal enterprise and fully focussing on her activism, she publicized discrimination against Black people in Harlem and the often illegal tactics employed in the name of justice. She died in 1969, at age 72; **Top right:** Bumpy Johnson, St. Clair's enforcer; **Above right:** Dutch Schulz, St. Clair's main rival for control of the Harlem Numbers Game.

KAZUO TAOKA THE GODFATHER

Above: Known as the "Godfather of Godfathers," Taoka was third *kumicho* (boss) of the Yamaguchi-gumi, Japan's largest yakuza organization, from 1946 to 1981; **Top left:** Taoka pictured with his daughter in the 1960s; **Top right:** In 1957 Taoka set up and registered Kobe Geinosha (Kobe Performing Arts Promotion) under his own name. The Yamaguchi-gumi had become Japan's largest organized crime gang, and they quickly become the most powerful showbiz brokers in Japan.

Kazuo Taoka, often referred to as the "Godfather of Godfathers" within the Yakuza community—the Japanese mob—was born on March 28, 1913, in Tokushima Prefecture, Japan. Delving into the world of crime at a young age, Taoka began his journey as a street hustler and quickly earned a reputation for his tenacity and fearlessness.

Leadership of Yamaguchi-gumi

Taoka's ascension to power was marked by his takeover of the Yamaguchi-gumi in 1946, following the death of its previous leader. Under his leadership, the Yamaguchi-gumi transformed from a local gang into Japan's most dominant and formidable Yakuza syndicate. At its peak, the organization had a presence across Japan, with influence seeping into various sectors, from entertainment to politics.

Expanding Influence and Challenges

Over the decades, Taoka expanded the gang's

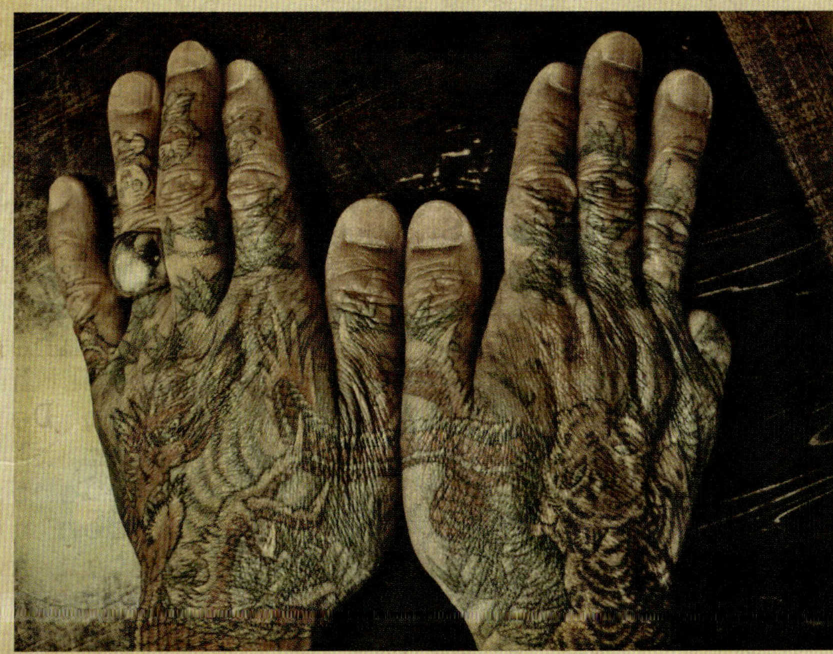

OF GODFATHERS

operations into diverse criminal ventures, including gambling, prostitution, and drug trafficking. However, his leadership wasn't without challenges. Throughout the 1960s and 1970s, the Yamaguchi-gumi faced internal strife and rival gang conflicts. Yet, Taoka's tactical genius and iron-fisted leadership style ensured the syndicate's supremacy in Japan's underworld.

Personal Life and Death

Despite being a feared figure in the world of organized crime, Taoka was known to have a charismatic personality and was fiercely loyal to his allies. He evaded numerous assassination attempts during his life but was severely wounded in 1978 when a rival gang member attacked him. While he survived the attempt, his health deteriorated over the subsequent years. On July 23, 1981, Kazuo Taoka passed away from a heart attack.

Legacy in the Yakuza World

Kazuo Taoka's influence on the Yakuza and organized crime in Japan is profound. Under his reign, the Yamaguchi-gumi rose to unparalleled prominence, setting the standard for other Yakuza groups. Even today, Taoka's strategies, leadership style, and legacy continue to shape the dynamics of the Yakuza world.

Top left: Hands of the Yakuza; **Top right:** Yakuza code is harsh and infractions by members are treated seriously—first offenders must cut off the top of the pinky. A second offence loses the the tip of the ring finger, and so on. The practice is dying out though, as police are more easily able to identify gang members; **Above:** The Godfather in his later years, surrounded by his people.

James Joseph Bulger Jr., known as "Whitey" due to his platinum blond hair, was born on September 3, 1929, in Boston, Massachusetts. Raised in a working-class family in South Boston, Bulger's youth was marked by poverty and hardship. His father worked as a laborer, and the family lived in cramped public housing. At an early age, Bulger demonstrated a proclivity for trouble, which eventually escalated into more serious criminal activities. He was arrested for the first time at age 14, and several times more over the years. Later in life, after serving nine years in federal prison for a 1956 arrest, Bulger claimed that he had been used as a test subject in the CIA's controversial MK-ULTRA program while incarcerated.

Rise to Infamy

In the 1970s, Bulger rose to prominence as a feared mobster and the leader of the Winter Hill Gang, an Irish-American organized crime syndicate based in Boston. The gang was involved in a range of criminal activities, including loan-sharking, bookmaking, extortion, and drug trafficking. Under Bulger's leadership, the Winter Hill Gang became one of the most powerful criminal organizations in New England. In a shocking twist, it was later revealed that Bulger had been an FBI informant since 1975, feeding information about the Italian-American Patriarca crime family, the Winter Hill Gang's main rivals. This relationship allowed him to evade law enforcement scrutiny for many years, as the Winter Hill Gang's activities were overlooked in exchange for the information Bulger provided.

Notable Crimes and Activities

Bulger was implicated in a litany of crimes, including drug distribution, extortion, armed robbery, and arms trafficking. However, it was his involvement in at least 19 murders that made him a particularly notorious figure. Some

JAMES "WHITEY" BULGER
A LIFETIME OF CRIME

of these killings were allegedly committed to eliminate potential witnesses or informants against him. Despite being one of America's most wanted criminals, Bulger successfully evaded capture for over 16 years. This period of his life was shrouded in mystery and involved numerous aliases and hideouts.

Capture and Imprisonment

Whitey Bulger's luck ran out in June 2011 when he was arrested in Santa Monica, California, along with his longtime companion, Catherine Greig. He was subsequently tried and convicted of 31 counts of racketeering, money laundering, extortion, and firearms violations, including his involvement in 11 murders. In November 2013, he was sentenced to two consecutive life terms plus five years.

Later Life and Death

Bulger's life came to a violent end on October 30, 2018, just a day after he was transferred to the U.S. Penitentiary, Hazelton, in West Virginia. Bulger, who by this time was 89 years old and in a wheelchair, was beaten to death by inmates. Some four years later, prisoners Sean McKinnon, Fotios Geas, and Paul DeCologero were eventually charged with conspiracy to commit his murder.

Legacy

Whitey Bulger's life has inspired several books, documentaries, and even Hollywood films, most notably "Black Mass," where Johnny Depp portrayed him. His story is not just a tale of criminal exploits but also an unsettling narrative about corruption within the ranks of the FBI. He remains a cautionary tale in the annals of American organized crime and law enforcement, showing how lines can blur dangerously when authorities make deals with criminals.

Above: Jack Nicholson and Matt Damon in *The Departed*, 2006, loosely based on Bulger's lifestory; **Top right:** Johnny Depp as Bulger in *Black Mass*, 2015; **Top left:** Bulger's police mugshot from March 1953; **Opposite, top:** Bulger in his early twenties; **Opposite, below:** Bulger's police mugshot from July 1956.

THE KRAY TWINS PSYCHOTIC MOB RULE IN THE EAST END

Top left: Reggie (left) and Ronnie Kray drinking tea at their mother Violet's house, circa 1966; **Top right:** The Blind Beggar on Whitechapel Road, after Ronnie Kray's shooting of rival gangster George Cornell; **Above:** In their teenage years the Kray twins were experienced and proficient boxers. Ronnie Kray is on the left.

Born just minutes apart on October 24, 1933, in London's East End, Reggie and Ronnie Kray were inseparable from the start. The twins grew up in a close-knit family but were exposed early to London's gritty underbelly. Their maternal grandfather introduced them to boxing at an early age, because their father was often absent, dodging military service and engaging in petty crimes. This environment made an impression on the young twins, shaping their future in ways unimaginable at the time.

Climbing the Criminal Ladder

In their late teens and early twenties, the Krays dabbled in various illicit ventures, from running protection rackets to engaging in organized brawls. Quickly gaining a reputation for ruthlessness, they leveraged their charisma and toughness to build the notorious criminal enterprise known as "The Firm." With a mix of brute force and keen business acumen, they established themselves as dominant figures in London's underworld.

Activities and Criminal Exploits

Rather than being mere gangsters, the twins fashioned themselves as celebrities of the criminal world, socializing with politicians and stars alike. Their activities spanned a variety of illegal enterprises, including armed robbery, arson, and protection rackets. Yet, it was their involvement in the darker aspects of crime—like murder—that made headlines. While Reggie was often considered the more level-headed of the two, Ronnie was diagnosed as a paranoid schizophrenic, adding an unpredictable element to their operations. One of their most infamous acts was the killing of George Cornell, a rival gangster, at the Blind Beggar pub on Whitechapel Road, executed without emotion by Ronnie.

Daily Mirror

GUILTY OF MURDER

The Kray Firm's 'directors' . . Reginald, left, and his twin brother Ronald. Picture by DAVID BAILEY

The Kray twins will be sentenced today

THE Kray Firm is finally out of business. The twin "directors," Ronald and Reginald Kray, were convicted last night of murder.

Gallery

Turn to Back Page

BACKGROUND TO MURDER

See Pages 4 and 5 and MIRRORSCOPE Pages 15-18

The Krays' biographer argues that their mother was responsible for the malignant narcissism the twins would display as adults by encouraging them to think of themselves as extraordinary, whilst also pandering to their every whim.

Legal Reckoning and Imprisonment

In 1968, after years of eluding the law, the Kray twins were finally arrested and charged with an array of offenses, including murder. The trial captivated the nation and ended in both twins being convicted. They were sentenced to life imprisonment, with a recommended minimum of thirty years. Ronnie was incarcerated at Broadmoor Hospital for the criminally insane, while Reggie spent most of his time in various mainstream prisons.

Endings and Aftermath

Ronnie Kray died of a heart attack in Broadmoor Hospital on March 17, 1995, while Reggie, after being diagnosed with bladder cancer, was released on compassionate grounds in 2000. He lived for a mere five weeks after his release, eventually succumbing to his illness.

Eternal Infamy

Their story continues to captivate the public imagination, cementing their status as icons of 20th-century British crime history. The lives and misdeeds of the Kray twins have inspired numerous books, documentaries, and films, including the movie "Legend," starring Tom Hardy in dual roles as both twins. The Kray twins' saga serves as a compelling study in the psychology of crime, the lure of power, and the complexities of sibling relationships. Even in death, their infamy endures, turning them into dark legends who continue to haunt the collective consciousness of Britain.

Top, left to right: George Cornell; Jack "the hat" McVitie, a Krays associate who was stabbed to death by Reggie Kray; Daily Mirror front page from Wednesday, March 5, 1969, the morning after the Kray Twins had been found guilty at The Old Bailey; **Center:** Ronnie and Reggie Kray with their mother Violet; **Left:** The twins snapped leaving their apartments at Cedra Court; **Above:** A promotional still for the movie *Legend* (2015), with Tom Hardy as Ronnie (foreground) and Reggie, in a recreation of the well-known David Bailey portrait of the twins.

JOHN GOTTI
LUCKY AND SMART: THE TEFLON DON

Above. Gotti in court, 1990, listening to the opening arguments; **Top left:** John D'Amico (left), John Gotti, and Peter Gotti (right); **Top right:** A smiling Gotti, arriving in court...again.

John Joseph Gotti Jr. was born on October 27, 1940, in the Bronx, New York City, into a family struggling to make ends meet. The fifth of 13 children, Gotti grew up in a household where financial hardship and an unreliable father shaped his early experiences. Moving to Brooklyn at a young age, Gotti was exposed to the enticements and hazards of street life, a crucible that would harden him for his future role as a notorious mob boss.

Ascent Through the Ranks

Gotti's involvement with the Gambino crime family began in the 1950s when he became a protégé of capo Carmine Fatico. Starting off with small burglaries and carjackings, he quickly graduated to more serious crimes. Arrested multiple times but never convicted, Gotti gained a reputation for being both "lucky" and "smart," traits that would serve him well in his criminal pursuits.

The Teflon Don

Gotti's audacious leadership style reached its apex when he orchestrated the murder of his own boss, Paul Castellano, in 1985. With Castellano out of the picture, Gotti ascended to the top of the Gambino family. Dubbed the "Teflon Don" for his ability to evade legal consequences, Gotti reveled in his public persona, often appearing in expensive suits and engaging openly with the media—a marked departure from the traditional low profile maintained by Mafia bosses.

Criminal Exploits and Operations

Under Gotti's reign, the Gambino family soared in both wealth and power, deeply involved

in racketeering, loan-sharking, illegal gambling, and drug trafficking. Despite his high-profile status and repeated run-ins with the law, Gotti managed to escape conviction until the early 1990s. His bravado wasn't just for show; it was a calculated risk that, for a time, seemed to pay off.

Downfall and Conviction

Gotti's empire began to crumble when his underboss, Salvatore "Sammy the Bull" Gravano, turned informant. For years, Gravano had been one of Gotti's most trusted associates, but the prospect of a life sentence—and Gotti's attempts to shift the police's attention onto him—pushed him to cooperate with the FBI. With Gravano's testimony, Gotti was arrested and charged with five murders, racketeering, and other crimes. In 1992, he was convicted on all counts and sentenced to life imprisonment without the possibility of parole. He spent most of his time in solitary confinement.

Final Years and Legacy

In 1998, John Gotti's health deteriorated due to throat cancer. He was transferred to the United States Medical Center for Federal Prisoners in Springfield, Missouri, where he had surgery and radiation treatments and then was transferred back to prison. He went back to the hospital when the cancer returned and died on June 10, 2002. Although Gotti was undeniably a criminal mastermind responsible for countless unlawful activities, his life story has fascinated the public and media for decades. The audacity with which he operated and his flair for the dramatic have made him an enduring symbol of Mafia culture in America.

Cultural Impact

From documentaries to feature films, Gotti's life continues to captivate, contributing to the larger narrative about organized crime in America. He remains a controversial figure—both a charismatic anti-hero and a ruthless criminal—who has left an indelible mark on the American cultural landscape.

Above left: Gotti's mugshot from February 1968; **Top right:** Gotti arrives at Manhattan Supreme Court in 1986, where he is on trial on charges of conspiracy and assault for the shooting of a carpenters' union official. (Photo by Willie Anderson, New York Daily News); **Above right:** John Travolta as John Gotti, in the 2018 movie *Gotti*.

Kenichi Shinoda, also known as Shinobu Tsukasa, was born on January 25, 1942, in Ōita, Japan. He embarked on a life of crime early on, gradually making his way up the ranks of Japan's formidable Yakuza crime syndicate. Shinoda eventually became the sixth *kumicho* of the Yamaguchi-gumi, the largest and most powerful Yakuza organization in Japan.

Leadership and Expansions

Under Shinoda's stewardship, the Yamaguchi-gumi expanded its influence, both domestically and internationally. Their criminal activities ranged from gambling, drug trafficking, and loan-sharking to legitimate ventures in real estate and finance. Shinoda's leadership was characterized by a mix of traditional Yakuza values and modern business tactics.

Legal Troubles and Incarceration

Like many figures in organized crime, Shinoda faced his share of legal troubles. In 2005, shortly after assuming leadership of the Yamaguchi-gumi, he was imprisoned on gun possession charges and was released in 2011. Despite his incarceration, Shinoda's influence over the syndicate remained strong, showcasing his indomitable grip on the organization. In 2012, The United States imposed sanctions on Shinoda and his second in command, Kiyoshi Takayama, as well as several other high-ranking members of international organized crime groups, in an attempt to restrict their ability to operate on American soil.

KENICHI SHINODA THE SIXTH GODFATHER

The Yamaguchi-gumi
Japan's largest Yakuza organization is named after its founder Harukichi Yamaguchi. Its origins go back to a Kobe dockworkers' union before the Second World War. The Yamaguchi-gumi are among the world's wealthiest gangsters, bringing in billions of dollars annually from the sex industry and Internet pornography, extortion, gambling, arms trafficking, drug trafficking, real estate and construction kickback schemes. The organization is also involved in stock market manipulation. Its headquarters are in Kobe, but it operates across Japan, and Shinoda has declared an expansionist policy, even making inroads into Tokyo—historically not Yamaguchi territory. Immediately after the Kobe earthquake of 1995, the Yamaguchi-gumi started a large-scale relief effort for the victims, helping with essential food and supplies distribution. Incredibly, in 2013, the Yamaguchi-gumi started its own magazine, keeping members updated and including articles on the group's opinions and traditions—as well as columns on angling! The editorial section of the magazine is contributed by *Boss Shinoda*.

Main image above, and opposite top, left and right: Boss Shinoda back in 2011 on his release from prison; **Opposite, below:** A rare picture of Shinoda.

GRISELDA BLANCO THE BLACK WIDOW

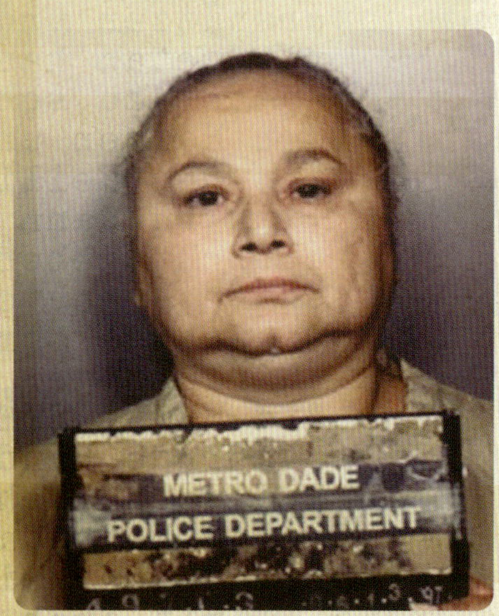

Top left: Blanco's mugshot from 1985; **Top right:** Griselda, circa 1980; **Above:** Blanco's mugshot from 1997.

Griselda Blanco was born on February 15, 1943, in Cartagena, Colombia. Raised in a slum outside Bogotá, Blanco's early life was marked by extreme poverty and domestic violence. By her pre-teen years, she had already engaged in criminal activities, including pickpocketing and petty theft. These early experiences helped shape her into one of the most notorious figures in the world of organized crime.

Rise to Infamy

Blanco moved to the United States in 1964, settling in Queens, New York. She soon began setting up a vast and intricate drug trafficking network, responsible for importing massive amounts of cocaine into the United States. Her operations extended from Colombia to South Florida, California, and New York, eventually earning her the moniker "La Madrina." Blanco was innovative in her drug smuggling techniques, which reportedly included a clothing factory that produced lingerie with hidden compartments. Her criminal empire rapidly expanded, and at the height of her power, she was reportedly making up to $80 million per month.

Notable Crimes and Activities

Griselda Blanco was no stranger to violence. She is said to have ordered the murders of multiple rivals, business partners, and even family members—earning her another nickname, the "Black Widow." Her ruthlessness and capacity for violence were well-documented, with estimates suggesting that she may have been responsible for up to 200 murders. One of her most notorious acts was the initiation of the "Miami Drug War," which resulted in dozens of killings in the late 1970s and early 1980s.

Capture and Imprisonment

Blanco's empire began to crumble in 1975 when

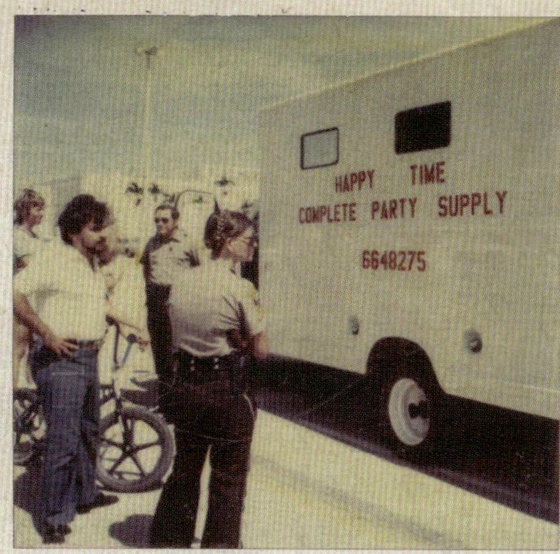

she was indicted on federal drug conspiracy charges but managed to evade arrest by fleeing back to Colombia. She returned to the United States and settled in Miami, only to be arrested in 1985. Blanco served 13 years in a U.S. prison before being deported to Colombia in 2004.

Later Life and Death

After her deportation, details about Blanco's life are sketchy. She was said to have led a relatively quiet life, although she never completely severed her ties with the criminal underworld. On September 3, 2012, her life came to an end in the way she had lived it—marked by violence. She was assassinated by a gunman in Medellín, Colombia, at the age of 69.

Legacy

Griselda Blanco remains a controversial and fascinating figure, symbolizing the excesses and ruthlessness of the drug trade. Her life story has been covered in multiple documentaries, biographies, and feature films. She has also been cited as an influence on the portrayal of female drug lords in the media, often serving as the archetype of a ruthless woman in a male-dominated criminal world. Her brutal reign left an indelible mark on the history of organized crime and the international drug trade, serving as a cautionary tale about the consequences of unfettered ambition and a complete disregard for human life.

Her ruthlessness and capacity for violence were well-documented, with estimates suggesting that she may have been responsible for up to 200 murders...

Top images: July 11, 1979: Miami, Florida. A shootout between members of rival Colombian drug cartels in broad daylight at Dadeland Mall is widely seen as the beginning of the "Cocaine Wars" in South Florida. Police say two men in a panel van painted with "Happy Time Complete Party Supply" were enforcers for the Medellín drug cartel "Cocaine Godmother" Griselda Blanco. They shot and killed a rival dealer and his bodyguard inside Crown Liquors. Photo by David Poller © David Poller/ZUMAn; **Above:** The Black Widow after her release from prison, made up for a photo shoot on her lawn, circa 2004.

PABLO ESCOBAR
COCAINE OVERLORD

Top left: Barrio Pablo Escobar, Medellín, where the cocaine overlord built over 3000 houses for the poor; **Top right:** Escobar, circa 1991; **Above:** Escobar police mugshot from 1976.

Pablo Emilio Escobar Gaviria was born on December 1, 1949, in Rionegro, Colombia, to Abel de Jesús Dari Escobar, a farmer, and Hermilda Gaviria, a schoolteacher. He grew up in a modest environment and quickly realized the power that money held in a class-divided society.

Rise to Infamy

Pablo Escobar began his criminal career in his teens with petty street crimes before moving into the drug trade in the early 1970s. He founded the Medellín Cartel, which soon monopolized the cocaine trade in the United States, Europe, and other parts of the world. At the height of its power, the cartel was responsible for up to 80% of the world's cocaine supply. Escobar became one of the world's richest men, with an estimated net worth of $30 billion at the time of his death. His success wasn't solely down to business acumen; Escobar was ruthlessly violent and didn't hesitate to eliminate rivals or threats to his operation. He pioneered a model of business known as "plata o plomo," which translates to "silver or lead," meaning either accept a bribe or face death.

Notable Crimes and Activities

Escobar's reach extended far beyond drug trafficking. He was involved in various criminal enterprises, from contract killings to bombings. His most notorious act was perhaps the bombing of Avianca Flight 203 in 1989, killing all 107 passengers on board in an attempt to assassinate presidential candidate César Gaviria, who was not on the flight.

Capture and Imprisonment

Due to escalating violence and international pressure, the Colombian government was forced to act. After a long manhunt, Escobar surrendered and was imprisoned in 1991 in a luxurious private prison he designed, known as La Catedral. However, this arrangement allowed him to continue his criminal activities from behind bars. The government decided to transfer him to a more secure facility in 1992, but he escaped.

Above left: La Catedral, the luxurious prison that Escobar was allowed to design for himself after his capture and imprisonment in 1991. He was even able to continue his criminal activities there; **Above right:** The bombed-out ruins of Escobar's "Finca Manuela" vacation home on the shore of Peñol-Guatape Reservoir, Guatape, Antioquia, Colombia; **Left:** Members of New Liberalism, c. 1979. From left: Iván Marulanda, Luis Carlos Galán, Rodrigo Lara, Nancy Restrepo de Lara, Gabriela White de Vélez, and Hernán Vieira. Galán, Lara, and White were assassinated—either by the People's Army (FARC), or more likely, on the orders of Escobar. Lara, together with Galán, publicly denounced the drug cartels, especially in Medellín, where the cartel was led by Escobar; **Below:** The predictable end for Escobar, killed in December 1993, after a rooftop shootout with Colombian Police, aided by U.S. intelligence—and rival cartel members.

Later Life and Death

After his escape, Escobar was on the run for more than a year. During this time, he lost significant power and influence. The relentless pursuit by Colombian police, aided by U.S. intelligence and rival cartels, led to his discovery in a safe house in Medellín. On December 2, 1993, the day after his 44th birthday, Pablo Escobar was killed in a rooftop shootout with police.

Legacy

Pablo Escobar remains a controversial figure in Colombia and around the world. To some, he was a Robin Hood-like character who built hospitals, schools, and housing for the poor. To others, he was a ruthless criminal who brought untold suffering to thousands through drugs, violence, and corruption. Pablo Escobar's life has been the subject of numerous films, documentaries, and the highly successful TV series, "Narcos." Despite the decades that have passed since his death, interest in his life remains high, and his legacy as one of the world's most infamous criminals endures.

DAWOOD IBRAHIM
DRUGS, ARMS, BOMBS, EXTORTION

Top, left to right: Images of the immediate aftermath of the Mumbai bombings in March 1993. Photos by Fawzan Husain; **Above:** Dawood Ibrahim around the time of the Mumbai bombings.

Dawood Ibrahim was born on December 26, 1955, in Ratnagiri, Maharashtra, India, to a police constable, Ibrahim Kaskar, and his wife, Amina Bi. Raised in the Dongri neighborhood of Mumbai, his upbringing was far from privileged, which perhaps laid the groundwork for his criminal inclinations.

Rise to Infamy

Ibrahim started his criminal career as a member of don Baashu Dada's gang, initially involving himself in activities like smuggling and illegal trading. Eventually, he and his older brother Shabir Ibrahim Kaskar broke away and formed the criminal organization known as the D-Company, an organized crime syndicate that has been linked to various illicit activities such as drug trafficking, arms smuggling, and extortion. By the late 1980s and early 1990s, Ibrahim had become one of Asia's most feared underworld figures. He is also believed to have significant connections with terrorist organizations and has been designated as a global terrorist by India, the United States, and the United Nations. The D-Company's operations are not limited to India; it has been reported to have bases in several countries, including the United Arab Emirates and Pakistan.

Notable Crimes and Activities

Ibrahim is most notoriously linked to the 1993 Mumbai bombings, a series of 12 bomb explosions in Mumbai, India, that resulted in over 250 fatalities and more than 700 injuries. The attacks were believed to be orchestrated by Ibrahim as retaliation for the destruction of the Babri Masjid and subsequent widespread

riots that engulfed parts of India. Over the years, he has been connected to various criminal enterprises ranging from counterfeiting and narcotics to targeted killings. Despite the grave charges against him, he has managed to elude capture and continues to operate his criminal empire.

Capture and Imprisonment

As of 2023, Dawood Ibrahim remains a fugitive. He has successfully evaded capture by law enforcement agencies and is believed to be residing in Pakistan, although the Pakistani government has consistently denied this. His name appears on the wanted list of several organizations, including Interpol. Numerous attempts to extradite him to India for trial have been unsuccessful.

Legacy

Dawood Ibrahim continues to be an emblem of organized crime in South Asia. His network and influence serve as a reminder of the international reach that such criminal enterprises can achieve. The constant failure to apprehend him has led to significant public interest and media speculation, contributing to his almost mythical status in the underworld. While Ibrahim's life has been covered in various journalistic accounts, documentaries, and fictional adaptations, the man himself remains elusive, making him one of the most enigmatic and dangerous criminals in the world today.

Above: Indian security forces put parts of the city into lockdown after the bombings, in which over 250 people were killed, with over 700 injured. Ibrahim was designated a global terrorist by India and the United States, with a reward of US$25 million on his head for his suspected role in the 1993 Mumbai bombings. In 2011, he was named second on "The World's 10 Most Wanted Fugitives" by the U.S. Federal Bureau of Investigation.

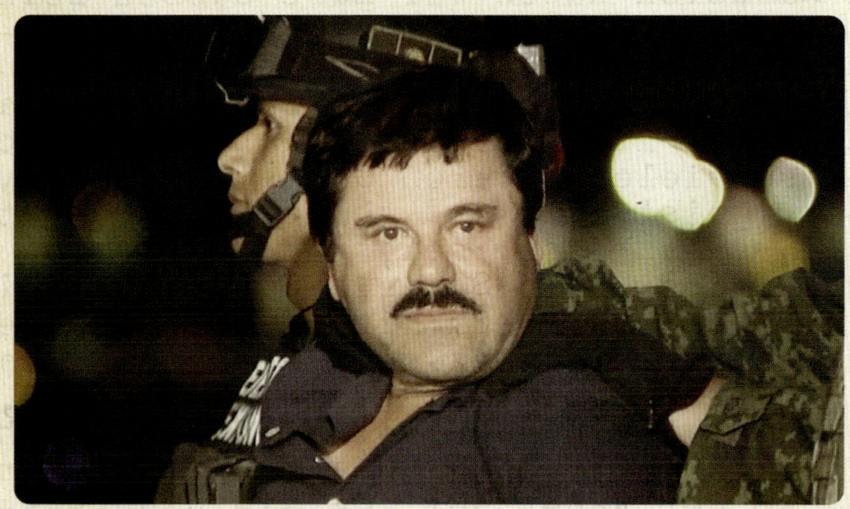

JOAQUIN "EL CHAPO" GUZMÁN THE MEXICAN SINALOA CARTEL

Top left: Guzmán is escorted by soldiers after his capture in 2016; **Top right:** Guzmán in a helicopter after his capture in 2016; **Above:** Guzmán after his arrest in 1993.

Joaquín Archivaldo Guzmán Loera, commonly known as "El Chapo," was born on April 4, 1957, in La Tuna, a small village in the state of Sinaloa, Mexico. Born into a poor farming family, Guzmán had limited educational opportunities and reportedly dropped out of school by the third grade to help support his family.

Rise to Infamy

Guzmán entered the world of organized crime in the late 1970s, initially working under Miguel Ángel Félix Gallardo, the head of the Guadalajara Cartel. When the cartel was disbanded, Guzmán took control of its lucrative drug trafficking routes and established the Sinaloa Cartel, a criminal enterprise that would become one of the most powerful and feared drug cartels in the world. The Sinaloa Cartel specializes in the smuggling and distribution of narcotics, primarily cocaine, marijuana, and heroin. Under Guzmán's leadership, the cartel used a range of sophisticated methods for drug trafficking, including tunnels across the U.S.-Mexico border, airplanes, and submarines.

Notable Crimes and Activities

Throughout his criminal career, El Chapo gained notoriety for his audacious prison escapes. In 2001, he escaped from the Puente Grande maximum-security prison in Jalisco, reportedly hidden in a laundry cart, and remained at large for 13 years. He was recaptured in 2014 but escaped again the following year through an elaborate tunnel leading out of his prison cell. Guzmán's activities were not limited to drug

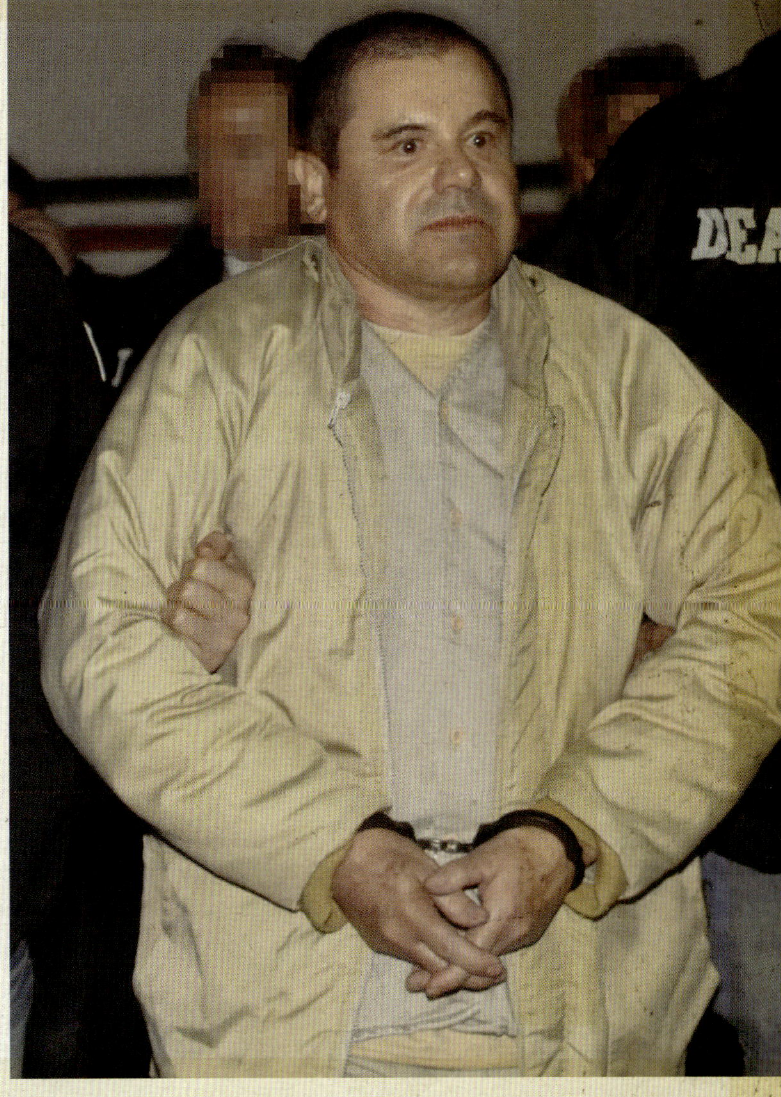

trafficking; he was also involved in organized crime on various fronts, including money laundering, arms smuggling, and extortion. His organization was responsible for numerous deaths, either through direct assassinations or as a result of the brutal drug wars he led against rival cartels.

Capture and Imprisonment

After his second escape, Guzmán was captured in January 2016 in a military operation in the coastal city of Los Mochis, Sinaloa. He was extradited to the United States in 2017. In July 2019, he was convicted on multiple counts, including drug trafficking, money laundering, and involvement in organized crime. He was sentenced to life imprisonment plus 30 years and is currently incarcerated in the ADX Florence supermax prison in the United States.

Later Life

Guzmán's conviction marked the end of a lengthy and infamous criminal career. His capture and imprisonment were seen as a significant victory for both Mexican and U.S. law enforcement agencies.

Legacy

El Chapo's life has been the subject of numerous books, documentaries, and a popular TV series. While he is reviled for the pain and suffering his activities caused, his ability to elude capture for many years and his audacious escapes have made him a larger-than-life figure in the realm of organized crime. He remains a symbol of the ongoing drug war and the challenges of combating organized crime on a global scale.

Top left: Guzmán being escorted after his capture in 2014; **Above left:** A U.S. Border Patrol agent surveilling the Mexican bank of the Rio Grande; **Above:** Guzmán effected a second escape from prison in 2015, but was recaptured in a military operation in Los Mochis the following January. The picture shows his extradition to the U.S. in 2017. He was found guilty of charges related to his leadership of the Sinaloa Cartel and was sentenced to life imprisonment. Guzmán is currently incarcerated in ADX Florence, Colorado.

CHAPTER FOUR
KILLERS

In the world of true crime, few figures are as simultaneously feared and fascinating as the murderer. This chapter examines the individuals whose actions have left indelible scars on the fabric of society; not only their crimes, but also the complex psychological, environmental, and sometimes inexplicable factors that led these individuals down a path of violence.

The killers featured here are as diverse as the motives behind their crimes. Some act alone, driven by deep-seated rage, twisted desires, or cold calculation. Others were part of groups, their actions the result of twisted ideologies or misplaced loyalties.

From serial killers who stalked their victims with chilling precision to mass murderers whose rampages left communities in shock and mourning, each story offers a glimpse into the abyss of human capability. As we recount their crimes, we strive to understand the methodology and madness behind their actions, the impact on their victims, and the terror they sowed among the innocent.

Rumors began circulating in the late 1590s about Báthory's cruel treatment of young servant girls at the castle...It was also rumored that she believed that bathing in the blood of virgins would grant her eternal youth, leading to whispers of vampirism...

ELIZABETH BÁTHORY THE BLOOD COUNTESS OF HUNGARY

Countess Elizabeth Báthory of Hungary, often dubbed the "Blood Countess," is one of history's most infamous female serial killers. Born on August 7, 1560, into one of the wealthiest and most powerful families in Hungary, her life would take a dark and macabre turn, leading to legends of vampirism and blood rituals.

Early Life and Marriage

Báthory was raised in the renowned Báthory family, which held vast estates in Hungary. At the age of 15, she was married to Ferenc Nádasdy, a union that further solidified her social status. The young couple resided at Čachtice Castle, where Elizabeth would later commit many of her heinous crimes.

The Beginning of a Dark Legacy

Rumors began circulating in the late 1590s and early 1600s about Báthory's cruel treatment of young servant girls at the castle. Stories spread of torture, beatings, and other unspeakable acts. It was also rumored that she believed that bathing in the blood of virgins would grant her eternal youth, leading to whispers of vampirism.

Investigation and Imprisonment

In 1610, following numerous complaints and increasing suspicion, King Matthias II ordered an investigation into the Countess's alleged crimes. Led by György Thurzó, the inquiry uncovered a litany of horrors. Witnesses recounted tales of girls being beaten, burned, mutilated, and even bitten by Báthory herself. While it's known that she had

accomplices, the exact number of her victims remains uncertain. Estimates range from 30 to 650, based on varying testimonies and accounts. Due to her noble status, she was never formally tried in a court of law. Instead, in 1611, she was placed under house arrest at Čachtice Castle. Her accomplices, however, faced public trials and were executed for their roles in the crimes. Elizabeth Báthory spent her remaining years confined to a set of rooms within the castle, with windows and doors bricked up, leaving only small slits for ventilation and the passing of food. She died on August 21, 1614.

Legacy and Cultural Impact

The legend of Elizabeth Báthory has persisted through the centuries, evolving and intertwining with vampire lore. Her supposed quest for eternal youth through the blood of virgins has cemented her place in history as one of the most notorious female killers. Her life, and the tales surrounding her have inspired numerous books, films, and artworks. While the extent of her crimes and the motivations behind them remain topics of debate, her dark legacy as the "Blood Countess" endures, serving as a chilling reminder of the depths of human cruelty and the myths that can arise from genuine horror.

Opposite: A 1590s portrait of the infamous Countess Elizabeth Báthory. The hair-raising local rumors that she bathed in, and drank, the blood of virgins from the surrounding villages led to stories which have endured down the centuries; **This page, top left:** An aerial view of the mid-13th century Čachtice Castle, which was the residence (and later the prison) of the Countess. The now-ruined castle is in the Trnava region of present-day Slovakia; **Above:** Ingrid Pitt stars as Countess Báthory in the 1971 British Hammer movie, *Countess Dracula*, which weaves its plot directly from the stories of the Countess Báthory; **Top right:** The Countess, after her "treatments," is restored to her fulsome beauty, and **(center)**, the blood of the village virgins no longer has the desired effect, and the Countess has reverted back to her dotage.

The infamous East End murders in the fall of 1888...

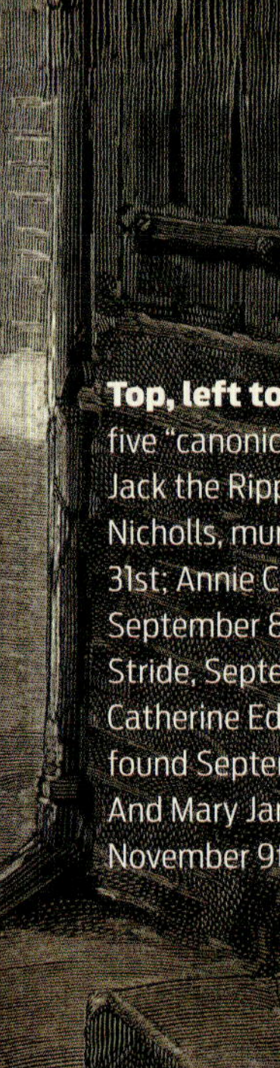

Top, left to right: The five "canonical murders" of Jack the Ripper: Mary Ann Nicholls, murdered August 31st; Annie Chapman, September 8th; Elizabeth Stride, September 30th; Catherine Eddowes, also found September 30th; And Mary Jane Kelly, November 9th.

JACK THE RIPPER
GOTHIC HORROR IN WHITECHAPEL

A Shadow in London's Fog

The name "Jack the Ripper" evokes chilling images of gaslit cobblestone streets, fog-drenched alleys, and a merciless killer who eluded capture. This unidentified serial killer terrorized the Whitechapel district of London in 1888, and his heinous acts have since become the stuff of legend, sparking countless theories, investigations, and media adaptations.

A Series of Grisly Murders

Between August and November 1888, the Ripper claimed at least five victims, all women, many of whom were prostitutes. The brutality of the murders was unprecedented. The victims were not just killed; they were mutilated with chilling precision. The nature of the wounds suggested that the killer had a knowledge of human anatomy, leading to speculation that he could be a doctor or a butcher.

Letters from the Abyss

During the spree, various letters were sent to the police and newspapers, purportedly from the killer himself. The most famous of these is the "From Hell" letter, which was sent with a piece of a human kidney. While many of these letters are believed to be hoaxes, they added a psychological dimension to the Ripper's terror, making it clear that he was not just killing but also taunting the authorities and the public.

Investigations and Suspects

The Ripper case was one of the first to attract massive media attention. Newspapers of the day were filled with accounts of the murders, sketches of possible suspects, and theories about the killer's identity. The Metropolitan Police, led by Commissioner Sir Charles Warren and detectives Frederick Abberline, Henry Moore, and Walter Andrews, were under immense pressure to solve the case. Over the years, many suspects have been proposed, including Montague John Druitt, a barrister and schoolteacher; Aaron Kosminski, a Polish barber; and even Walter Sickert, a prominent painter. However, none were definitively proven to be the Ripper.

The Ripper's Enduring Legacy

Jack the Ripper's killing spree lasted only a few months, but his shadow has loomed large for over a century. The mystery surrounding his identity and the nature of his crimes have made him one of history's most infamous killers. The Ripper case laid bare the grim realities of Victorian London — the poverty, the vice, the desperation, and the stark contrasts between the haves and the have-nots. It's a world that has been vividly captured in literature, film, and television, making the Ripper not just a killer but a cultural icon.

Theories and Continued Fascination

The allure of the Ripper case lies in its unsolved status. Who was Jack the Ripper? Why did he kill? And why did he stop? These questions have spawned an entire field of study, known as "Ripperology." Books, documentaries, movies, and TV shows continue to delve into the mystery, each proposing its own theory. Today, the story of Jack the Ripper stands as a testament to society's enduring fascination with the macabre, the unsolved, and the depths of human depravity.

SO JUST WHO WAS JACK THE RIPPER?

Besides the barrister Montague Druitt and barber Aaron Kosminski, several gentlemen of Victorian society were, at one time or another, suspected of being the Ripper. A somewhat unlikely candidate was Mr Lewis Carroll, author of *Alice's Adventures in Wonderland*—he preferred to take photographs of naked young girls. Sickert came under lingering suspicion when his dark canvases of Camden Town prostitutes were exhibited. Sir William Withey Gull, physician and surgeon to Queen Victoria has been many armchair detectives' choice for a long time, now, but he is another unlikely candidate—in his seventies and in ill-health at the time of the crimes. He was to die just 13 months later. A more plausible candidate was James Maybrick **(above)**. The last of the so-called "Leather Apron" murders was either December 1888, or September 1889, and Maybrick died by poison, administered by his wife Florence in 1889, believing her husband to be the Ripper.

LIZZIE BORDEN
THE FALL RIVER MYSTERY

Top left: A young Lizzie Borden, 1889; **Top right:** A crime scene photograph of Lizzie Borden's stepmother Abby Gray Borden; **Above:** 92 Second St, Fall River, MA—the Borden house—as it appeared in 1892.

Born on July 19, 1860, in Fall River, Massachusetts, Lizzie Andrew Borden was a figure who would soon become the epicenter of one of America's most enduring true crime mysteries. Fall River, a prosperous town during the 19th century, provided the backdrop for a crime that juxtaposed its serene environs.

The Borden Household

The Borden family was well-established in Fall River. Lizzie's father, Andrew Borden, was a successful businessman who accumulated wealth through real estate and banking. However, despite their wealth, the Bordens led a relatively austere lifestyle. Lizzie's mother, Sarah, passed away when Lizzie was just a child, and Andrew remarried Abby Durfee Gray a few years later.

The Infamous Crime

On the morning of August 4, 1892, a heinous crime shattered the tranquility of Fall River. Andrew and Abby Borden were found brutally murdered in their home, having been struck multiple times with a hatchet. The brutality of the act was in stark contrast to the quiet and seemingly peaceful household.

Accusations and Trial

Lizzie, being one of the few people present at the home at the time of the murders, quickly became the prime suspect. Her inconsistent statements to the police, coupled with reports of family disputes over property and money, cast a shadow of suspicion. Furthermore, Lizzie's attempt to purchase prussic acid, a deadly poison, from a local drug store just a day before the murders, further intensified

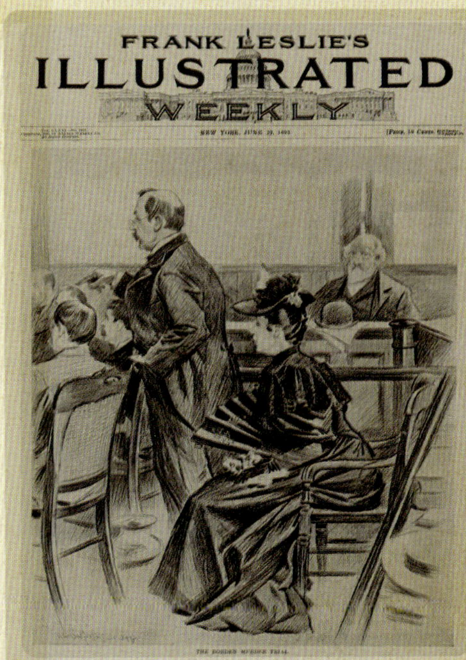
FRANK LESLIE'S
ILLUSTRATED
WEEKLY

Top left: Lizzie Borden, circa 1892; **Top and center:** *Bewitched* star Elizabeth Montgomery as Borden in *The Legend of Lizzie Borden*, 1975; **Above:** *Frank Leslie's Illustrated Weekly*, with the front page devoted to an artist's impression of the Borden trial.

the suspicions against her. When the trial began on June 5, 1893, the courtroom was packed, with the case drawing national attention. Evidence against Lizzie was largely circumstantial. Key points of contention during the trial included the potential murder weapon, a hatchet found in the basement, Lizzie's burning of a dress shortly after the murders, and her peculiar behavior in the days following the crime. However, the defense effectively cast doubt on the prosecution's case. They argued that the police investigation was flawed and highlighted the lack of physical evidence linking Lizzie to the crime. The possibility of an intruder committing the murders was also proposed.

Acquittal and Later Life

After a trial lasting 14 days, the jury deliberated for just 90 minutes before acquitting Lizzie Borden of the murders. Despite her acquittal, suspicions lingered, and Lizzie became a figure of intrigue and speculation. Many in Fall River continued to believe in her guilt, leading Lizzie and her sister, Emma, to move to a new home, where they lived in relative seclusion. Lizzie Borden passed away on June 1, 1927. The mystery surrounding the Borden murders remains unsolved, with Lizzie's guilt or innocence still a topic of debate.

Legacy and Cultural Impact

The Lizzie Borden case has taken on a life of its own in American folklore. The story has been the subject of countless books, films, plays, and even a chilling children's rhyme. Lizzie Borden remains an enigmatic figure in American history, embodying the fascination with true crime and the seductive allure of unsolved mysteries.

HENRY H. HOLMES THE MAZE OF HORROR

Top left: Henry Howard Holmes's; **Top right:** 63rd Street, Chicago—the "Murder Castle," as it became known to locals; **Above:** The vast classical splendor of the World's Columbian Exposition of 1893 in Chicago.

Herman Webster Mudgett, better known by his alias H. H. Holmes, stands as one of America's first documented serial killers. Born on May 16, 1861, in Gilmanton, New Hampshire, Holmes would go on to devise one of the most elaborate and horrifying killing sprees in history.

A Dubious Upbringing

From a young age, Holmes exhibited troubling behavior. He was reportedly fascinated by death and would often perform surgical experiments on animals. As he grew older, Holmes developed a knack for con artistry and fraud, leading him to pursue a degree in medicine as a means to further his scams.

The "Murder Castle"

Holmes arrived in Chicago in the late 1880s, a burgeoning city bustling with opportunity, and soon to host the upcoming 1893 World's Columbian Exposition. Seizing the moment, he constructed a three-story building which locals dubbed the "Castle." On the surface, it was a mix of commercial and residential spaces. However, unbeknownst to all, the building was a labyrinthine structure of trap doors, hidden passages, soundproof rooms, and a basement designed for torture and body disposal. As visitors flocked to Chicago for the exposition, Holmes lured many to his "Castle," often under the pretense of offering employment or accommodations. Once inside, his victims found themselves trapped in a maze of horror. Holmes would torture, kill, and often dissect the bodies, selling the skeletons and organs to medical schools.

Crimes and Capture

Holmes's reign of terror came to an end in 1894 when he was arrested for a separate

fraud case. As authorities delved deeper into his background, the ghastly details of his murder spree began to emerge. While Holmes confessed to 27 murders, the true count remains unknown and is speculated to be much higher. Some estimates place the number closer to 200.

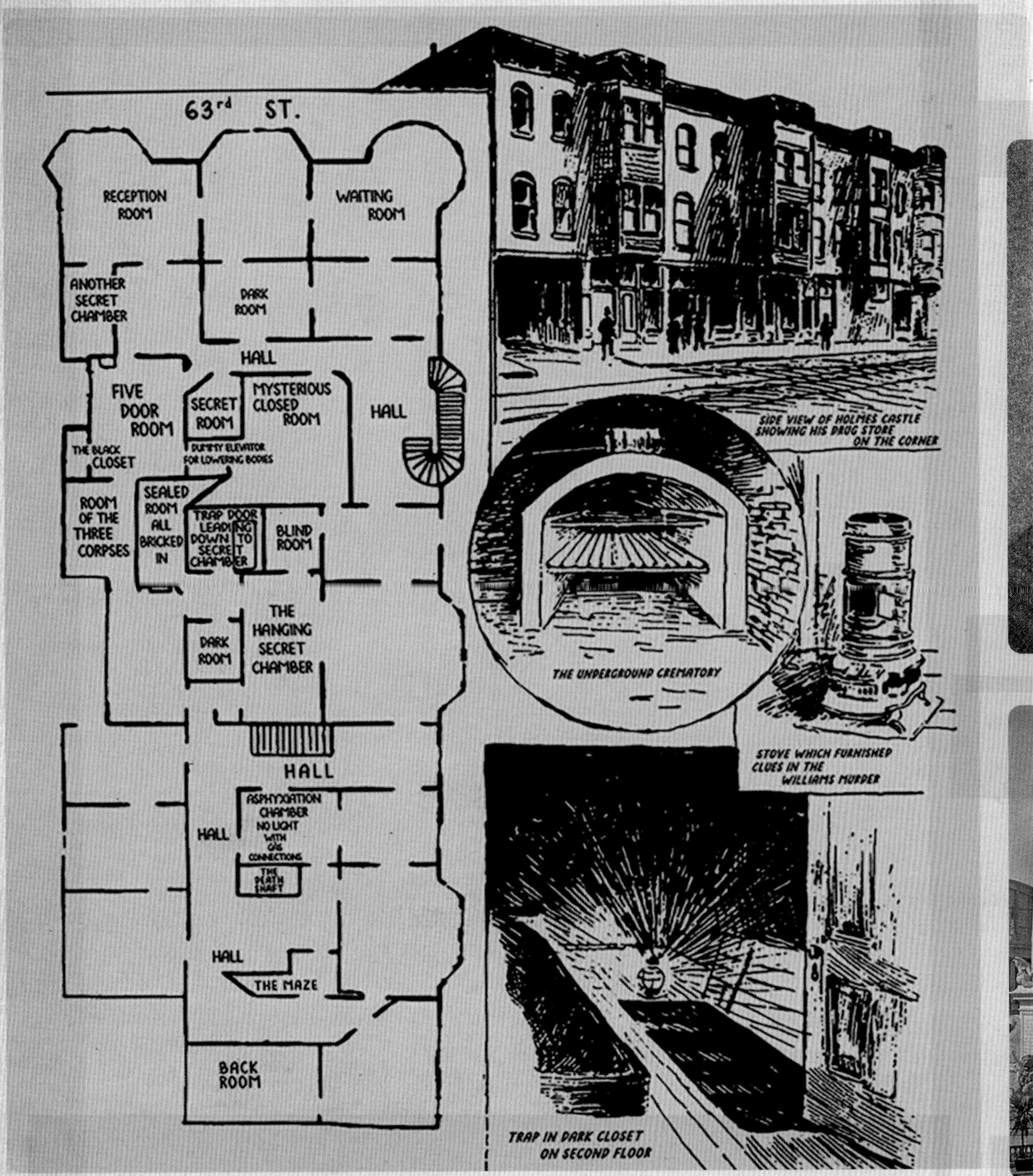

Trial and Execution

The trial of H. H. Holmes was a national sensation, with media outlets across the country covering the chilling details of his crimes. In 1896, he was found guilty of murder and sentenced to death. Holmes met his end on May 7, 1896, when he was hanged at Moyamensing Prison in Philadelphia.

Legacy of Horror

The story of H. H. Holmes remains one of the most chilling chapters in American crime history. His calculated cruelty, combined with his architectural ingenuity, created a unique and terrifying narrative that has both horrified and captivated the public for over a century. Holmes's life and crimes have been the subject of numerous books, documentaries, and fictionalized accounts, cementing his place as one of America's most notorious killers.

Above left: A plan of Holmes's "Murder Castle," published in the *Chicago Tribune*, August 18, 1895; **Top:** Another photo of Holmes; **Above:** More of the magnificent "White City," as the Chicago World's Columbian Exposition site became known around the world.

ALBERT FISH
TORTURE, MURDER AND CANNIBALISM IN NEW YORK

Above: Experienced homicide detectives pick over evidence at the murder location in New York State where "The Boogey Man" Albert Fish killed Grace Budd.

Hamilton Howard "Albert" Fish was born on May 19, 1870, in Washington, D.C. His early years were marred by tragedy—his father passed away when Albert was just five years old, leading to his placement in an orphanage. It was a childhood marked by horror. Fish was exposed to regular beatings and sadistic acts, which he later claimed instilled a perverse pleasure in pain.

Dark Descent into Crime

As Fish grew older, his sadistic tendencies intensified. He moved to New York, where he began preying on young children. His crimes escalated from molestation to murder. Fish was not just content with killing; he often tortured his victims, indulging in cannibalism and other gruesome acts. He described the acts in horrifying detail, leaving no doubt about the depth of his depravity.

Notorious Crimes and Capture

Albert Fish's most infamous crime was the kidnapping and murder of Grace Budd in 1928.

Above: The victim who got him caught—an embellished photo of the 10-years old Grace Budd. Six years after murdering and eating the child, Fish sent a letter to her parents, which led police straight to him; **Left:** A weary and disconsolate Albert Fish during his trial; **Below:** Fish is helped into court by officials; **Bottom:** Albert Fish about to experience "the supreme thrill," as he is strapped into the electric chair at Sing Sing.

Under the pretense of offering employment for her brother, Fish lured the 10-year-old to his home, where he killed her. Six years later, in a twisted act of cruelty, he sent a letter to Grace's parents, graphically detailing the murder and his subsequent cannibalization of her body. This letter was the beginning of the end for Fish. The envelope's emblem led the police to the rooming house where Fish was staying. When confronted with the evidence, Fish confessed not only to the murder of Grace Budd but also to the killings of several other children.

Trial and Execution

Albert Fish's trial began in March 1935. His defense centered on his obvious insanity, with numerous psychiatrists testifying to his myriad of sexual fetishes and mental disorders. Fish himself provided chilling testimonies of his crimes, seemingly oblivious to the horror they evoked. Despite his apparent insanity, the jury found Fish sane and guilty after a mere 10 days of trial. The reasoning was clear: someone who could plan and execute his crimes in such a methodical manner was fully aware of his actions. On January 16, 1936, Albert Fish was executed in the electric chair at Sing Sing Correctional Facility. His last words were a testament to his twisted psyche, claiming that his impending electrocution would be "the supreme thrill."

Legacy and Cultural Impact

Albert Fish remains one of the most notorious figures in the annals of American crime. His heinous acts and apparent pleasure in them make him stand out even among other serial killers. His story has been the subject of numerous documentaries, films, and books, each trying to delve into the mind of a man whose actions seem beyond comprehension. Fish's legacy serves as a chilling reminder of the depths of human depravity. His story underscores the dark potential that lies within, awaiting the right combination of circumstances to be unleashed.

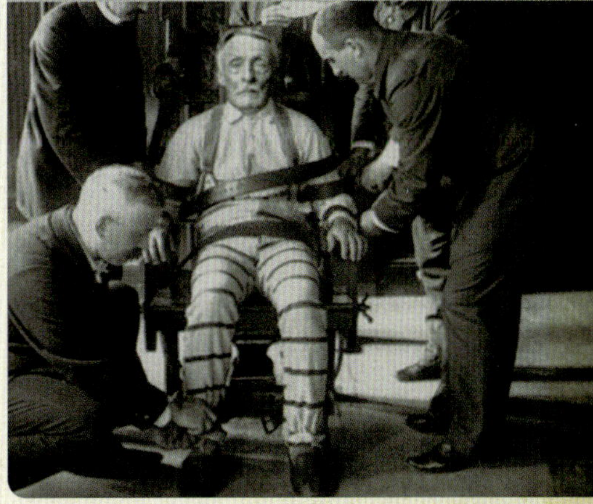

LEONARDA CIANCIULLI THE SOAP MAKER

Born on April 18, 1894, in Montella, Avellino, Italy, Leonarda Cianciulli's early life was interspersed with hardships and personal challenges. The psychological strain on her was evident from her youth, marked by multiple suicide attempts. Her familial ties were further strained when she chose to marry Raffaele Pansardi in 1917, a decision her parents strongly disapproved of.

Married Life and Motherhood

Leonarda's marriage to Raffaele was fraught with heartbreak. The couple conceived 17 children, but only four survived to adulthood. This immense loss, coupled with a haunting prediction by a fortune teller that she would lose all her children young, deeply affected Leonarda. Another soothsayer's prediction that Leonarda would outlive her children further exacerbated her anxieties.

Deep-seated Superstitions

Cianciulli's actions were heavily influenced by her superstitions. The idea of losing her remaining children, especially her most beloved son, Giuseppe, was unbearable. When the Second World War beckoned, and the possibility of Giuseppe being conscripted arose, Cianciulli's fears reached a fever pitch. She believed that human sacrifices could act as a protective measure to ensure his safety.

The Grisly Murders

Between 1939 and 1940, Leonarda Cianciulli executed a series of macabre murders. Three women—Faustina Setti, Francesca Soavi, and Virginia Cacioppo—fell prey to her. Each victim was lured under different pretexts: Faustina with the promise of a husband, Francesca with a job at a school, and Virginia with a job in a town far away. Once they were in her clutches, Cianciulli drugged them, leading to their deaths. Post-murder, Leonarda's actions became even more gruesome. She dissolved their bodies in caustic soda. In a grotesque twist, she transformed the drained bodily fluids into soap, which she freely distributed among her unsuspecting neighbors. Furthermore, she used the victims' blood to make tea cakes, which she consumed and shared with acquaintances.

Arrest and Legal Proceedings

Leonarda's heinous activities came to light when Virginia Cacioppo's sister-in-law grew suspicious of her sudden disappearance and reported it. Investigators soon turned their attention to Cianciulli, who denied any wrongdoing. It wasn't until the investigators began to suspect her son Giuseppe that Cianciulli finally confessed, providing a chilling, detailed confession of her crimes to protect her son. During her 1946 trial, Cianciulli's testimonies were clinical and devoid of remorse, amplifying the horror of her actions. Recognizing the gravity of her crimes and her unstable mental state, the court sentenced her to thirty years in prison, followed by three years in a criminal asylum. Her life came to an end in the confines of the asylum in 1970.

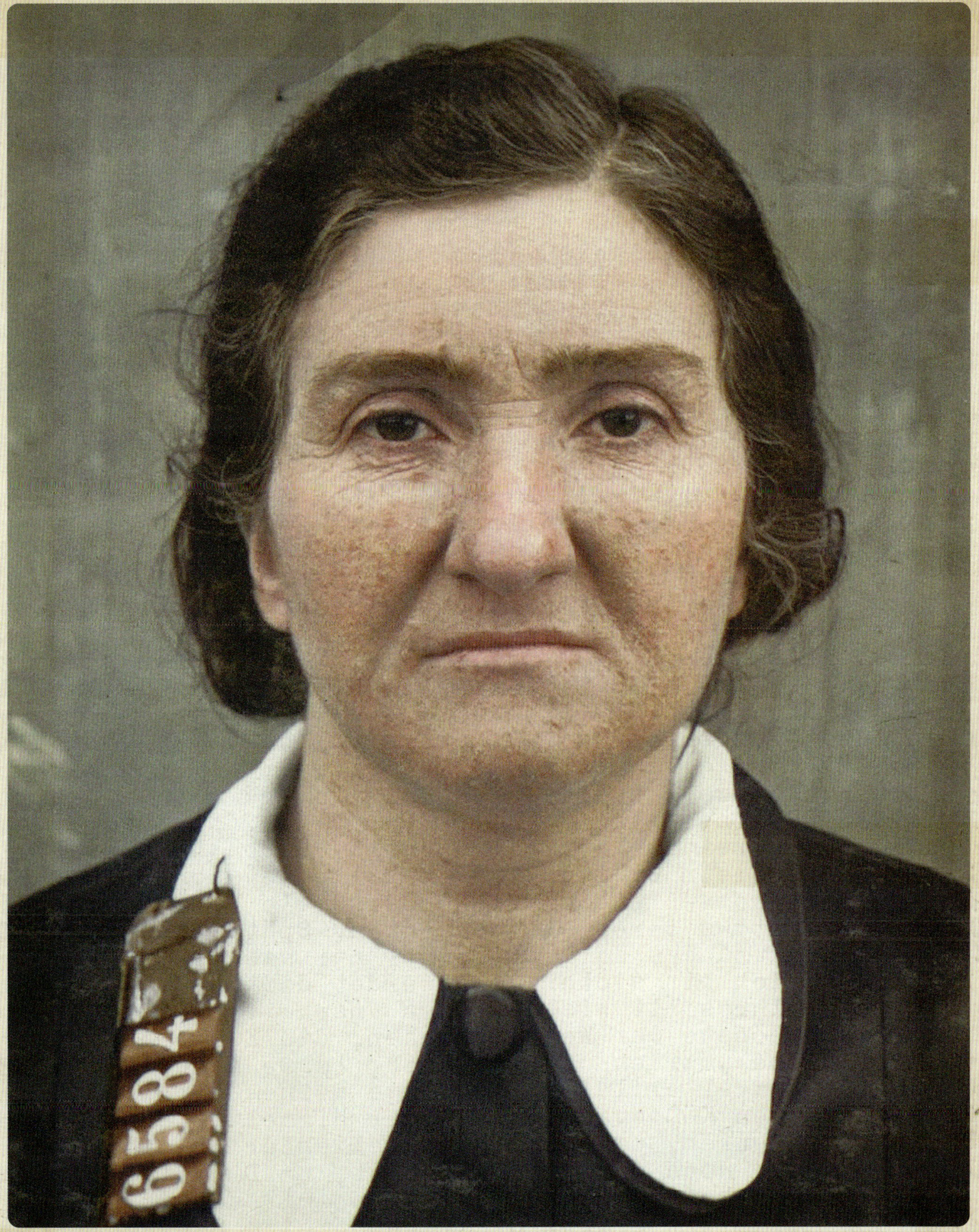

Above: Leonarda Cianciulli's mugshot. (Colorizing by Lorenzo Folli); **Opposite, top:** Faustina Setti, the spinster looking for a husband, was Cianciulli's first victim; **Opposite, center:** Francesca Soavi, who visited Cianciulli to talk about a job at a girls' school, was her second; **Opposite, below:** Virginia Cacioppo, Cianciulli's third and final victim. All three were murdered in identical fashion—given drugged wine, then killed with an axe.

The loss of his overbearing mother, to whom he was obsessively attached, triggered his descent into madness...

ED GEIN THE BUTCHER OF PLAINFIELD

Born on August 27, 1906, in La Crosse, Wisconsin, Ed Gein would become one of the most notorious figures in criminal history. His heinous crimes not only shocked the nation but also inspired several major horror films and novels.

Troubled Upbringing

Ed Gein's early life was marred by a dysfunctional family environment. His father was an alcoholic, and his mother, Augusta, was domineering and fanatically religious. She instilled in her sons a deep fear of women and the outside world, often preaching about the immorality of society. Gein's father died in 1940, followed by his brother in 1944, leaving him alone with his mother until her death in 1945. The loss of his overbearing mother, to whom he was obsessively attached, triggered Gein's descent into madness.

Horrifying Discoveries

In 1957, the small town of Plainfield, Wisconsin, was rocked by the discovery of the gruesome crimes committed by one of its residents. Following the disappearance of a local store owner, Bernice Worden, authorities visited Gein's isolated farmhouse. What they found inside was the stuff of nightmares: human body parts turned into household items, including chairs upholstered with human skin, skulls used as bowls, and masks made from faces. While Gein admitted to robbing graves, he also confessed to the murders of two women: Bernice Worden and Mary Hogan. The brutality and macabre nature of his actions earned him the moniker "The Butcher of Plainfield."

Trial and Commitment

Deemed mentally unfit for trial, Gein was sent to Central State Hospital for the Criminally Insane. It wasn't until 1968, after nearly a decade, that he was found competent to stand trial. Ultimately, Gein was found guilty of first-degree murder but was also deemed mentally insane. As a result, he was committed to the hospital where he would spend the rest of his life.

Death and Legacy

Ed Gein passed away on July 26, 1984, from respiratory difficulties and heart failure. While

The Minneapolis Tribune reported that Adeline Watkins, 50, said that during a 20-year romance with Gein 'he was so nice about doing things I wanted to do...I loved him and still do.'

he was directly linked to only two murders, the macabre nature of his crimes and the horrors found in his home left an indelible mark on the American psyche. Gein's story has been the inspiration for various dark strands in popular culture—most notably the motion pictures *Psycho* (1960), *The Texas Chainsaw Massacre* (1974), and *The Silence of the Lambs* (1991). His life and crimes serve as a grim reminder of the depths of human depravity—and the horrors that can hide in seemingly innocent and apparently civilized corners of the world.

Opposite, top to bottom: Ed Gein arriving in court on November 21, 1957; Gein on his way to a lie-detector test about other murders; A Plainfield police officer looks over Gein's dilapidated home; **This page, top:** The Gein house, boarded up after Gein had been committed to a hospital for the criminally insane; **Center:** Adeline Watkins, who remarkably came forward and told reporters she'd had "a 20-year romance" with the killer; **Above, left and right:** Before it was boarded up, the Gein house was a magnet for ghoulish sightseers—who even *dressed* as Gein and his friend Adeline Watkins—and took photos at the crime scene. Apparently, reports in the local news outlets at the time of Gein's crimes had started a humorous fad for "Geiners."

GEIN'S LEGACY OF HORROR IN POPULAR CULTURE

Ed Gein's gruesome deeds formed the model for many popular slasher movies and novels. His career as a killer, necrophile, and grave robber gave rise to such characters as Norman Bates in *Psycho* (1960), top; Leatherface in *The Texas Chainsaw Massacre* (1974), center; and Buffalo Bill (Jame Gumb) in *The Silence of the Lambs* (1991).

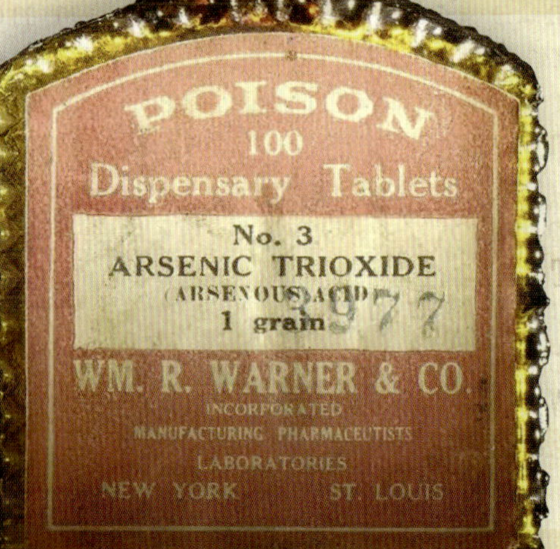

NANNIE DOSS

A SPITEFUL POISONER

Nannie Doss, colloquially known as "the Giggling Granny" or "the Jolly Black Widow," was an American serial killer responsible for the deaths of 11 people, including four of her husbands, two children, her two sisters, her mother, a grandson, and a nephew.

Early Life and Turbulent Marriages

Born on November 4, 1905, in Blue Mountain, Alabama, Doss's early life was marred by a strict and often abusive upbringing. This tumultuous childhood led her to seek solace in romance novels and daydream about her ideal husband. However, her real-life relationships were far from the romantic fantasies she cherished. Over the years, Doss married five times, with four of those marriages ending in the deaths of her spouses.

A Trail of Death

While Doss's initial killings were motivated by insurance money or property, it seems that as time went on, she killed out of spite or for perceived slights against her. Her victims were usually poisoned with arsenic or rat poison, both of which she slipped into their food or drink. The death toll began with two of her children from her first marriage, followed by her two husbands from her second and third marriages. She didn't stop at spouses and children; she also poisoned her mother, her sister Dovie, and even her grandchildren. Despite the unusual number of deaths surrounding her, Doss managed to evade suspicion for years. It was only after the death of her fifth husband, Samuel Doss, that authorities began to connect the dots.

Samuel's doctor, suspecting foul play due to the sudden onset of his illness, ordered an autopsy. The examination revealed a substantial amount of arsenic in his system.

Capture and Confession

Following the discovery of poison in Samuel Doss's body, authorities arrested Doss in 1954. During her interrogation, she not only confessed to his murder but also detailed the deaths of her previous victims. Her nonchalant demeanor and occasional giggles during the confession earned her the nickname "The Giggling Granny."

Imprisonment and Death

Nannie Doss was convicted of the murder of Samuel Doss in 1955 and was sentenced to life imprisonment. She was never tried for her other crimes. Doss spent the rest of her life in the Oklahoma State Penitentiary and died of leukemia on June 2, 1965.

Legacy

Nannie Doss's crimes stand out due to the sheer audacity with which she operated, eliminating anyone she perceived as an obstacle or annoyance. Her story serves as a chilling reminder that killers can sometimes hide behind the most unassuming facades, and that the face of evil is not always what one might expect.

Top line photos, and main image above: Nannie Doss, almost always with a smile on her face. She was getting away with murder; **Opposite, bottom left:** Doss's mugshot, October 29, 1954. The mysterious deaths come to an end as she is finally arrested on charges of murdering her fifth husband, Samuel. A wry smile even here though.

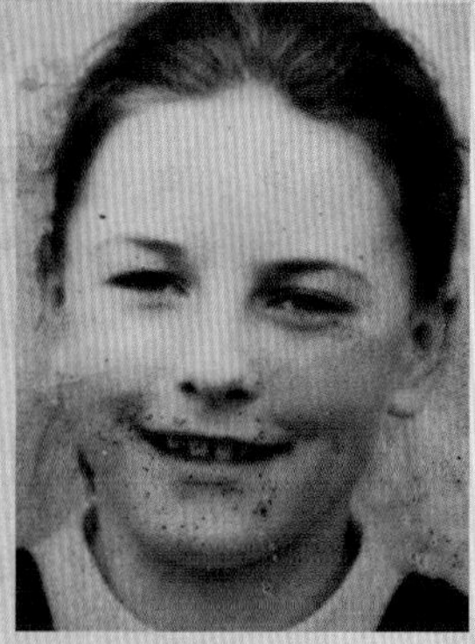
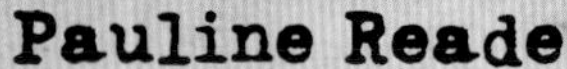
Pauline Reade

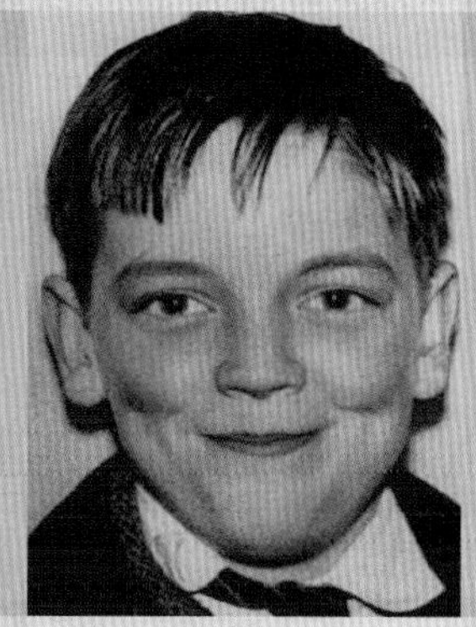
John Kilbride

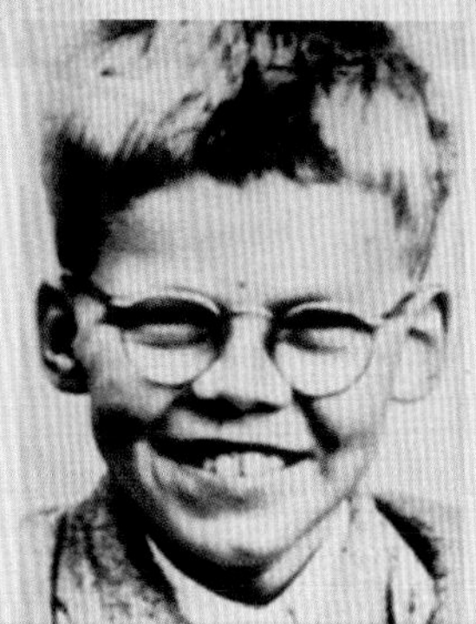
Keith Bennett

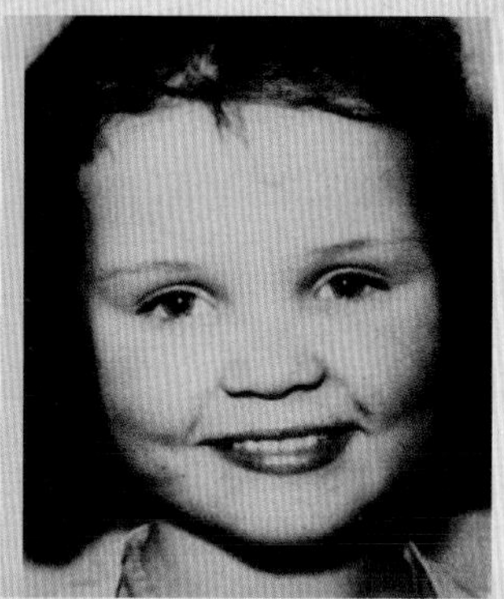
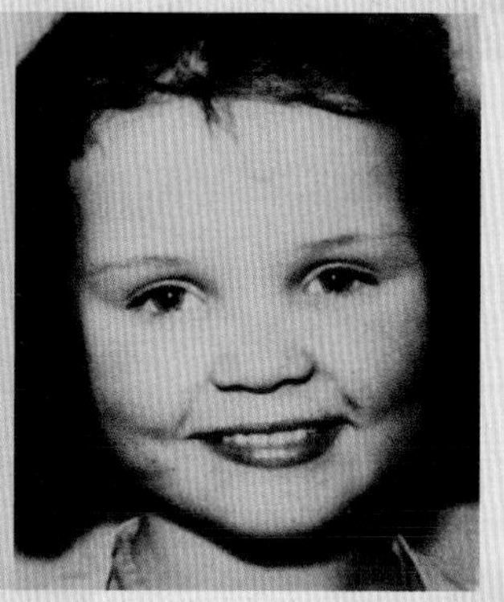
Lesley Ann Downey

Edward Evans

IAN BRADY & MYRA HINDLEY THE MOORS MURDERERS

Above: Police and members of the public search Saddleworth Moor in May 1966 for the bodies of the murdered children after Brady and Hindley's revelations. (Photo Trinity Mirror/Mirrorpix); **Top, the young murder victims, from left:** 16-year-old Pauline Reade, 12-year-old John Kilbride, Keith Bennett, also 12 years old, and 10-year-old Lesley Ann Downey. Their final victim **(top right)** was 17-year-old Edward Evans, killed in their house by an axe blow to his head. This last ghastly crime was witnessed by Hindley's brother-in-law, David Smith, who immediately left and called the police. His statement led to the discovery of Edward's body at the house. Of the four victims buried on Saddleworth Moor, Keith Bennett's remains have yet to be found.

Ian Brady was born on January 2, 1938, in Glasgow, Scotland, as Ian Duncan Stewart. His childhood was marred by neglect and a lack of supervision, leading him to a life of petty crime at a young age. Myra Hindley was born on July 23, 1942, in Crumpsall, a district of Manchester, England. Hindley's father was a violent alcoholic, and she experienced other traumas in her youth, including the early death of a close friend.

Their Relationship

The two met in 1961 while working at a chemical distribution company in Manchester. The pair quickly bonded over shared interests, including a fascination with Nazi ideology. As their relationship developed, so did their descent into darker obsessions, fueled in part by Brady's interest in sadism and the macabre.

The Moors Murders

Between 1963 and 1965, Brady and Hindley committed a series of heinous crimes that would soon be dubbed the "Moors Murders." They targeted children and teenagers, luring them with various ruses. The victims were then sexually assaulted, tortured, and murdered.

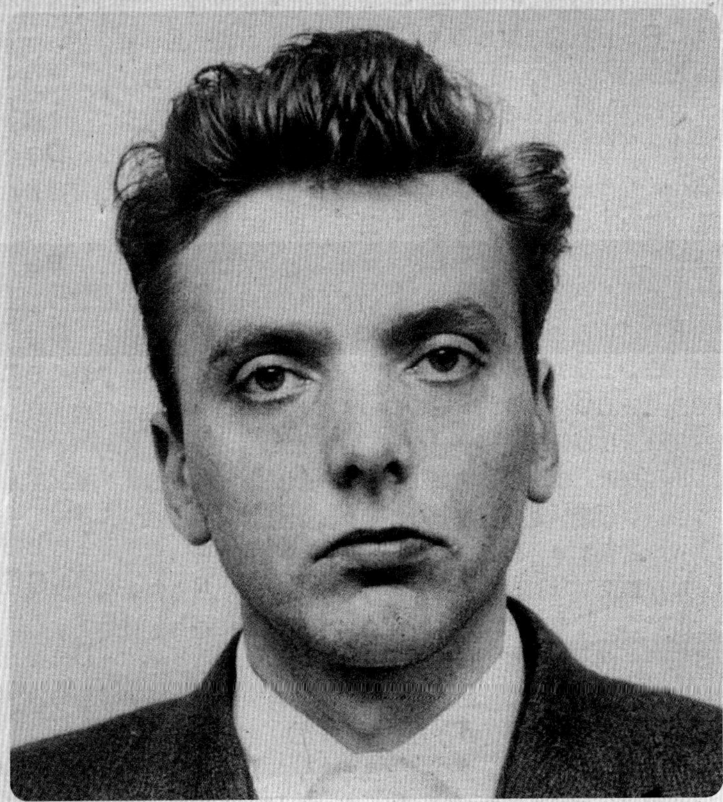

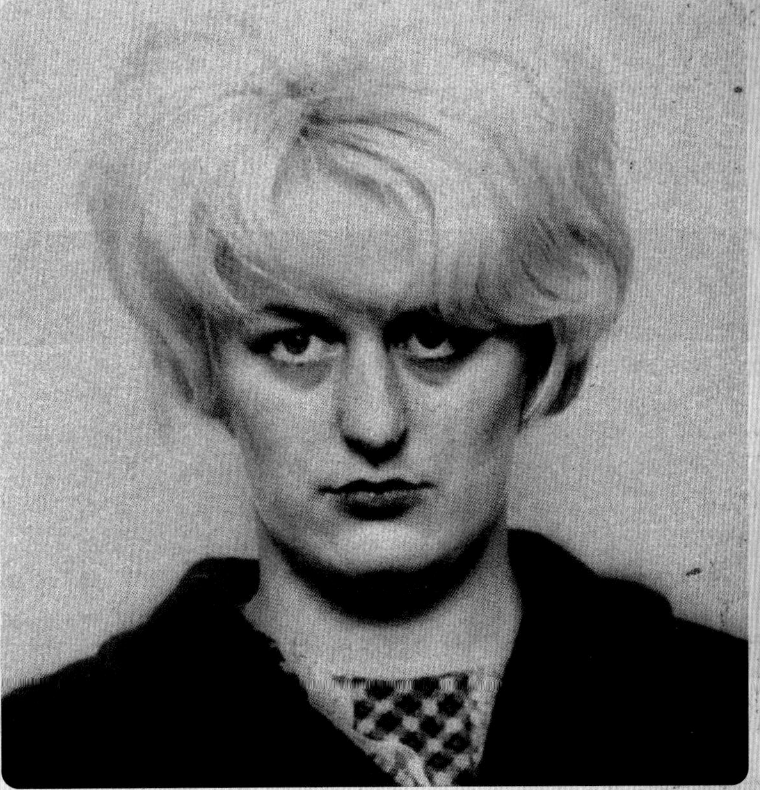

Their bodies were buried on Saddleworth Moor, a vast and desolate part of the Pennine hills near Manchester. The victims included Pauline Reade, John Kilbride, Keith Bennett, Lesley Ann Downey, and Edward Evans. The discovery of photographs and an audiotape detailing the abuse of one of their victims, Lesley Ann Downey, provided chilling evidence of their cruelty.

Capture and Trial

The duo's crime spree came to an end in October 1965 when Hindley's brother-in-law, David Smith, witnessed the murder of Edward Evans. Shocked and horrified, Smith went to the police, leading to their arrest. The trial, held in 1966, was a major media event. The evidence presented was both grim and compelling, including the haunting tape-recording of Lesley Ann Downey's final moments. Both Brady and Hindley were found guilty. Brady was convicted of three murders and Hindley of two, with both receiving life sentences.

Later Years and Deaths

While incarcerated, Brady was declared criminally insane in 1985 and transferred to Ashworth Hospital. He remained there until his death in 2017. Hindley, on the other hand, made several attempts to secure her release, asserting that she had reformed. These efforts were in vain, and she died in prison in 2002.

Legacy

The Moors Murders stand as one of the most notorious cases in British criminal history. The cold and calculated nature of Brady and Hindley's crimes, combined with their lack of remorse, has made them figures of enduring infamy. The case prompted significant media coverage and public discourse, challenging societal perceptions of evil and the nature of psychopathy. Ian Brady and Myra Hindley's actions have left an indelible mark on the British psyche, serving as a bleak reminder of the depths of human depravity and the vulnerability of society's youngest members.

Main images, top: The iconic mugshots of Ian Brady (left), and Myra Hindley; **Right:** October 28, 1965: Lesley Ann Downey's uncle is restrained by police as the two accused are separately driven away from the court in Hyde, Manchester, after the charges are laid.

RICHARD SPECK THE CHICAGO NURSE SLAYINGS OF 1966

Top: Richard Speck's mugshot taken by the Sheriff's Department, in Dallas, Texas, January 4, 1965, 18 months before the Townhouse Invasion in Chicago; **Above:** Student nurses at South Chicago Community Hospital, July 1966. Four of the group were murdered days later by Speck: Mary Ann Jordan (left), Suzanne Farris (third left), Nina Jo Schmale (fourth left), and Pamela Wilkening (right); **Opposite, top:** The eight student nurse victims of Speck, from top, left to right: Pamela Wilkening, Valentina Pasion, Pat Matusek, and Gloria Davy; second row, left to right: Suzanne Farris, Nina Jo Schmale (courtesy of the Schmale family), Merlita Gargullo, and Mary Ann Jordan.

Richard Benjamin Speck was born on December 6, 1941, in Kirkwood, Illinois. His upbringing was marked by instability, primarily due to familial issues. After the death of his father when Speck was just six, his mother remarried, introducing a stepfather into Speck's life who was known for his aggressive and often abusive behavior.

Transition to Criminality

As Speck entered his late teens and early twenties, he accumulated a series of minor criminal offenses. From forgery to theft, his infractions hinted at a deeper, burgeoning criminal inclination. With each passing year, his criminal engagements escalated in severity, often accompanied by substance abuse.

The Chicago Murders

On the night of July 13, 1966, Speck's criminal trajectory reached its horrifying zenith. He broke into a townhouse in Chicago that was occupied by nine student nurses. Over the course of the night, Speck brutalized, assaulted, and murdered eight of the young women in a spree of violence that shocked the nation. Only one nurse, Corazon Amurao, managed to survive by hiding under a bed.

Capture and Trial

The lone survivor, Amurao, played a crucial role in identifying Speck. With her testimony and the investigative efforts of the police, Speck was apprehended a few days later. His trial in 1967 was one of the most closely-watched events of the year. The evidence against him, combined with Amurao's brave testimony, led to his conviction. He was initially sentenced to death, but this was later commuted to life in prison after the U.S. Supreme Court abolished the death penalty in certain cases in 1972.

Incarceration and Death

Speck's life in prison was largely uneventful, although an illicit video surfaced in the 1980s, revealing him using drugs and engaging in inappropriate activities with another inmate. The video spurred discussions about prison oversight and conditions. Richard Speck died of a heart attack on December 5, 1991, a day before his 50th birthday.

Legacy

Richard Speck's crimes were so heinous that they remain etched in the collective American memory. His name is often cited in discussions about criminal psychology, specifically regarding what drives individuals to commit such extreme acts of violence. His case prompted a reevaluation of security measures in shared housing facilities and became a focal point in the broader dialogue about the nature of evil and the capacity for human cruelty.

Above left: Corazon Amurao, who survived Speck's attack. She was able to identify him, and later was a key witness for the prosecution; **Above:** Speck is surrounded by newsmen after receiving the death sentence.

CHARLES WHITMAN THE TEXAS UNIVERSITY TOWER SHOOTINGS

Above: Charles Whitman. On the surface, a wholesome all-American boy; **Above right, and right:** A formal Whitman family portrait, and Whitman's wedding day, marrying Kathleen Leissner on August 17, 1962; **Top right:** The Tower of the Texas University at Austin, where, from the observation deck, Whitman held the entire campus in the grip of terror.

Charles Joseph Whitman was born on June 24, 1941, in Lake Worth, Florida. Growing up in a Catholic household, Whitman's childhood was fraught with tension, primarily due to his father's violent tendencies and strict disciplinary measures. Drawn to military life and eager to escape his abusive father, Whitman enlisted in the U.S. Marine Corps at 18. His intelligence and sharpshooting abilities were quickly recognized, leading him to win a scholarship to study mechanical engineering at the University of Texas. However, his time in the university was punctuated by poor academic performance and disciplinary issues, leading to a return to active duty.

Marriage and University Life

In 1962, Whitman married Kathleen Leissner, and the couple settled in Austin, Texas. He resumed his studies at the University of Texas, but his life was anything but stable. Plagued by personal and financial struggles, Whitman began to show signs of psychological distress.

The Tower Shootings

On August 1, 1966, Whitman's growing turbulence culminated in a chilling act of violence. In the early hours, he murdered his wife and mother, leaving behind notes that explained his mental turmoil in great detail. Later that day, armed with an assortment of firearms, he ascended the University of Texas Tower. From the tower's observation deck, Whitman opened fire on unsuspecting individuals below. For nearly two hours, he held the campus in a grip of terror, indiscriminately shooting at people. By the time the ordeal ended, with Whitman being shot by police officers, he had killed 14 people and wounded over 30.

Posthumous Discoveries

The aftermath of the shooting prompted a deep dive into Whitman's life and mindset. In his notes, he had requested an autopsy to determine if there was a reason for his violent tendencies. The subsequent autopsy revealed a tumor in his brain, leading to speculation about its potential influence on his actions. However, medical opinions on whether the tumor could have directly caused his violent outburst remain divided.

Legacy and Impact

The University of Texas Tower shooting was one of the first mass shootings to occur in a public space in the U.S., receiving extensive media coverage. The event spurred debates on various issues, including gun control, campus security, and the need for better mental health interventions. Whitman's actions left an indelible mark on the University of Texas community and the nation as a whole. His case is frequently studied in criminology and psychology fields, serving as a tragic reminder of the complex interplay of factors that can lead to such catastrophic events.

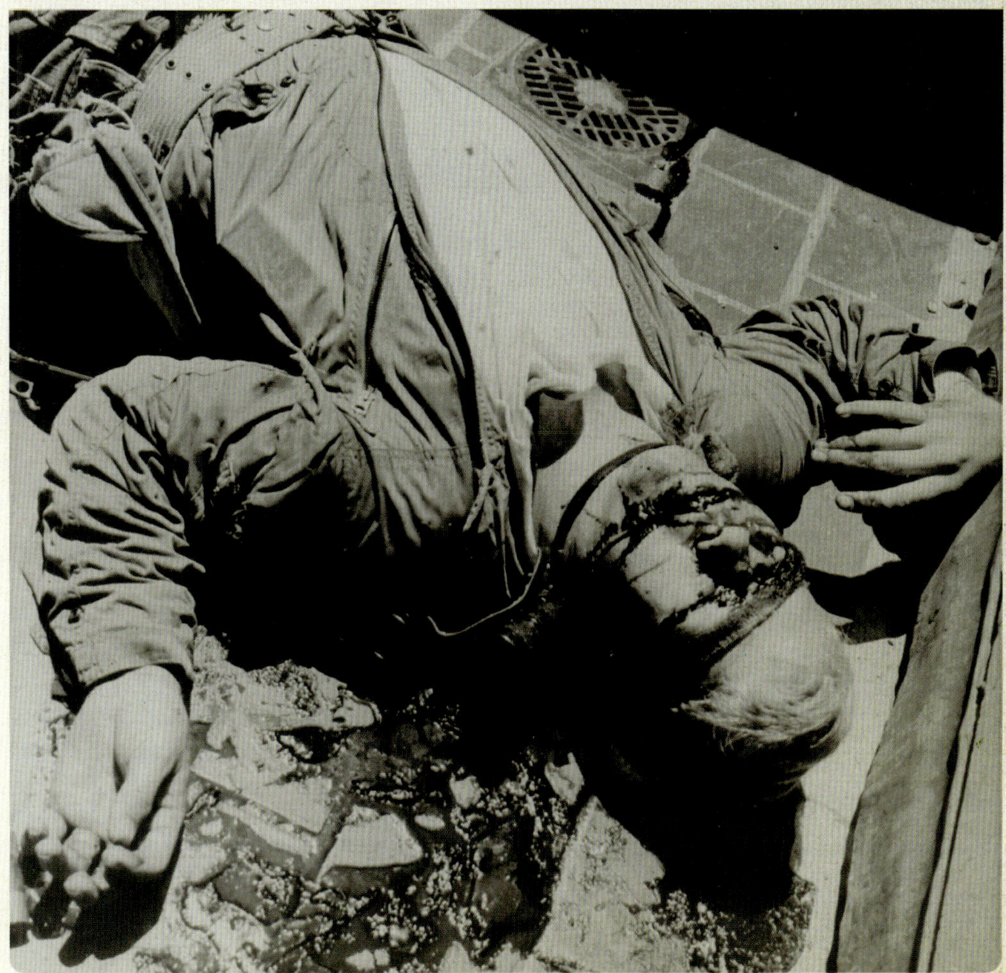

Top: An Austin policeman is carried to a waiting ambulance after being critically wounded by Charles Whitman on the 24th floor of the University of Texas Tower, August 1, 1966 (Associated Press); **Right:** The bloody corpse of Whitman after his shooting by police marksmen. The local *Troy Record* newspaper splashed the tragedy across its front page—and ran a prescient headline which read, "Psychiatrist predicts More Mass Murders"...

JOHN WAYNE GACY
KILLER CLOWN

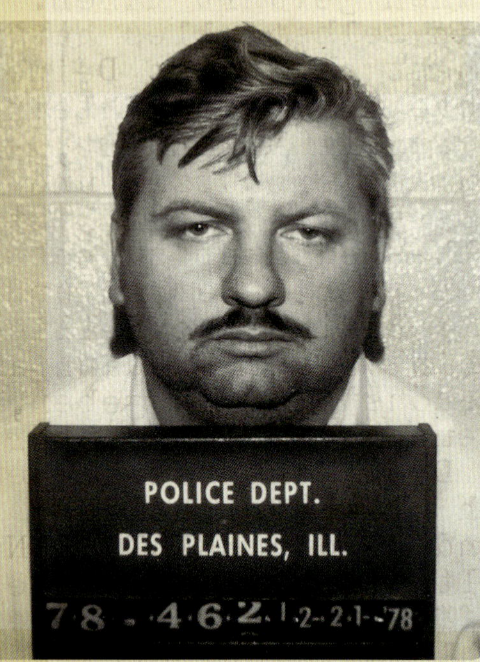

Top: Police and forensics take out the body bags; **Above:** Gacy's Des Plaines Police mugshot, after his arrest, dated as December 21, 1978.

Gacy's criminal record began in his early twenties when he was convicted of sexually assaulting two teenage boys in Iowa. After serving 18 months of a 10-year sentence, he was released on parole with the condition that he would relocate to Chicago. Once back in his hometown, Gacy seemed to settle into a normal life, starting a construction business and becoming involved in local Democratic Party politics, even having his picture taken with the First Lady at the time, Rosalynn Carter.

Crimes

However, beneath this facade of community involvement, Gacy's dark side persisted. Between 1972 and 1978, he sexually assaulted and murdered at least 33 young men and boys. Gacy lured his victims to his home with promises of work or by posing as a police officer, then overpowered them, sexually assaulted them, and ultimately strangled them. He buried 29 of his victims in the crawl space of his home, as well as elsewhere on his property, and dumped four others in the Des Plaines River.

Capture

The investigation into Gacy's crimes began when 15-year-old Robert Piest went missing on December 11, 1978. Piest was last seen leaving work to meet Gacy about a potential job. Initial police enquiries then led to the surveillance of Gacy, and a first search of his house took place. Continuing its surveillance on him, Des Plaines police then decided to arrest Gacy—for fear he might attempt suicide. This happened on December 21, 1978, and later that day a second search of his home finally did uncover evidence of his crimes—personal belongings of the missing boys…and the unmistakable stench of decaying bodies emanating from the crawl space, via a heating duct.

Trial and Death

Gacy confessed to over 30 murders. His trial began on February 6, 1980, and he was charged with 33 murders. His counsel attempted an insanity defense but this was described by the prosecution as "a sham," and on March 13, 1980 the jury found Gacy guilty on all 33 counts of murder, also finding him guilty of sexual assault and taking indecent liberties with a child. The

jury's recommendation was he be put to death. After spending 14 years on death row, Gacy was finally executed by lethal injection on May 10, 1994, at the Stateville Correctional Center in Crest Hill, Illinois.

Legacy

Gacy has since become known as the "Killer Clown," due to his habit of dressing up as "Pogo the Clown" for children's parties and charitable events—an eerie juxtaposition to his crimes. Gacy's life and crimes have been extensively examined in the context of criminal psychology, and his case has influenced both law enforcement techniques and the American legal system.

Top: Ten of Gacy's victims; **Above, center left:** Gacy (second left), pictured with Marlynn Myers, his first wife (left) at the 1967 Waterloo Jaycees Christmas party; **Above left:** Gacy poses with First Lady Rosalynn Carter on May 6, 1978. At the time this photo was taken, Gacy had perpetrated almost all of his crimes—he was a serial killer hidden in plain sight; **Above:** Gacy, as "Pogo the Clown." (Photo courtesy Martin Zielinski)

What made Rader's reign of terror even more unnerving was his ability to lead a seemingly normal life. He was married, raised two children, and was active in his church...

DENNIS RADER
BIND, TORTURE, KILL

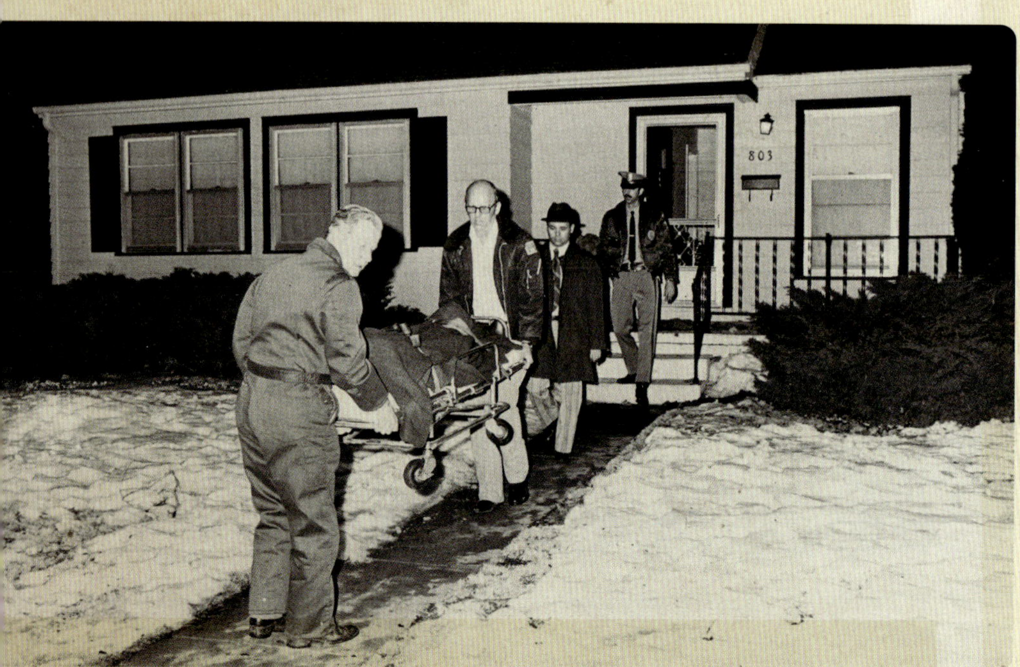

Top: Dennis Rader; **Above:** 1974. The body of an Otero family member is removed from their home in Wichita. All four members of the Otero family were assiduously stalked, then killed, by Rader. They were his first murders. (Picture by Associated Press)

The chilling acronym "BTK" stands for "Bind, Torture, Kill," a modus operandi and a self-chosen name for one of the most infamous serial killers in U.S. history, Dennis Rader.

Early Life and Obscured Darkness

Born on March 9, 1945, in Pittsburg, Kansas, Dennis Rader grew up in Wichita. Outwardly, Rader's upbringing seemed typical of mid-century America. However, from a young age, he harbored dark fantasies, often involving bondage and torture. These early inclinations would foreshadow the terror he'd later unleash.

A Series of Heinous Crimes

Rader's killing spree began in 1974 when he brutally murdered four members of the Otero family in their home. His crimes were characterized by a chilling mix of premeditation and opportunism. He would stalk potential victims, often observing them for weeks before striking. Rader's victims ranged in age, indicating his lack of a specific 'type.' Over the

years, he evaded capture, killing ten people between 1974 and 1991. Throughout this period, Rader taunted law enforcement and media with letters describing the details of his crimes, and often offering chilling narratives.

Double Life

What made Rader's reign of terror even more unnerving was his ability to lead a seemingly normal life. He was married, raised two children, and was active in his church. Rader also held various jobs, including a stint as a compliance officer. This double life allowed him to elude suspicion for decades.

Capture and Confession

Rader's own hubris led to his downfall. In 2004, he resumed communication with the media, sending letters and packages. In one such correspondence, he sent a floppy disk, which authorities were able to trace back to a computer at Rader's church. This critical lead allowed them to arrest him in February 2005. After his arrest, Rader shockingly confessed to all the BTK killings, providing gruesome details with a chilling detachment. He seemed to relish recounting his crimes, showing no remorse for the lives he'd taken.

Sentencing and Imprisonment

Given the weight of evidence and his own confession, Rader was swiftly brought to trial. In August 2005, he was sentenced to ten consecutive life terms without the possibility of parole, as Kansas had no death penalty at the time of his crimes. Rader is currently incarcerated at the El Dorado Correctional Facility in Kansas.

Legacy

The BTK killings and subsequent capture underscore the unsettling reality that sometimes, monsters hide in plain sight. Rader's ability to compartmentalize his life, being a family man by day and a ruthless killer by night, remains a dark testament to the complexities of human psychology. The case serves as a chilling reminder of the depths of depravity that can lurk behind the most ordinary facades.

Above: Rader in chains for the remainder of his life; **Top left:** Rader poses with his daughter, showing his pleasant, public, "everyday good guy" persona; **Top right:** The chilling image of Rader in private—attempting sexual gratification by assuming the role of his victims in peril. Dressed in a blond wig and painted mask, and hands tied behind his back to a chair, Rader's picture is reported to have been taken by him in 1991—after he had killed Dolores Davis. Psychologists believe it is an attempt to recreate the murder scene in order to achieve sexual release.

TED BUNDY THE CHARISMATIC PSYCHOPATH

Top and above: In his trial in Miami for the Chi Omega homicides in June 1979, Bundy conducted his own defense, and in so doing exhibited some of the psychologically-profiled traits of the serial killer—sensation seeking, narcissism and grandiosity.

Ted Bundy, born Theodore Robert Cowell on November 24, 1946, in Burlington, Vermont, had a complicated early life. Raised believing his grandparents were his parents and his mother was his sister, Bundy's discovery of the truth may have influenced his later actions.

Deceptive Charm

Bundy was academically gifted and notably charismatic. He enrolled in various colleges, studying psychology and law, and even showed promise in politics. To those who knew him, Bundy seemed like a promising individual with a bright future. However, beneath this facade lurked a darker nature.

A Terrifying Spree

Bundy's early criminal activities were relatively minor, consisting of theft and burglary. However, in the early 1970s, he escalated to kidnapping, sexual assault, and murder as he embarked on a series of heinous crimes across several states, including Washington, Utah, and Colorado. He used his charm to lure young women, often feigning injury to elicit sympathy or posing as an authority figure. Once he gained their trust, he would overpower and sexually assault them before killing them, typically by bludgeoning or strangulation. Bundy's modus operandi wasn't consistent; he employed various means, making it challenging for authorities to link the crimes initially. This unpredictability, combined with his ability to change his appearance, allowed him to evade capture multiple times.

Arrests and Escapes

Bundy was first arrested in 1975. He managed to escape custody twice in 1977; first by jumping from a second story window, and later by losing about 30 pounds in order to fit through a small opening in the ceiling of his cell. The latter escape was successful, and Bundy fled to Chicago, then Florida. Bundy committed several more murders and assaults during a violent crime spree while on the run in Florida before his

Left: A montage of some of Bundy's victims published in a UK tabloid. **Top row, left to right:** Kimberly Leach; Caryn Campbell; Margaret Bowman; Debra Kent. **Second row:** Laura Ann Aime; Roberta Parks; Georgann Hawkins; Donna Manson. **Third row:** Lynda Healy; Janice Ott; Denise Naslund; Susan Rancourt. **Fourth row:** Katherine Devine; Melissa Smith; Brenda Ball; Lisa Levy. *In 2002, Katherine Devine was ascertained to have been murdered by William Cosden—not Bundy.

final arrest in 1978. The most infamous of these was his attack on the Chi Omega Sorority house, killing two women and injuring two others.

Confessions and Execution

After his capture in Florida, Bundy was tried and received three death sentences in two separate trials. While on death row, he confessed to 30 murders, though the actual number remains unknown and could be much higher. During this time, Bundy was interviewed extensively by criminologists and psychologists who were eager to understand the motivations behind his crimes. Bundy offered varying explanations, sometimes blaming pornography and at other times hinting at a compulsion he couldn't control. On January 24, 1989, Bundy met his end in the electric chair at Florida State Prison.

Legacy and Cultural Impact

Ted Bundy's life and crimes have been the subject of countless articles, documentaries, movies, and books. He stands out in the annals of criminal history because of the juxtaposition of his charm and brutality. To many, he exemplifies the idea that monsters can hide behind the most ordinary, even charming, faces.

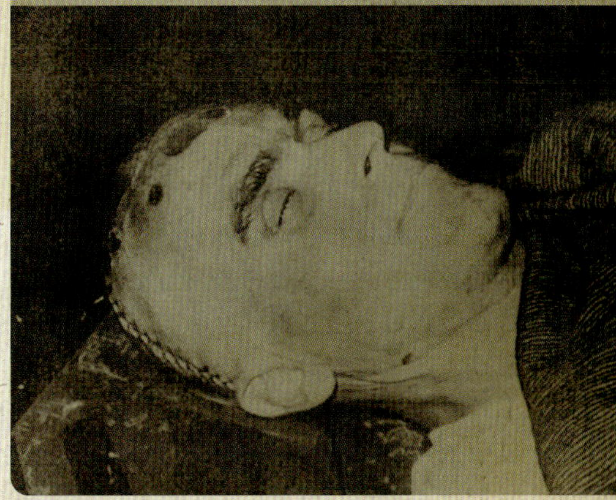

Top: Bundy delivers a stare at the photographer during his final trial in Florida; **Center:** An archive photo of one of the first "electric chair" executions; **Above:** The charismatic psychopath was executed in the Florida State Prison electric chair on January 24, 1989.

ANDREI CHIKATILO THE BUTCHER OF ROSTOV

SOVIET AND NAZI BRUTALIZATION

Top left: Chikatilo's "killing kit"; **Top center:** The memorial to Irina Karabelnikova, Chikatilo's seventh victim, at the site of her murder; **Top right:** A hysterical Chikatilo after his capture by Soviet police; **Above:** The serial killer responsible for the deaths of at least 52 people was kept in a cage during his trial.

Andrei Romanovich Chikatilo was born on October 16, 1936, in Yabluchne, a village in the heart of the Ukrainian SSR, during a time of widespread hardship under Stalin's regime. The son of a PoW and a mother who was a victim of the famine and hardship of the era, Chikatilo grew up in a climate of extreme deprivation. This period of Soviet history, marked by Nazi invasion, would cast a long shadow over Chikatilo's psychological development. He was a chronic bedwetter, and his mother berated him for his condition, further contributing to his feelings of inadequacy and isolation. Despite these challenges, Chikatilo was a model student, though socially awkward and often bullied by his peers.

Above left: The bridge over the Grushevka River, where the body of Yelena Zakotnova was found, on Christmas Eve, 1978; **Above:** Andrei Chikatilo photographed in the 1970s. After being convicted of 52 murders, he was executed with a shot to the back of his head.

Crimes

Chikatilo's criminal activities spanned from 1978 to 1990, during which he committed at least 52 murders, making him one of the most prolific serial killers in modern history. His victims, mostly young women and children, were lured under various pretenses to secluded areas where they were then brutally assaulted, murdered, and mutilated. Chikatilo's method of killing involved stabbing and slashing his victims, leading to his moniker, "The Butcher of Rostov." His crimes were not only marked by their brutality but also by the sexual nature of the assaults, reflecting his deeply troubled psyche.

Capture and Trial

Chikatilo's arrest on November 20, 1990, was the culmination of one of the most extensive and exhaustive manhunts in the USSR. The investigation was hampered by the Soviet authorities' reluctance to acknowledge the possibility of a serial killer, a stance that delayed the apprehension of Chikatilo for years. His capture was eventually facilitated by a combination of forensic evidence and surveillance, following a pattern of behavior that linked him to the locations where victims had been abducted. During his trial, which began in April 1992, Chikatilo was kept in a specially constructed iron cage for his protection. The proceedings were marked by his erratic behavior, including outbursts and confessions to the gruesome details of his crimes. On October 15, 1992, Chikatilo was convicted of 52 murders and sentenced to death. After a lengthy appeals process, he was executed by a gunshot to the back of the head on February 14, 1994.

Legacy

Andrei Chikatilo's case had a profound impact on Russian society and its criminal justice system. It exposed the inadequacies of Soviet police work and forensic methods, leading to significant reforms in how serial crimes were investigated and prosecuted in post-Soviet Russia.

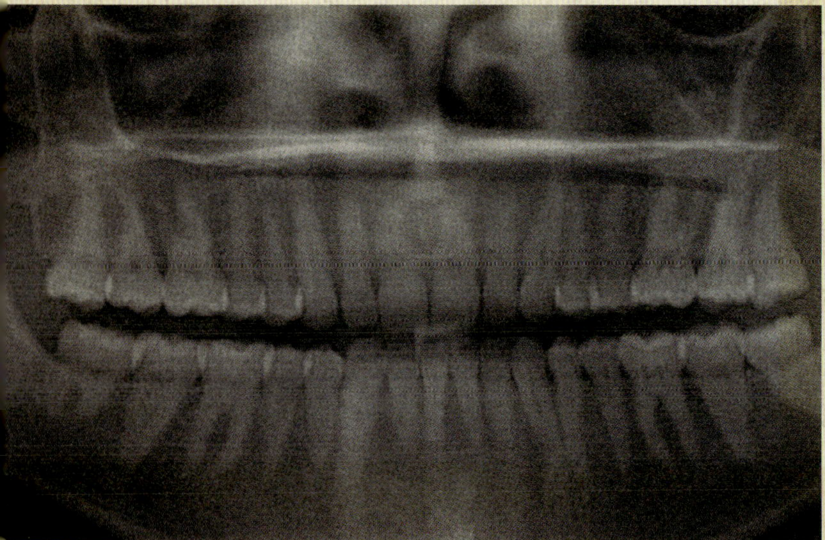

NIKOLAI DZHUMAGALIEV METAL FANG THE KAZAKHSTANI CANNIBAL

Nikolai Dzhumagaliev was born in 1952 in Uzynagash, a small town near Almaty, Kazakhstan, during the period when it was part of the Soviet Union. Little is known about his early life or family background, but his later behavior would suggest a disturbed psyche from a young age.

Mental Health and Early Indications

Dzhumagaliev had lost a couple of teeth in a fight in his youth and they had been replaced with white metal prosthetics, earning him the chilling nickname "Metal Fang." At age 18 he was conscripted into the Soviet army, where he served as a cadet for several years. After completing his military service, Dzhumagaliev had a number of jobs in the construction and electrical trades, even working as a sailor, before joining the city of Almaty firefighting service. Medical records researched after his arrest state that around this time he was diagnosed with schizophrenia.

String of Murders

Starting in the late 1970s, Dzhumagaliev embarked on a killing spree that would terrorize Kazakhstan. His modus operandi was consistent: he preyed on women, often luring them into secluded areas. Once isolated, he would brutally kill them, dismembering their bodies with precision. Disturbingly, Dzhumagaliev engaged in acts of cannibalism, consuming parts of his victims and, on at least one occasion, serving their remains to unsuspecting friends. His meticulous method of disposing of the bodies made it challenging

for the authorities to estimate the total number of his victims. Although he was convicted for 10 murders, some believe the actual number might be higher.

Capture and Institutionalization

Dzhumagaliev's reign of terror came to an end in 1980. His ninth murder, involving the dismemberment of a victim during a party he had hosted at his home, led to his initial capture in December 1980. However, due to the police's shock at catching Dzhumagaliev in the act of eating a corpse, he managed to escape briefly before he was apprehended the next day. The nature and gruesomeness of his crimes led to public outrage, demanding swift justice. However, given his clear signs of mental illness, he was deemed unfit for a traditional trial. Instead, Dzhumagaliev was declared insane and remanded to a special treatment center for eight years. In August 1989, he escaped from the mental hospital and was on the run for several years, during which he was suspected of committing more murders. In 1991, Dzhumagaliev was recaptured in Fergana after staging a theft and turning himself in. He was then returned to a psychiatric hospital in Kazakhstan. As of the last update, he remains incarcerated in a specialized psychiatric clinic, with the question of his discharge still open. In 2014, he was convicted of another murder committed in 1990 in Aktobe. Rumors of his escape circulated in 2016, but these were found to be false.

Later Years

Dzhumagaliev's confinement wasn't without incident. He managed to escape from the facility on multiple occasions, causing widespread panic each time. However, he was always recaptured. Details about his later life are scant, but he remains one of the most notorious figures in the annals of crime in Kazakhstan, a stark embodiment of the blend of mental illness and violence.

Opposite, top left: Dental X-ray; **Opposite, top right:** Nikolai Dzhumagaliev during his incarceration; **Opposite, bottom left:** Dzhumagaliev, after his arrest, December 1980; **This page, top left:** A unit of Soviet army cadets in Moscow, 1972. This would be how Dzhumagaliev spent his basic training and inculcation into the Soviet Communist system; **This page, top right:** Kazakhstani firefighters. Dzhumagaliev began his murders some 18 months after joining the Almaty firefighting service; **Above:** Dzhumagaliev (second left) is captured after fleeing the scene of his cannibalism, late December 1980.

JEFFREY DAHMER

SERIAL KILLER. NECROPHILE. CANNIBAL.

Jeffrey Lionel Dahmer, infamously dubbed the "Milwaukee Cannibal" or the "Milwaukee Monster," was born on May 21, 1960, in Milwaukee, Wisconsin. As a child, Dahmer displayed unsettling interests, such as a fascination with dead animals. His early life was further complicated by his parents' troubled marriage and eventual divorce, factors that some speculate may have contributed to his dark evolution.

Initial Offenses

Dahmer's first arrests—in 1981 and 1982—were for drunk and disorderly conduct and indecent exposure, followed by more arrests for similar offenses over the years. His first murder, however, was committed several years earlier. In 1978, Dahmer lured hitchhiker Steven Hicks to his home, then killed him, dissected his body, and eventually buried him in the back yard.

A String of Horrifying Crimes

Between 1978 and 1991, Dahmer committed a series of gruesome murders, claiming 17 male victims in total. His modus operandi was chilling. Often luring young men to his apartment, Dahmer would drug, assault, and eventually murder them. But death was only the beginning of the horror. Dahmer's

crimes included acts of necrophilia and cannibalism. He kept trophies, such as skulls or photographs of the mutilated bodies, further showcasing his morbid obsession. On two occasions, Dahmer came within moments of being caught, only to talk his way out of police scrutiny. In May of 1991, 14-year-old Konerak Sinthasomphone—a Lao teenager Dahmer had been keeping prisoner in his apartment—escaped, and the police were called. Dahmer was able to convince the police that Sinthasomphone was his intoxicated boyfriend, however, even leading the officers into his apartment where a decomposing body was hidden at the time. The police returned Sinthasomphone to Dahmer's custody and left, labeling the incident a domestic dispute. On another occasion, Dahmer was pulled over for reckless driving with a garbage bag full of human remains in the back of his car, but convinced the police to let him go with a warning.

Capture and Confession

Dahmer's reign of terror concluded on July 22, 1991, when one of his intended victims managed to escape and alert the police. Officers arriving at Dahmer's apartment discovered a scene straight out of the darkest nightmares: human remains in his refrigerator, photographs of dismembered bodies, and an environment rife with evidence of his horrific acts. Upon arrest, Dahmer confessed in exacting detail to the murders. He displayed a candidness that both helped investigators and further shocked the public, providing insight into the twisted psyche of one of America's most notorious serial killers.

Trial and Death

In 1992, Dahmer was put on trial. Given the overwhelming evidence and his own confession, the primary focus of the trial was his mental state. His defense argued that he was insane, driven by uncontrollable urges, while the prosecution painted him as an evil individual fully aware of his crimes. Dahmer was found guilty and sentenced to 16 life terms in prison. However, Dahmer's time behind bars was short-lived. On November 28, 1994, he was killed by a fellow inmate, Christopher Scarver, at the Columbia Correctional Institution in Portage, Wisconsin.

Legacy and Continuing Fascination

The name Jeffrey Dahmer has become synonymous with the archetype of the deranged serial killer. His crimes have been analyzed in countless documentaries, books, and films, attempting to understand the man behind the monstrous deeds. Dahmer's case continues to fascinate criminologists, psychologists, and the public, serving as a grim reminder of the depths of human depravity. His life and actions challenge our perceptions of evil, prompting questions about the origins of such dark impulses: are they born out of inherent malevolence, societal failures, psychological defects, or a harrowing mix of all these factors?

Opposite, top left: Dahmer is led into court for arraignment; **Opposite, top right:** The South 2nd Street district of Milwaukee, where he alighted on most of his 17 known victims; **Opposite, bottom left:** Dahmer as a three-year-old toddler—already displaying a disregard for other lives; **This page, top left:** The Oxford Apartments, where Dahmer lived, January 1992; **This page, top right:** Dahmer's charges are laid out in the County Circuit Court, August 7th, 1991; **Inset above:** Four of his luckless victims, clockwise from top left: **Stephen Hicks, 18,** killed June 18, 1978; **James Doxtator, 14,** January 16, 1988; **Richard Guerrero, 22,** March 24, 1988; **Anthony Sears, 24,** March 25, 1989.

LUIS GARAVITO LA BESTIA

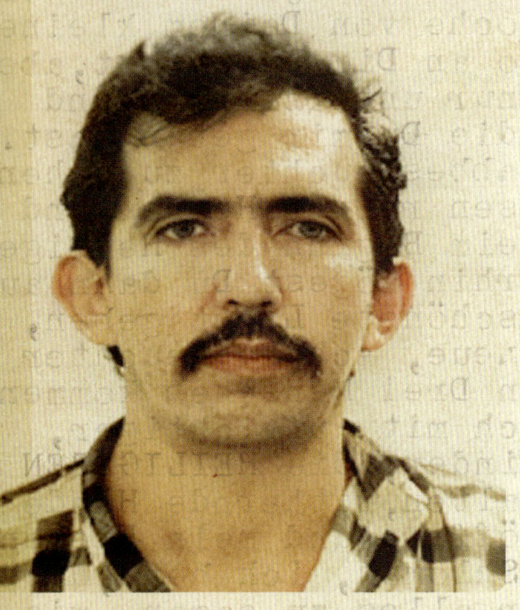

Above: Garavito's mugshot, after his capture in April 1999; **Top:** Garavito interviewed in prison, circa 2000. He cooperated with Colombian police in locating the remains of some of his victims; **Opposite, all pictures:** Colombian police and forensic teams at a death site bag up remains of Garavito's young victims.

Luis Alfredo Garavito Cubillos, born on January 25, 1957, in Génova, Quindío, Colombia, grew up in a poverty-stricken and abusive household. He was the oldest of seven, and often bore the brunt of his father's alcoholic rages. Garavito's childhood was marred by physical and emotional abuse, and he also claimed to have been a victim of sexual abuse, although these claims remain unverified. The toxic environment of his early years is believed to have played a significant role in shaping his later actions. Despite his troubled upbringing, little in Garavito's early life could have indicated the extreme violence he would go on to perpetrate.

Crimes

Luis Garavito is considered one of the most prolific serial killers in history. His crimes were committed over a span of 19 years from 1980 to 1999, during which he preyed on young boys between the ages of six and 16. Garavito's victims were primarily street children, orphans, or children from impoverished backgrounds whom he lured away with small gifts or the promise of money. Once isolated, the children were subjected to torture, rape, and ultimately murder. Garavito's method of killing involved slitting the throats of his victims and often dismembering their bodies. The sheer number of his victims, which he confessed to be over 100, and potentially as many as 300, earned him the nickname "La Bestia"—The Beast.

Capture and Confession

Garavito's capture on April 22, 1999, was somewhat fortuitous. He was initially apprehended for attempted rape against an adolescent boy, which led to a broader investigation. The breakthrough came when detectives found a mass grave with the bodies of numerous children, all bearing similar signs of torture and murder. Garavito's glasses were found at a crime scene, which, along with survivor accounts, led to his arrest. Under

interrogation, Garavito confessed to the murders, providing detailed accounts of his crimes and leading police to the gravesites of his victims.

Trial and Imprisonment

In 1999, Garavito was charged with the murder of 138 children, though the actual number of his victims is believed to be much higher. He was found guilty and sentenced to 1,853 years and 9 days in prison, the lengthiest sentence in Colombian history. However, due to Colombian law, which does not allow imprisonment for more than 40 years, and because Garavito helped police find victims' bodies and was considered to have shown "good behavior," his sentence was later reduced to 22 years. He developed eye cancer and leukemia while imprisoned and died in October of 2023.

ISSEI SAGAWA
A CANNIBAL IN PARIS

Issei Sagawa was born on April 26, 1949, in Kobe, Hyōgo Prefecture, Japan, into a wealthy family. Afflicted with a disease that stunted his growth, Sagawa grew up physically frail but intellectually curious. He exhibited an early interest in literature and the arts but also harbored darker fantasies that would later shape his life's tragic trajectory.

Educational Journey

Sagawa attended Wako University in Tokyo where he studied English literature. Following his graduation, he moved to France to pursue doctoral studies in comparative literature at the Sorbonne in Paris. It was here that he grew increasingly isolated and his cannibalistic fantasies intensified.

The Crime

On June 11, 1981, Sagawa invited his classmate Renée Hartevelt to his apartment under the pretext of translating German poetry for a school project. Once she had her back to him, he shot her in the neck with a rifle. Sagawa then proceeded to sexually assault her corpse and consume various parts of her body over the course of two days. He captured the act through photographs and even attempted to preserve some of her remains.

Capture and Legal Outcome

Sagawa attempted to dispose of Hartevelt's remains in a lake in the Bois de Boulogne, but was seen in the act and subsequently arrested by French police. After his arrest, Sagawa was held in French custody, where he underwent extensive psychological evaluations. Psychiatrists declared him legally insane, finding him unfit to stand trial, and he was ordered to be held indefinitely in a

Left and top left: Sagawa in the custody of the French police after his arrest in Paris on June 15, 1981; **Top, and opposite:** Sagawa was a constant source of fascination for journalists and filmmakers around the world, and he conducted many interviews; **Above:** Sagawa the outsider, alone in Tokyo.

mental institution. However, in a controversial decision in 1984, Sagawa was deported to Japan due to a request by his wealthy father and a loophole in the extradition agreement between France and Japan. Upon his return, Japanese authorities found themselves in a legal bind; French courts had sealed the case files and deemed Sagawa unfit for trial, leaving Japan with no grounds to charge him. Consequently, after a brief period in a Japanese mental hospital, Sagawa was released in August 1985, having spent a total of approximately five years in custody without ever being convicted of his crime.

Aftermath and Legacy

Following his release, Sagawa became a minor celebrity in Japan and, to some extent, internationally. He has written books, including a memoir detailing the murder and cannibalism of Hartevelt, appeared in films and documentaries, and even contributed to magazines and public discussions on his crime. Sagawa's case has sparked debates on mental health, the justice system, and the nature of celebrity culture that seemingly rewards infamy. Despite the public's fascination, Sagawa's freedom has been a source of outrage and sorrow. In the late 2010s, Sagawa's health began to deteriorate significantly. He was hospitalized with various illnesses, including diabetes and heart issues, and died in November of 2022.

RICHARD RAMIREZ THE NIGHT STALKER

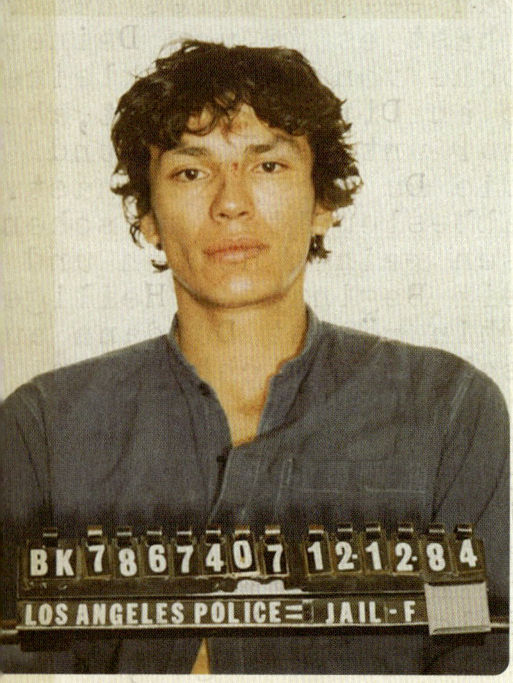

Top left: Ramirez departs after an early court appearance, September 1985; **Top right:** Ramirez flashes the pentagram scrawled on his palm during his trial; **Above:** Ramirez's mugshot from December 1984, taken after his arrest for auto theft.

Richard Ramirez, born Ricardo Leyva Muñoz Ramirez on February 29, 1960, in El Paso, Texas, grew up in a tumultuous household, the youngest of five children. His father, Julián Ramirez, a former police officer turned laborer, was prone to fits of anger that often resulted in physical abuse. From an early age, Ramirez was exposed to violence and criminal behavior, notably through his cousin Miguel, a Vietnam War veteran who shared graphic stories and photographs of wartime atrocities and taught Ramirez military skills like stealth and killing. This exposure, combined with a head injury at age five and subsequent epileptic seizures, contributed to Ramirez's disturbed adolescence, marked by petty theft, drug use, and an increasing interest in Satanism.

Crimes

Richard Ramirez's reign of terror, which earned him the nickname "The Night Stalker," spanned from June 1984 to August 1985. During this period, Ramirez committed a series of brutal home invasion crimes in California that included at least 13 murders, 11 sexual assaults, and 14 burglaries. His victims ranged in age from nine to 83, reflecting a chilling indifference to human life. Ramirez's method of operation varied, but his crimes were characterized by exceptional brutality and often included satanic symbols left at crime scenes. He utilized a variety of weapons, including handguns, knives, a tire iron, and a hammer, demonstrating a chilling adaptability and lack of remorse.

Capture and Trial

Ramirez's capture on August 31, 1985, was as dramatic as his crime spree. After his latest stolen car was identified and his fingerprints were matched to those found at multiple crime scenes, his picture was released to the media. Recognized by residents in East Los Angeles, Ramirez was pursued and captured by a group of civilians until the police arrived to arrest him. His trial, which began on July 22, 1988, was a

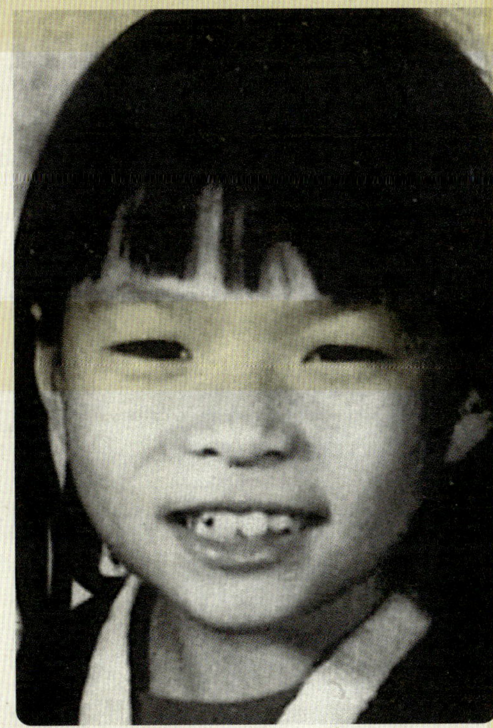

media circus, notable for Ramirez's outbursts and the pentagram he occasionally displayed on his hand. On September 20, 1989, Ramirez was convicted of all charges, including 13 counts of murder, five attempted murders, 11 sexual assaults, and 14 burglaries. He was sentenced to death.

Death

Richard Ramirez died of complications related to B-cell lymphoma on June 7, 2013, while on death row at San Quentin State Prison in California. At the time of his death, he was 53 years old and had been awaiting execution for over 23 years, during which he had attracted a following of admirers and even married one of his supporters in 1996.

Top left: Two of the Night Stalker's victims, Lela and Maxon Kneiding; **Above left:** The earliest—and youngest—of Ramirez's victims, nine-year-old Mei Leung—although Ramirez wasn't identified as her killer until 2009; **Above:** Ramirez adopts his psychotic stare during his trial. He was found guilty and convicted of all charges—13 counts of murder, five attempted murders, 11 sexual assaults, and 14 burglaries, and sentenced to death.

His methodical approach—moving from table to table and engaging victims in brief conversation before shooting them—added a chilling dimension to the massacre...

CAMPO DELGADO THE POZZETTO MASSACRE

Top: A younger Delgado; **Above:** The Pozzetto Restaurant in Bogotá; **Opposite:** Snippets from the internet—clockwise from top left: The death scene at Pozzetto Restaurant in the aftermath; police arrive during Delgado's violence; outside Pozzetto after the event; taking out the dead; and Delgado's passport.

Campo Elias Delgado Morales was born on May 14, 1934, in Chinácota, Colombia. His early years were marked by tragedy when he witnessed his father's suicide. This event had a profound impact on his psychological well-being, and forever damaged his relationship with his sister and mother, who he blamed for his father's death. Delgado later served in the U.S. military, rising to the rank of Sergeant first class, before being honorably discharged. Although he claimed to have fought in Vietnam, the time period during which he was enlisted makes this unlikely.

Return to Colombia

After his military service, Delgado returned to Colombia. He lived a relatively isolated life, residing in Bogotá with his aging mother, who he resented and blamed for his inability to connect with others. Acquaintances described him as a withdrawn man of few words, and he often expressed disillusionment with society. There were signs of his deteriorating mental state as he occasionally shared unsettling stories about his alleged time in Vietnam, oscillating between moments of clarity and intense paranoia.

BOG-1 BOGOTA, 5 (ap) El cadaver de Campo Elías Delgado, de 52 años, aparece en la gráfica portando un cinturón con caryuchos de bala que utilizó para matar ayer a 21 personas en dos ataques contra un edificio de apartamentos y un restaurante. A su lado cadáveres de algunas de sus víctimas. Delgado, al parecer exveterano de Vietnam, sufrió un ataque de locura. RDP AP. 5/12/86. Sstringer Gonzalez./ FOTO CARLOS GONZALEZ S.

The Massacre

On December 4, 1986, Delgado's simmering tensions culminated in a horrifying act of violence. He began his killing spree by murdering a mother and daughter who had once hired him to provide tutoring in English. He then returned to his apartment to kill his own mother, before setting the apartment on fire and continuing his rampage through the building. After killing 10 people in the apartment building, he visited the upscale restaurant Pozzetto, where he systematically killed 20 diners in the establishment. His methodical approach—moving from table to table and engaging victims in brief conversation before shooting them—added a chilling dimension to the massacre. Police eventually stormed the restaurant, leading to a standoff that resulted in Delgado's death.

Aftermath and Speculations

The reasons behind Delgado's violent outburst remain a topic of speculation. Some point to the trauma he experienced during his military service, combined with his challenges in reintegrating into society, as significant contributing factors. Others believe underlying psychological issues, potentially exacerbated by the early loss of his father and his isolated lifestyle, played a role. The massacre had a profound impact on Colombian society. The Pozzetto Massacre, as it came to be known, remains one of the deadliest attacks by a lone gunman in Colombia's history. Delgado's case is often referenced in discussions related to the psychological scars of trauma and the need for comprehensive mental health support for veterans.

The Hungerford Massacre had significant repercussions. The sheer randomness of the attack, carried out in broad daylight in a peaceful community, led to rigorous debates in Britain about gun control...

MICHAEL RYAN
THE HUNGERFORD MASSACRE 1987

Top: Michael Ryan, the Hungerford shooter; **Above:** The tranquil and picturesque market town of Hungerford, Berkshire in 1987.

Michael Robert Ryan was born on May 18, 1960, in Marlborough, Wiltshire, England. His upbringing was relatively uneventful, growing up in a town known for its tranquility and community ties. Despite this serene backdrop, Ryan was often described as a loner, struggling with social interactions and exhibiting early signs of an obsessive personality.

Fascination with Firearms

As he transitioned into adulthood, Ryan developed a deep fascination with firearms. He amassed a collection of weapons, often spending beyond his means to purchase them. This obsession extended to military paraphernalia, and he was frequently seen donning combat attire, even though he had no military background.

The Hungerford Massacre

On August 19, 1987, Ryan's growing instability manifested in one of Britain's most notorious shooting incidents. Armed with a semi-

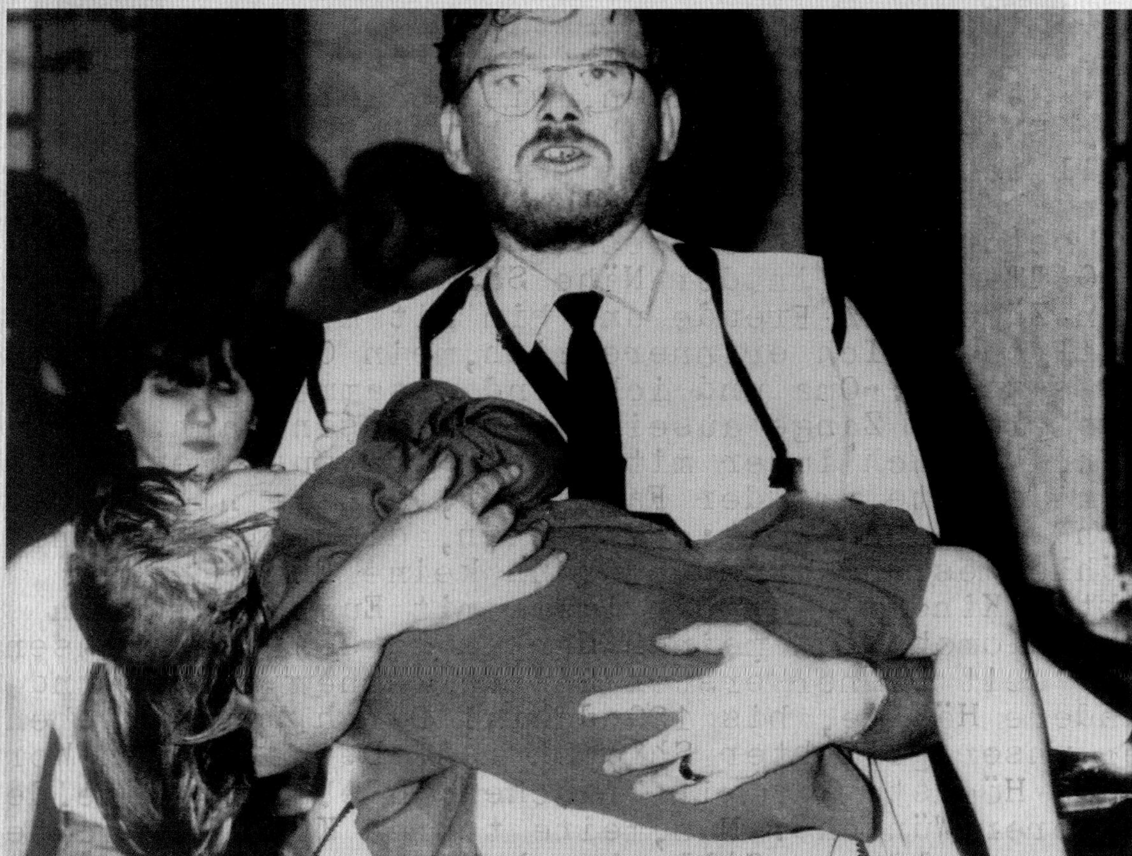

automatic rifle, he embarked on a shooting spree that began in the woods near Hungerford and culminated in the town itself. The rampage lasted several hours, during which Ryan methodically moved through the town, firing at residents, and burning down his family home as well as several others. By the time his reign of terror ended, 16 people had been killed, and more than a dozen others were injured. Ryan's motive behind the indiscriminate killings remains unclear. Some speculated that it was a culmination of personal grievances, while others pointed to his deteriorating mental health as a key factor. The massacre concluded when Ryan barricaded himself inside a school, eventually taking his own life.

Aftermath and Legacy

The Hungerford Massacre had significant repercussions. The sheer randomness of the attack, carried out in broad daylight in a peaceful community, led to rigorous debates in Britain about gun control, culminating in the Firearms (Amendment) Act 1988, which introduced stricter regulations related to gun ownership.

Personal Assessments

Multiple post-event assessments attempted to decipher the motivations behind Ryan's actions. Some pointed to a series of personal setbacks, including financial troubles and social isolation, as potential triggers. However, his exact reasons remain elusive, with no definitive explanations available. The tragedy stands as a grim reminder of the unpredictability of human actions and the profound impacts they can have on tight-knit communities. Ryan's name remains synonymous with one of the darkest days in Britain's recent history, a day when the serene town of Hungerford was plunged into unimaginable horror.

Main image, top left: Emergency services hurry away a child; **Top:** British Home Secretary Douglas Hurd talks to reporters in front of Ryan's burnt-out home; **Other pictures:** Police marksmen, barricades, and a visit by their regional and national top brass, in the wake of the shootings.

DOROTHEA PUENTE
DEATH HOUSE LANDLADY

Dorothea Puente was an American convicted serial killer who operated a boarding house in Sacramento, California. Though she appeared to be a caring and compassionate elderly woman, Puente's sinister side was hidden well beneath her benign exterior.

Early Life

Born on January 9, 1929, in Redlands, California, Dorothea's early life was riddled with hardships. She claimed to have been orphaned at a young age and spent time in an orphanage. As she grew older, she became involved in various illegal activities, including forging checks and committing fraud.

Sacramento Boarding House

In the 1980s, Dorothea operated a boarding house at 1426 F Street in Sacramento. The residence mainly catered to the elderly, disabled, and mentally ill. Though Puente projected the image of a kind-hearted landlady, things within the boarding house were far from idyllic. Dorothea had a criminal record, including arrests for theft, fraud, and treachery. She often administered drugs to her tenants, rendering them unconscious to rob them. However, her crimes escalated to murder, when she poisoned several of her tenants to continue collecting their Social Security checks.

The Grisly Discovery

The horrifying nature of Puente's crimes came to light in 1988 when a social worker became concerned about the sudden disappearance of a tenant named Alvaro Montoya, a mentally disabled man. This concern led the police to Puente's boarding house, where they discovered a freshly disturbed patch of soil. An

excavation revealed the body of Montoya, and subsequent digs unearthed the remains of six other victims.

Capture and Trial

Puente initially managed to evade the police by fleeing to Los Angeles, where she was later apprehended in a hotel. Brought back to Sacramento, she stood trial for her crimes. The trial was a significant media event, with many struggling to reconcile Puente's grandmotherly appearance with the heinous crimes she had committed. In 1993, after a lengthy trial, Dorothea Puente was found guilty of three murders. The jury couldn't reach a unanimous decision on the other six deaths. She was sentenced to life in prison without the possibility of parole.

Prison and Death

Dorothea spent the remainder of her life at the Central California Women's Facility in Chowchilla. During her time in prison, she maintained her innocence, claiming she had never murdered anyone. On March 27, 2011, Dorothea Puente passed away in prison at the age of 82. Dorothea Puente's story remains a chilling testament to the depths of human depravity and deception, showing that evil can sometimes reside where it's least expected.

Top, main images: opposite left: The "caring and compassionate" Dorothea Puente. In reality, a scheming and cold-hearted woman who went on the run when the body of Alvaro Montoya was discovered in her garden; **center:** "The Death House," Dorothea Puente's boarding house in Sacramento where the crimes took place; **right:** Puente in court; **Above:** Puente during her incarceration; **Opposite, bottom left:** Police and forensics take away one of the excavated bodies.

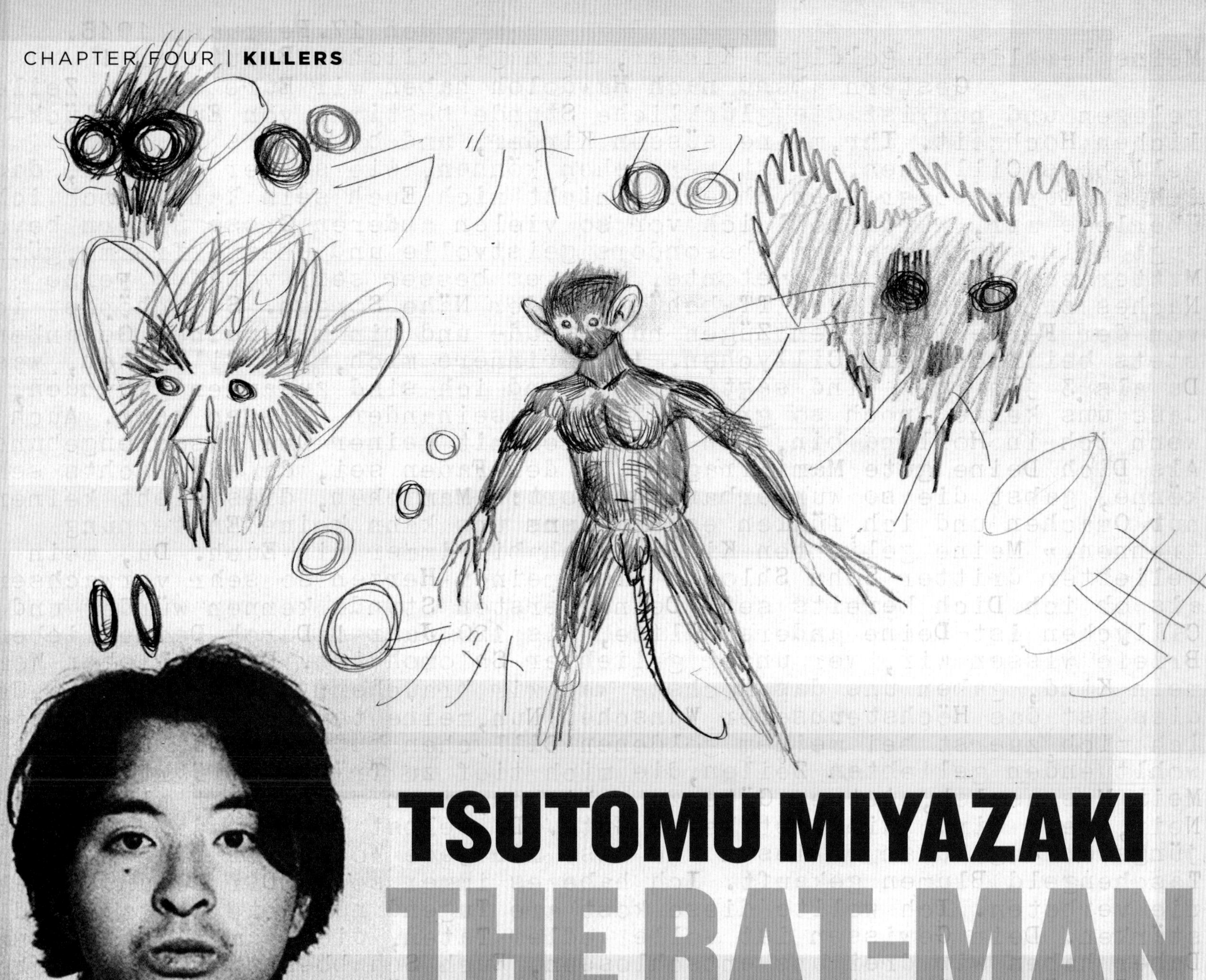

TSUTOMU MIYAZAKI THE RAT-MAN

He would often take photos of his victims, capturing their final moments. After committing the murders, Miyazaki engaged in post-mortem acts with the bodies, and in some cases even drank the victims' blood or ate parts of their remains...

Above: Miyazaki's mugshot, post-arrest; **Top:** A sheet of Rat-Man's sketches found in his apartment; **Opposite, top, right, and bottom left:** After the true horror of Miyazaki's crimes had come to light, Japanese police and forensics teams persuaded Miyazaki to lead them to his victims' burial sites; **Opposite, center left:** Miyazaki's hands. This photo, doing the rounds of the internet, looks to have been digitally distorted to amplify the extent of Miyazaki's deformities...or maybe not.

Tsutomu Miyazaki, variously referred to as "The Otaku Murderer," "The Little Girl Murderer," or "The Rat-Man," was a Japanese serial killer responsible for the abduction and murder of four young girls in the late 1980s. His crimes, combined with his bizarre behavior and obsession with anime and horror films, left a lasting scar on Japanese society.

A Troubled Beginning

Born on August 21, 1962, in Itsukaichi, Tokyo, Miyazaki's early life was marked by challenges. Born with deformed hands fused directly to his wrists, he faced difficulty in social situations and was often ostracized by his peers. This led to him seeking solace in anime and horror films, fostering an obsession that would later play a significant role in his crimes.

A Series of Grisly Acts

Between August 1988 and June 1989, Miyazaki abducted, killed, and mutilated four young girls aged between four and seven. He would often take photos of his victims, capturing their final moments. After committing the murders, Miyazaki engaged in post-mortem acts with the bodies and, in some cases, even drank the victims' blood or ate parts of their remains. His crimes extended beyond the act of murder. Miyazaki would send postcards to the families of the victims, describing the acts he committed in gruesome detail. These communications added a psychological terror aspect to an already horrifying series of events.

Capture and Trial

Miyazaki's reign of terror came to an end in July 1989 when he was caught trying to photograph a young girl. Upon his arrest, authorities found a trove of disturbing material in his home, including photos of his victims and a vast collection of violent anime and horror films. During his trial, Miyazaki's behavior was erratic. He often appeared disconnected from reality, sometimes blaming his actions on his alter ego or claiming he was under the influence of a "rat-man" figure. Despite attempts to plead insanity, Miyazaki was found to be of sound mind and was held fully responsible for his crimes.

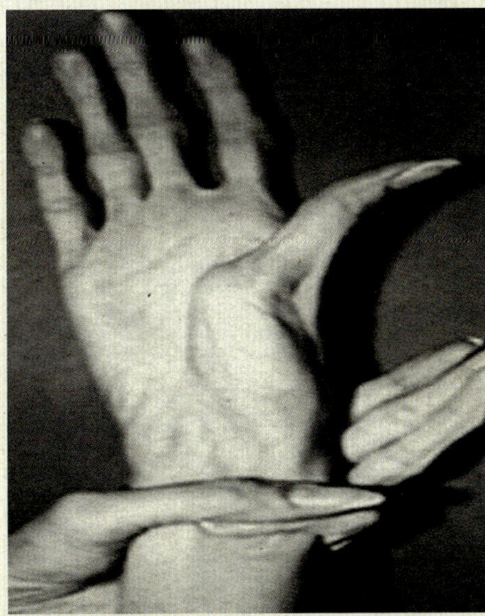

Execution

Tsutomu Miyazaki was sentenced to death in 1997. After several years of appeals and legal procedures, he was executed by hanging on June 17, 2008.

Impact on Japanese Society

Miyazaki's crimes sent shockwaves through Japanese society, leading to intense media scrutiny and public debate. His case brought attention to the potential dangers of extreme social isolation and the dark underbelly of otaku culture. The crimes led to increased censorship and regulations around explicit content in manga and anime. To this day, Tsutomu Miyazaki's name remains synonymous with some of Japan's most chilling and unsettling crimes.

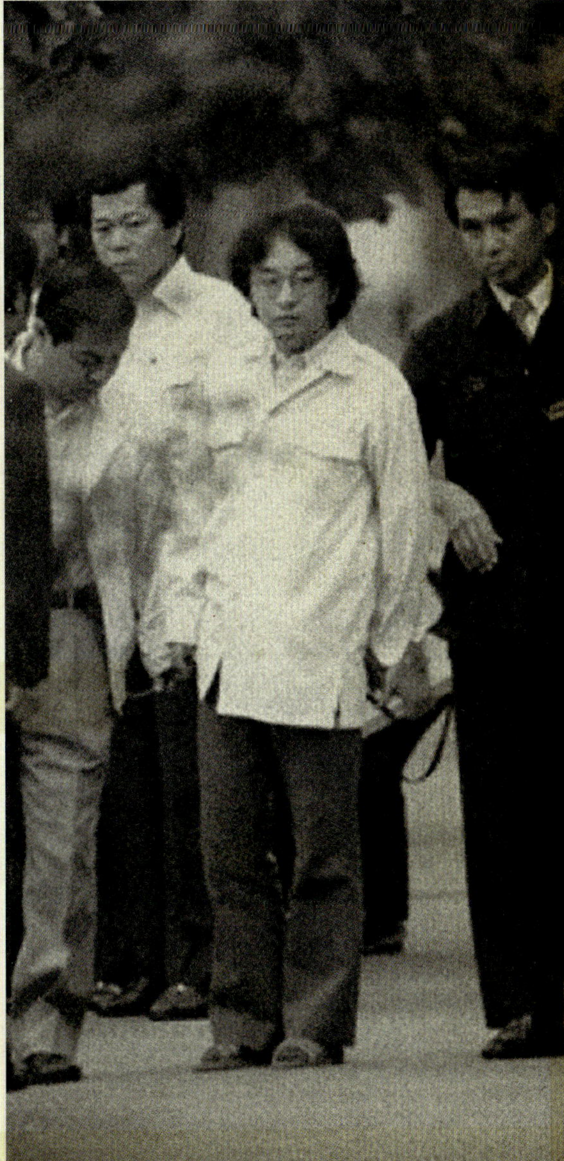

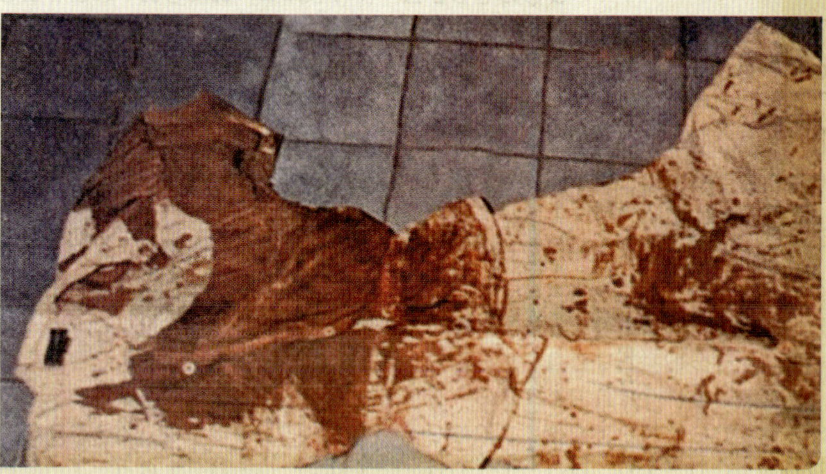

CLAUDIA MIJANGOS THE HYENA OF QUERETARO

Top left: The old *colonia*, neighborhood, of Querétaro; **Top right:** The bloodsoaked dress Mijangos was wearing on the night of the stabbings; **Above:** Mijangos in her late teenage years, when she was the beauty queen of her hometown of Mazatlán.

Claudia Mijangos was born in 1956 in Sinaloa, a city in northwest Mexico. Coming from a well-off family, she had access to education and the finer things in life. As she grew up, Mijangos was known to be charismatic and attractive, characteristics that made her popular in her community.

Marriage and Personal Turmoil

Mijangos met and married an engineer named Alfredo Castaños Gutiérrez, and after her parents died, she and Alfredo inherited a good deal of money. They moved to Querétaro, and were blessed with three children. The children were soon enrolled in the Catholic school Colegio Fray Luis de León, where Mijangos also worked as a catechism teacher. In the late 1980s the couple developed marital problems, and, according to relatives and friends, Mijangos began to display signs of emotional instability. Despite attending marriage counseling, they separated in 1989. Mijangos began exhibiting signs of psychological distress—often hearing voices and claiming to experience visions. Her mental health decline was exacerbated by the strained relationship with her husband.

The Tragic Event

On the night of April 23, 1989, in a fit of delusional rage after an argument with Castaños, Claudia attacked her three children in their sleep with a knife. Her daughters, aged 11 and nine, were killed, and her son, aged six, was also killed. When police arrived at the scene, they found Claudia in bed with bloody clothes and a knife.

Legal Proceedings and Confinement

Given the gravity of her actions and her evident psychological disturbances, Mijangos underwent a series of psychiatric evaluations. Medical professionals diagnosed her

with schizoaffective disorder, a condition characterized by delusions and auditory hallucinations. While she may not have been fully aware of what she had done, Claudia was sentenced to 30 years in prison—the maximum sentence allowed for her crimes in Mexico at the time. She was released in 2019, then subsequently admitted to a psychiatric facility for ongoing treatment.

Public Reaction and Legacy

The case of Claudia Mijangos sent shockwaves through Mexican society. The brutal nature of the crime, combined with Claudia's background as an educated and well-off individual, challenged the public's perception of what a "typical" criminal looked like. Her story was widely covered in the media and became the subject of numerous documentaries and investigative reports. Over the years, Claudia's case has been referenced in discussions about mental health awareness and the importance of early diagnosis and intervention in cases of severe psychological distress.

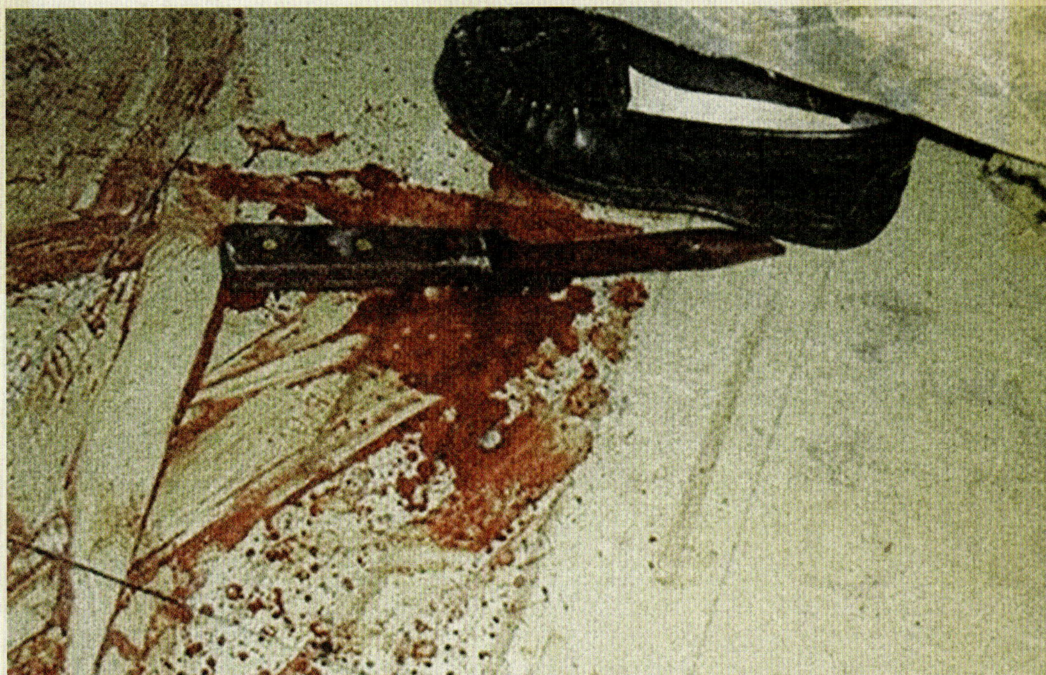

Top left: The bloodsoaked twin beds of her daughters. Much of the blood on the bed was her nine-year-old daughter Ana Belén's—she had been stabbed in the heart; **Center, left:** Claudia Mijangos, around the time of her crimes; **Above:** The bloody crime scene; **Top right:** A view of the tranquil old town of Querétaro.

THE MENÉNDEZ BROTHERS
MURDERING YOUR MOM AND DAD

Lyle Menéndez (born January 10, 1968) and Erik Menéndez (born November 27, 1970) were raised in an affluent household. Their father, Jose Menéndez, was a successful entertainment executive, while their mother, Kitty Menéndez, was a homemaker. On the surface, the Menéndez family appeared to epitomize the American dream. However, beneath the veneer of wealth and privilege lay a tumultuous family dynamic marked by allegations of abuse and dysfunction.

A Brutal Crime

On the evening of August 20, 1989, the lives of the Menéndez family changed irrevocably. Jose and Kitty Menéndez were found dead in their Beverley Hills mansion, having suffered multiple gunshot wounds. The brutality of the crime, combined with its setting in an upscale neighborhood, sent shockwaves throughout the nation.

Investigations and Shifting Narratives

Initially, Lyle and Erik, seemingly grief-stricken, were not considered suspects. They painted a picture of a robbery gone wrong

Opposite, main image: Lyle Menéndez (left) and his younger brother Erik, in court in 1990; **Opposite, below:** The young Menéndez brothers in suits, sat on their father's knee, circa mid-1970s; **Left:** The brothers appear in court again after spending time on remand in 1990. **Above:** Mom and dad Menéndez—the two murder victims.

and even speculated about potential ties to organized crime. In the weeks following the murders, the brothers embarked on a spending spree, purchasing luxury items and making lavish investments, leading investigators to question their innocence. The turning point in the investigation came when Erik, burdened by guilt, confessed to his therapist. Although confidentiality laws protected such confessions, the therapist's mistress, having overheard the admission, informed the police, setting the stage for the arrest of the Menéndez brothers in March 1990.

Trial and Media Frenzy

The trial of Lyle and Erik Menéndez began in 1993 and quickly became a media sensation. Court TV broadcast the proceedings, drawing millions of viewers. At the heart of the defense's argument was a shocking claim: Lyle and Erik had suffered years of physical, emotional, and sexual abuse at the hands of their parents, driving them to commit the murders in a desperate act of self-defense. The trial was a battleground of competing narratives. The prosecution painted the brothers as greedy, cold-blooded killers, motivated by the prospect of inheriting their parents' wealth. In contrast, the defense showcased a tale of trauma, manipulation, and fear.

Verdict and Sentencing

The first trial ended in 1994 with two deadlocked juries, leading to a mistrial. A second trial commenced in 1995, this time without cameras in the courtroom. In 1996, Lyle and Erik Menéndez were found guilty of first-degree murder and sentenced to life in prison without the possibility of parole.

Legacy and Continuing Debate

The Menéndez brothers' case remains a topic of fascination and debate. It delves into complex issues of family, abuse, morality, and the justice system. The trial, with its televised proceedings, also marked a turning point in the intersection of media and high-profile court cases, setting the stage for subsequent trials in the media spotlight. The case prompts questions about the veracity of the brothers' abuse claims, the ethics of broadcasting trials, and the influence of public perception on judicial outcomes. To this day, the Menéndez saga stands as a haunting reminder of the tragedies that can unfold behind closed doors, even in the most opulent of homes.

Above: Erik Menéndez gives evidence during the first trial; **Below:** The Menéndez brothers stand accused of murder.

Between 1989 and 1990, Florida's highways were the backdrop to a spate of male homicides, all of which had a common thread—middle-aged or older men, shot multiple times...

Top: Aileen Wuornos during her time on death row. Her mental health deteriorated waiting for her execution; **Above:** Richard Mallory, Wuornos' first victim—previously convicted of attempted rape. He had been shot in the chest several times. Wuornos asserted that Mallory tried to rape her and she shot him in self-defense.

Aileen Carol Wuornos was born on February 29, 1956, in Rochester, Michigan. From the outset, Wuornos' life was marred by tumult and tragedy. Born to a teenage mother and an incarcerated father diagnosed with schizophrenia, she never met her father, who hanged himself in prison. Wuornos stated that her grandfather sexually assaulted her as a child. At age 14, Wuornos became pregnant and gave the baby up for adoption after she was sexually assaulted by a family friend.

Descent into Crime

Wuornos was thrown out of her grandfather's house at age 15, shortly after dropping out of school, and began living in the woods near her childhood home. Over the years, she resorted to prostitution for survival. Her rap sheet grew over the years, including offenses from DUI and assault to armed robbery, and her mental health plummeted; Wuornos allegedly attempted to commit suicide six times in the span of eight years.

The Murders

Between 1989 and 1990, Florida's highways were the backdrop to a spate of male homicides, all of which had a common thread—middle-aged or older men shot multiple times. Wuornos's transition from criminal offenses to serial killer status began with the killing of Richard Mallory, previously convicted of attempted rape. She would go on to kill seven men in total, arguing that each killing was in self-defense against attempted rape or assault during her encounters as a prostitute.

Capture, Trial, and Execution

Suspicion soon fell on Wuornos and her then-girlfriend Tyria Moore, leading to Wuornos' arrest in January 1991. The subsequent trials drew significant media attention, due in part to the rarity of female serial killers, and Wuornos' open acknowledgment of her crimes. Although Wuornos claimed self-defense, the jury found her

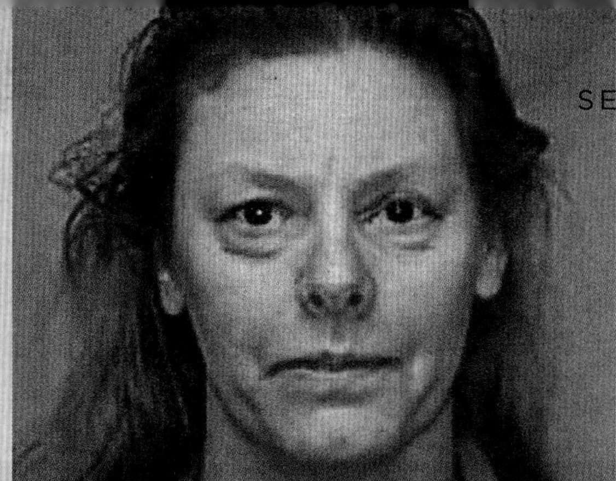

AILEEN WUORNOS

SERIAL KILLER AT LARGE IN FLORIDA

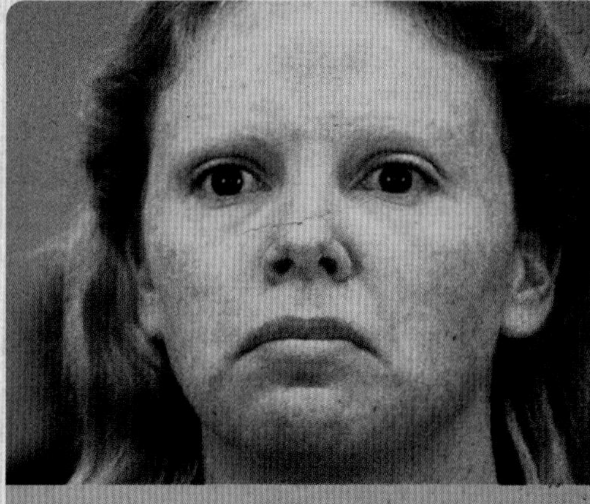

Top left: Wuornos' mugshot; **Top right:** David Spears, second victim of Wuornos; **Above, center:** Charlize Theron obscured her natural looks with prosthetics and make-up to play Wuornos in *Monster*, 2003; **Above:** Charlize Theron. She won that year's Oscar for Best Actress.

guilty, and she received six death sentences. Over the decade she spent on death row, her mental health visibly deteriorated. Appeals for clemency based on claims of mental illness and her turbulent upbringing were denied. On October 9, 2002, Aileen Wuornos was executed by lethal injection.

Media and Cultural Impact

Wuornos' life and crimes have been the subject of extensive media coverage, documentaries, and movies. The 2003 film *Monster*, in which Charlize Theron portrayed Wuornos, brought renewed attention to her story and won Theron an Academy Award. The public's fascination with Wuornos is rooted not only in the heinousness of her crimes but also in her narrative as a female serial killer, which challenged traditional gendered stereotypes about violence. Her background of abuse, coupled with claims of self-defense, made her a complex and controversial figure in debates about crime, punishment, and the justice system.

Legacy

The discourse surrounding Aileen Wuornos' crimes highlights the intersection of mental health, societal neglect, and the criminal justice system. She also remains that rarity—a female serial killer—her story serving as a grim reminder of the complexities of human nature and the systemic issues that can lead individuals down paths of extreme violence.

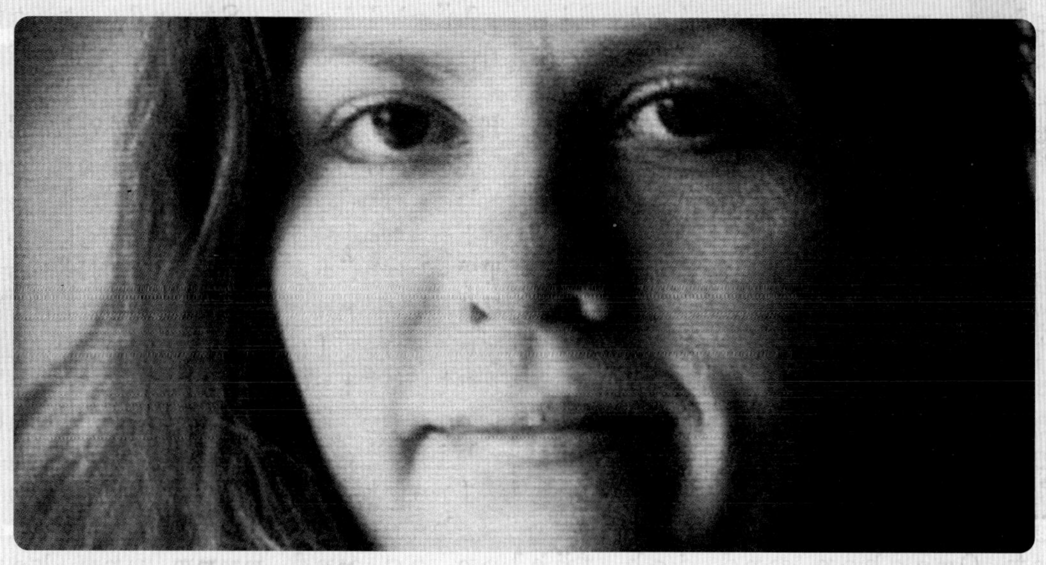

KRISTEN GILBERT ANGEL OF DEATH

Apart from the suspicious number of deaths during her shifts, her ex-boyfriend, James Perrault, a hospital security guard, testified against her. He recounted conversations where Gilbert allegedly confessed to some of the murders...

Kristen Heather Strickland, later known as Kristen Gilbert, was born on November 13, 1967, in Fall River, Massachusetts. From a young age, she displayed intelligence and ambition. However, she also exhibited signs of mental illness, frequently faking suicide attempts, and threatening other students with violence. As she grew, so did her interest in the medical field. This interest eventually led her to become a nurse. She was employed at the Veterans Affairs (VA) Medical Center in Northampton, Massachusetts.

A Trail of Suspicious Deaths

During Gilbert's tenure at the VA Medical Center between 1989 and 1996, an alarming number of patients mysteriously died. These deaths were particularly concentrated during her shifts. Colleagues began to notice a pattern: patients would go into cardiac arrest, and Gilbert would typically be present or nearby. Moreover, she often volunteered for emergency situations, even when not on duty.

Discovery of the Deadly Pattern

Suspicion arose when the hospital experienced an unprecedented increase in cardiac arrest deaths, especially during Gilbert's shifts. Further investigation revealed that a significant amount of the heart stimulant epinephrine was missing from the hospital's stock. When administered in high doses, epinephrine can lead to cardiac arrest. An anonymous tip-off to the VA's internal police led to a more in-depth investigation. It was suspected that Gilbert was administering unnecessary and lethal doses of epinephrine to patients, causing their deaths.

Trial and Conviction

Gilbert's trial began in 2000. Throughout the proceedings, the prosecution painted a portrait of a woman craving attention and excitement, who used her position as a nurse to play a deadly game. She would allegedly induce cardiac arrest in patients and then "heroically" attempt to resuscitate them, relishing the ensuing chaos. The evidence against her was mainly circumstantial but compelling. Apart from the suspicious number of deaths during her shifts, her ex-boyfriend, James Perrault, a hospital security guard, testified against her. He recounted conversations where Gilbert allegedly confessed to some of the murders. In March 2001, Kristen Gilbert was found guilty of three counts of first-degree murder, one count of second-degree murder and two counts of attempted murder. She was sentenced to four consecutive life sentences without the possibility of parole, narrowly escaping the death penalty.

Later Revelations and Impact

Following her conviction, further details emerged about Gilbert's personal life. She had tumultuous relationships and displayed signs of Munchausen syndrome, a mental disorder where a person acts as if they have physical or mental illnesses when they are not really sick. It's suggested she might have also had a form of Munchausen by proxy, causing harm to others to generate attention for herself. The case of Kristen Gilbert serves as a chilling reminder of the potential dark side of those entrusted with care. Her story has been featured in several documentaries and crime shows, underscoring the public's enduring fascination with the macabre and the unexpected perpetrators of heinous acts.

Opposite, top: Kristen Gilbert; **This page, main image:** The Veterans Affairs Medical Center in Northampton, Massachusetts; **Above:** Nancy Cutting with son Jeff. Gilbert killed husband and father Ken Cutting, a former serving soldier.

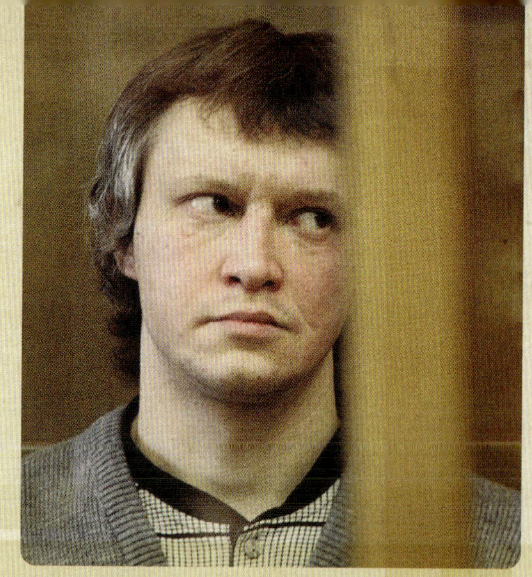

ALEXANDER PICHUSHKIN THE CHESSBOARD KILLER

Top left: Pichushkin (right), with his friend Mikhail Odïtchuk, who tragically was to become the serial killer's first victim, and **Top right:** Awaiting his sentence in 2007; **Above:** Pichushkin in jail in 2016; **Opposite, below right:** Pichushkin arrives in court for his trial; **Opposite, main image:** Pichushkin, against the background of Bitsa (or Bitsevski) Park, close to Moscow. It's a popular natural recreation space for Moscow residents. The parkland and forest is crossed by the Chertanovka and Bitsa Rivers, and extends for some seven miles from north to south. It's bounded by Balaklavsky Avenue from the north, and was an oft-used location for Pichushkin's crimes.

Born on April 9, 1974, in Mytishchi, Moscow Oblast, Russia, Alexander Yuryevich Pichushkin was an enigmatic figure from his early years. Often referred to as the "Chessboard Killer," his childhood revealed signs of a troubled psyche. As a young boy, a swing accident left him with a head injury, an event some speculate might have influenced his later actions. Pichushkin was notably introverted, showing a penchant for chess, which he played in Moscow's Bitsa Park, where many of his future crimes would occur.

Emergence of Violent Tendencies

Pichushkin's violent tendencies came to the fore in his late teens. He claimed that his initial urge to kill emerged around the age of 18. The vast, wooded expanses of Bitsa Park provided an ideal environment for his predatory instincts.

A String of Murders

Pichushkin's killing spree spanned from 1992 to 2006. Initially, he targeted homeless men, luring them with the offer of vodka. Once they were intoxicated, he would brutally murder them, often leaving a bottle of vodka sticking out of their skulls. As his confidence grew, his pool of victims expanded to include younger men, women, and children. Pichushkin was methodical, aiming to complete the squares on a chessboard with each murder, aspiring to have 64 victims. This gruesome goal earned him the moniker "Chessboard Killer."

Capture and Trial

The consistency in his modus operandi eventually led to Pichushkin's capture. In June 2006, following the murder of a woman in Bitsa Park, investigators found a metro ticket that led them to surveillance footage, putting Pichushkin at the scene. During his trial, which garnered significant media attention, Pichushkin was unapologetically proud of his actions, often detailing them with a chilling indifference. He was convicted of 48 murders and three attempted murders, although he claimed to have committed 60. In October 2007, he was sentenced to life imprisonment, with the first 15 years to be served in solitary confinement.

Psychological Analysis

Efforts to understand Pichushkin's psyche revealed a complex interplay of factors. Some experts attribute his violent tendencies to his childhood head injury, while others point to a deeply-rooted psychopathy. Pichushkin himself claimed that he killed to achieve fame, reveling in the power and control he exerted over his victims.

In 1993, Beverley Allitt was found guilty of four counts of murder, three counts of attempted murder, and six counts of causing grievous bodily harm with intent...

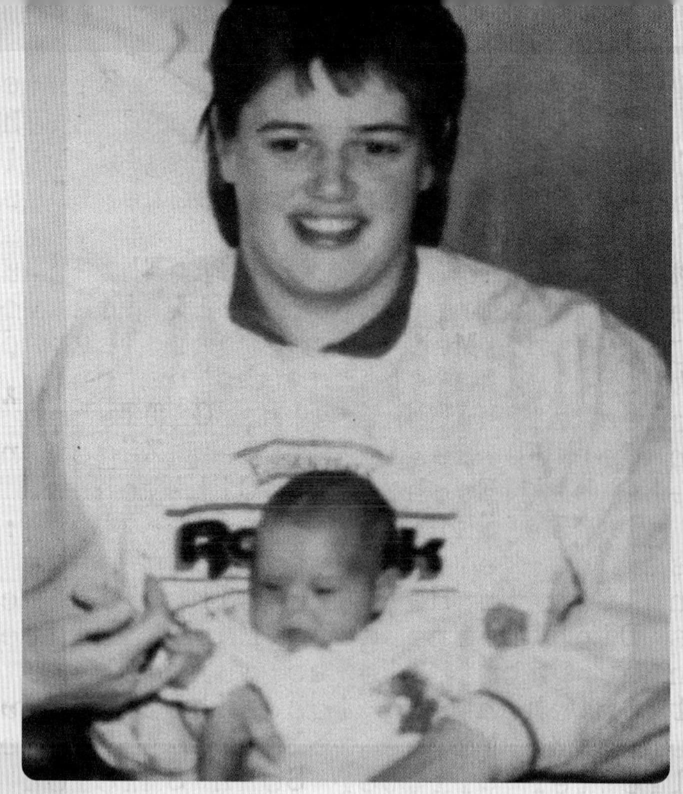

BEVERLEY ALLITT
ANGEL OF DEATH...No.2

Top: A hospital staff snap, showing Allitt with a newborn infant, some months before being arrested on suspicion of murder and attempted murder; **Above:** The former nurse Beverley Allitt is taken back to prison after the day's proceedings during her trial—a long lens picture by a press photographer.

Beverley Allitt, often referred to as "The Angel of Death," is a former pediatric nurse from the United Kingdom who was convicted of murdering four children and causing grievous bodily harm to several others under her care.

Background and Early Career

Born on October 4, 1968, in Corby Glen, Lincolnshire, Allitt showed signs of Munchausen syndrome from an early age, a disorder in which a person feigns illness or medical conditions for attention. This behavior escalated into Munchausen syndrome by proxy during her tenure as a nurse, where she would inflict harm on her patients to present herself as their savior when they experienced medical emergencies.

Crimes at Grantham & Kesteven Hospital

Between February and April 1991, an alarming number of pediatric patients at Grantham and Kesteven Hospital in Lincolnshire began to experience mysterious and life-threatening episodes. These events mainly occurred during Allitt's shifts. She used various methods to harm the children, including administering lethal doses of insulin, injecting air bubbles into their bloodstream, and tampering with medical equipment. Babies and children under Allitt's care would inexplicably stop breathing, suffer cardiac arrests, or experience unexplained seizures. While some of these young patients could be resuscitated, four children tragically lost their lives: Liam Taylor (aged 7 weeks), Timothy Hardwick (aged 11 years, suffering from cerebral palsy), Becky Phillips (aged 2 months), and Claire Peck (aged 15 months).

Investigation and Arrest

Suspicion soon fell on Allitt as the common factor in all these incidents. When a high number of insulin doses were reported missing from the hospital's storage, the investigation intensified. Authorities discovered that Allitt was the last person to be in contact with the

victims before their episodes. Forensic evidence, including traces of insulin and potassium found in the victims, as well as Allitt's partial fingerprint on a replacement cap for an insulin vial, further implicated her in the crimes.

Conviction and Life Imprisonment

In 1993, Allitt was found guilty of four counts of murder, three counts of attempted murder, and six counts of causing grievous bodily harm with intent. She was sentenced to 13 life terms in prison. The court recommended that she serve a minimum of 30 years behind bars. Allitt is currently incarcerated at Rampton Secure Hospital in Nottinghamshire, a high-security psychiatric facility. Reports suggest she has since been diagnosed with various personality disorders. Throughout her trial and subsequent incarceration, Allitt has shown little remorse for her actions, leaving the medical community and the public at large grappling with the chilling reality that someone who was supposed to care for and protect the most vulnerable instead chose to harm them.

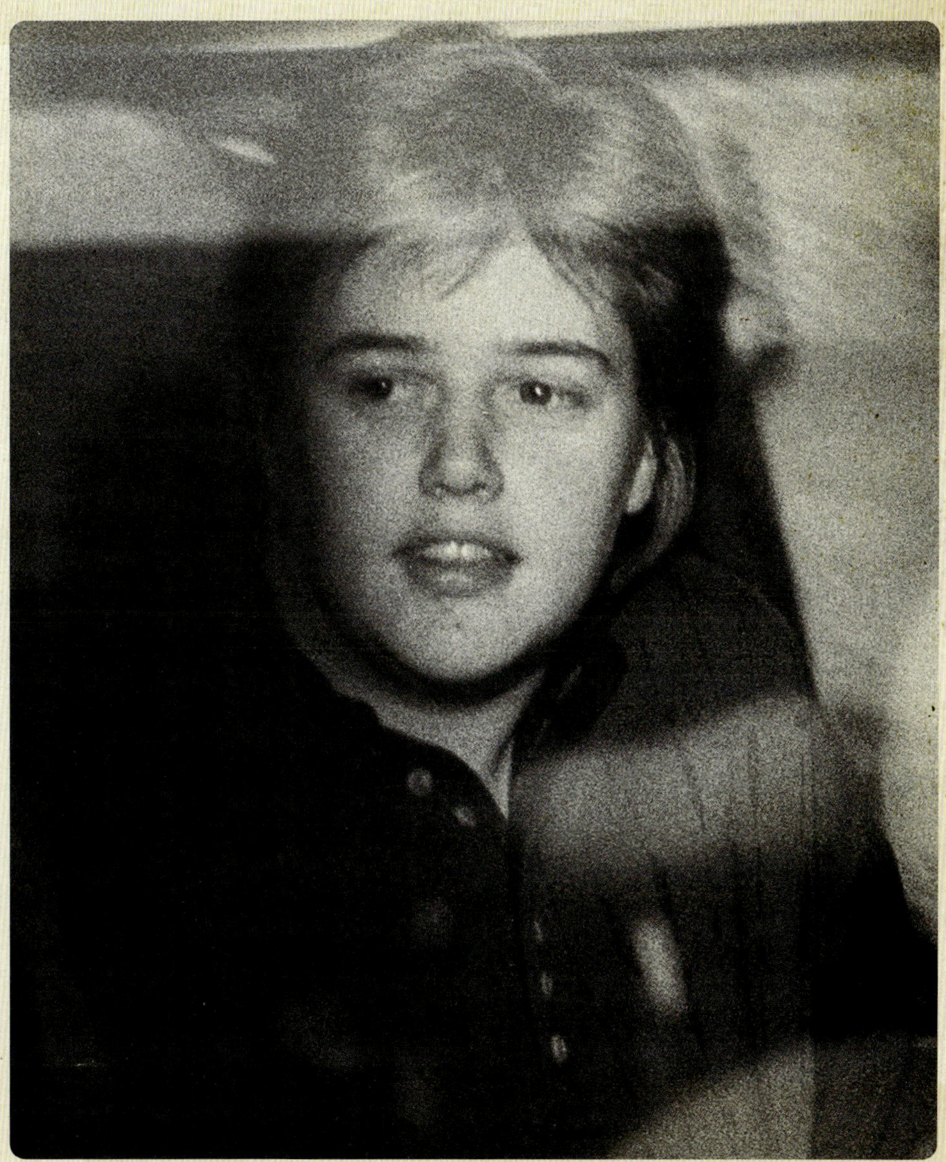

Top: A 2015 photograph of the old Grantham & Kesteven General Hospital. The hospital became part of the British National Health Service in 1948, and a Maternity Unit was added in 1972. The unit was closed down, as a result of very low birth rates in Grantham, by 2014. (Photo by Ian Grundy); **Right:** Another long lens shot by a press photographer as Allitt is transported in 1991.

OJ SIMPSON THE TRIAL OF THE CENTURY

Top: June 17, 1994: OJ Simpson's mugshot after he was arrested on suspicion of the murder of his ex-wife Nicole Brown Simpson and her friend Ron Goldman; **Above:** The famous demonstration that the murder gloves were "too small," leading Simpson's new lead defense counsel to assert: "If it doesn't fit, you must acquit."

Orenthal James "OJ" Simpson was born on July 9, 1947, in San Francisco, California. He rose to fame in the 1960s and 1970s as a record-breaking running back in both college football and the National Football League (NFL). Simpson's athletic talents earned him the prestigious Heisman Trophy in 1968, and he became one of the most celebrated athletes of his time. His fame on the field transitioned to a successful career in film and television, cementing his status as a household name.

A Marriage Marked by Tumult

In 1985, Simpson married Nicole Brown. They had two children together. However, their relationship was marred by reports of domestic violence. In 1992, the couple divorced, but their interactions remained a source of public and police attention.

The Murders and "Trial of the Century"

On June 12, 1994, Nicole Brown Simpson and her friend Ronald Goldman were brutally murdered

outside Nicole's home in Brentwood, Los Angeles. The nature of the crime, combined with Simpson's celebrity status, quickly made it headline news. Simpson became the prime suspect. A televised police chase, which saw Simpson as a passenger in a white Ford Bronco through Los Angeles highways with police in pursuit, further intensified media interest. Simpson eventually surrendered and was arrested.

The subsequent trial, often dubbed the "Trial of the Century," began in January 1995. Simpson's defense team, composed of prominent lawyers, argued that Simpson was the victim of a flawed police investigation and systemic racism. The prosecution pointed to compelling evidence, including DNA analysis, that linked Simpson to the crime scene. The trial was as much about racial tensions and the role of media as it was about the actual crime. After months of proceedings broadcast live to the nation, on October 3, 1995, Simpson was acquitted of both murders. The verdict was polarizing, with reactions deeply divided along racial lines.

Later Life and Legal Troubles

Although acquitted of the murders, Simpson's legal battles were far from over. In 1997, a civil court found him liable for the wrongful deaths of Brown and Goldman, ordering him to pay $33.5 million in damages to their families. Simpson's legal troubles continued. In 2007, he was arrested in Las Vegas for armed robbery and kidnapping after attempting to retrieve sports memorabilia he claimed belonged to him. In 2008, he was found guilty on multiple counts and sentenced to 33 years in prison. He was granted parole in 2017 after serving nine years.

Legacy and Cultural Impact

OJ Simpson's life and trial have left an indelible mark on American society. The case highlighted systemic racial biases, the role of media in the legal system, and public perceptions of celebrity. Simpson's fall from grace—from revered athlete to a central figure in a murder trial—remains a testament to the unpredictable and multifaceted nature of fame. His story has been the subject of numerous documentaries, films, and discussions, underscoring its enduring impact on American culture. OJ Simpson died of prostate cancer on Wednesday April 10, 2024. He was 76 years old.

Above, left: For years, Simpson was the TV face of Hertz; **Above:** The two murder victims, Nicole Brown Simpson and Ron Goldman; **Below:** 13 years after his famous acquittal, Simpson was back on trial, this time for robbery.

ANDREW CUNANAN A VERY UNBALANCED INDIVIDUAL

Born on August 31, 1969, in National City, California, Andrew Phillip Cunanan grew up in an environment of contrasts. His Filipino father and Italian-American mother strived to provide a comfortable upbringing, sending him to a prestigious private school, The Bishop's School in La Jolla. Here, Cunanan's intelligence quickly became evident. However, despite his apparent privileges, there were early indications of a darker side, including a propensity for deceit.

Life in San Diego and San Francisco

As Cunanan transitioned into adulthood, his father abandoned his family and fled the country to avoid being arrested for embezzlement. Cunanan soon dropped out of college and moved to San Francisco, where he became a well-known figure in the LGBTQ+ community. He was known for his charismatic persona and relationships with older, wealthier men. Cunanan often boasted about his extravagant lifestyle, funded by his affluent companions. However, beneath the glamor,

Opposite, main image: Gianni Versace's Miami home. Cunanan shot Versace twice in the head on the steps, using the gun of his first victim, and lover, Jeffrey Trail. (Photo: Clive Limpkin/Alamy); **Opposite, inset:** The FBI transmitted this photograph of Cunanan across the United States as a nationwide manhunt got underway; **Opposite, below:** Cunanan the privately-educated schoolboy.

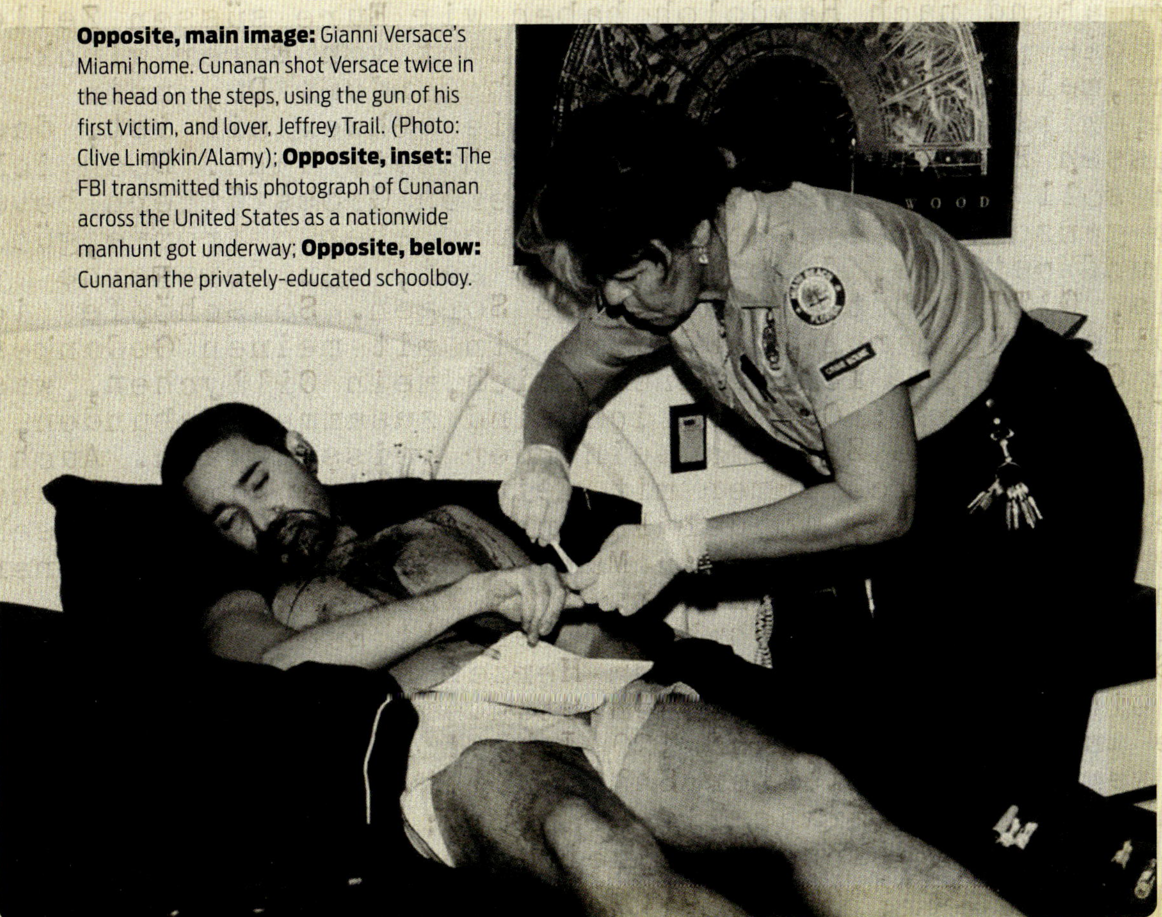

Above: Gianni Versace—the tragic final victim of Andrew Cunanan...before Cunanan ended his own life **(left)** on a luxury Miami houseboat; **Below:** Cunanan as a child, circa 1975.

there were rumblings of his escalating drug use and increasingly erratic behavior.

The Murders

In the first half of 1997, Cunanan's life took a dark turn. Over three months, he committed a series of murders across the United States. The killings began in Minneapolis with Jeffrey Trail, a former naval officer and friend of Cunanan, followed by David Madson, an architect and a former romantic partner. His spree continued with the murders of real estate mogul Lee Miglin in Chicago and cemetery worker William Reese in New Jersey.

The Assassination of Versace

On July 15, 1997, Cunanan committed his final and most high-profile murder, fatally shooting renowned fashion designer Gianni Versace on the steps of his Miami mansion. This brazen act triggered an intensified nationwide manhunt. However, the chase would not last long.

Cunanan's End

On July 23, 1997, just over a week after killing Versace, Cunanan ended his life inside a Miami Beach houseboat. Despite exhaustive investigations, the motives behind his killings, especially that of Versace, remained shrouded in mystery.

Investigations and Public Impact

The FBI and various local law enforcement agencies delved deep into Cunanan's background, seeking to understand the catalyst for his violent spree. Despite thorough investigations, a clear motive was elusive. Some pointed to potential personal vendettas, while others speculated about financial motivations or a desire for infamy. Cunanan's murder spree, particularly the assassination of Versace, attracted enormous media attention. The series of events highlighted challenges in cross-state criminal investigations and sparked debates on issues ranging from gay rights in the '90s to the nature of fame. Cunanan's life and crimes remain a subject of intrigue and speculation. While various theories attempt to decipher his actions, the true motivations of Andrew Cunanan may never be fully understood.

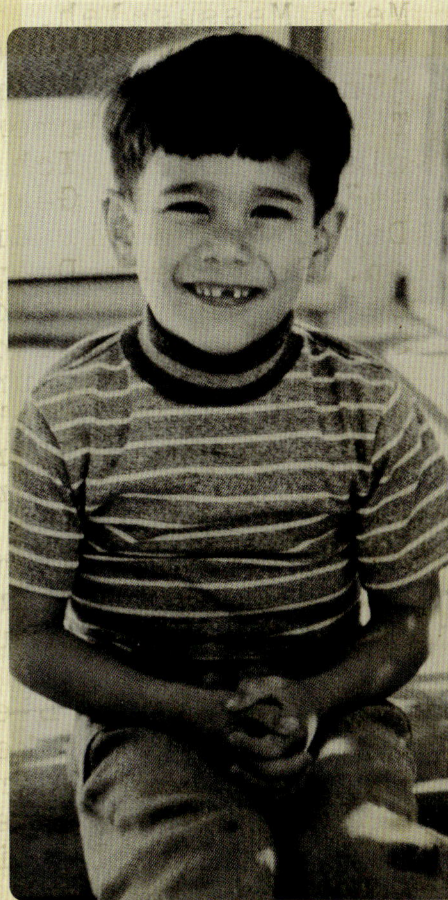

KATHERINE KNIGHT
CHILDHOOD TRAUMAS... NOW VIOLENTLY UNSTABLE

Top left: Katherine Knight and David Kellett on their wedding day in 1974; **Top right:** A photo of Knight; **Above:** John Price's house on the outskirts of Aberdeen, New South Wales, in the immediate aftermath of Knight's gruesome crime there—Australian police discovered his head simmering in a pot on the stove.

Katherine Mary Knight was born in Tenterfield, New South Wales, Australia, on October 24, 1955. Her upbringing was far from ordinary. Born into a tumultuous family environment, Katherine witnessed aggressive disputes between her mother and various partners. Her mother, Barbara Roughan, abandoned her marriage to initiate a relationship with Ken Knight, a coworker of her then husband, resulting in ostracization by the local community. Raised in this dysfunctional environment, Katherine was exposed to tales of familial rape and abuse. These traumatic episodes arguably laid the groundwork for the violent tendencies she manifested in adulthood.

Early Relationships

Katherine's personal relationships, starting with her teenage years, mirrored the volatility of her childhood. She married David Kellett in 1974, a union formed under the shadow of her domineering nature. David was often at the receiving end of her violent outbursts, but

Left: Knight and John Price, snapped at a get-together; **Below:** A young Katherine Knight; **Bottom:** The unfortunate John Price—stabbed to death, decapitated, dismembered...and cooked by Katherine Knight.

the couple still managed to have two children. Despite their familial expansions, the couple's relationship deteriorated over time due to Katherine's violent nature. After parting ways with Kellett, Knight started a relationship with David Saunders. This relationship, like its predecessor, was fraught with violent episodes. In one infamous incident, she killed Saunders' two-year-old dingo out of rage, an act eerily predictive of her future crime. Their tumultuous relationship ended, but not before they had a child together. John Chillingworth entered her life next, and they had a child. However, her most notorious and fatal relationship was the one she shared with John Charles Thomas Price.

The Gruesome Crime

By 1998, Knight and Price's relationship was a known roller coaster of passion and violence. Though Price was deeply enamored with Knight, he couldn't overlook her violent tendencies. Their disagreements escalated until February 2000 when Price attempted to get a restraining order against her, fearing for his life. Knight's retaliation was swift and brutal. On the evening of February 29, 2000, in a fit of rage, she stabbed Price 37 times, ensuring his demise. The aftermath was chilling. She skinned his body and hung the skin on a hook. Displaying a macabre culinary inclination, she cooked parts of his body before setting the table and attempting to serve them to Price's children.

Capture and Imprisonment

The subsequent police investigation unveiled a crime scene that shocked even the most seasoned officers. Price's head was found simmering in a pot on the stove, a grim testament to Knight's brutality. The court trial that followed showcased Knight's violent past and her unstable nature. In 2001, she received a life sentence without the possibility of parole. With this verdict, she made history as the first Australian woman to receive such a sentence. The tale of Katherine Knight remains one of the darkest chapters in Australian criminal history, a chilling reminder of the depths of human depravity.

In April 2003, the remains of Laci and her unborn son, Conner, washed ashore in San Francisco Bay—near the area Peterson claimed to have been fishing...

SCOTT PETERSON
MURDER—A MEANS TO AN END

Scott Lee Peterson was born on October 24, 1972, in San Diego, California. Growing up in a middle-class setting, Peterson attended California Polytechnic State University. It was during his college years that he met Laci Rocha. The two quickly fell in love and married in 1997. They settled in Modesto, California, where Scott worked as a fertilizer salesman and Laci as a substitute teacher. By all appearances, they were a happy couple eagerly anticipating the birth of their first child.

Disappearance and Growing Suspicions

On Christmas Eve 2002, Laci, eight months pregnant at the time, was reported missing. Scott claimed that he had been fishing at the Berkeley Marina the day his wife disappeared. As days turned into weeks with no sign of Laci, the media descended on Modesto, turning the missing person case into a nationwide sensation. The initial outpouring of sympathy for Scott began to wane as details of his personal life emerged. The revelation of his extramarital affair with Amber Frey, a massage therapist, painted a picture of a man leading a double life. Frey

cooperated with the authorities, even recording phone conversations with Scott, further casting doubt on his innocence.

Discovery and Arrest

In April 2003, the remains of Laci and her unborn son, Conner, washed ashore in San Francisco Bay—near the area Peterson claimed to have been fishing on the day of Laci's disappearance. This grim discovery shifted the narrative from a missing person case to a homicide investigation. Scott was arrested shortly afterward. He had bleached his brown hair blonde, and his car was packed with a significant amount of cash, camping equipment, and clothes, suggesting a potential plan to flee. The trial that ensued captivated the nation.

Trial and Conviction

The trial began in June 2004. The prosecution argued that Scott's affair and his desire for freedom from family responsibilities motivated the murder. Although the evidence against Peterson was largely circumstantial, the cumulative weight of his lies, the location of Laci's body, and his suspicious behavior were compelling. In November 2004, Scott Peterson was found guilty of first-degree murder for Laci's death and second-degree murder for the death of their unborn son. He was sentenced to death in March 2005 and in October 2022, he was transferred from San Quentin State Prison's death row to Mule Creek State Prison.

Aftermath and Legacy

The Scott Peterson case has left an indelible mark on American crime history. It underscores the unpredictable nature of crime and how ordinary individuals can become central figures in harrowing tales of deceit and tragedy. Peterson's trial also raised numerous questions about the role of media in shaping public opinion and its influence on the legal process. Documentaries, movies, and books exploring the case have proliferated over the years, reflecting a continued public fascination with the events. The Scott Peterson murder case serves as a somber reminder that, frequently, deeply haunting stories unfold in the most ordinary settings, challenging our perceptions of trust, relationships, fidelity and guilt.

Opposite, above left: Peterson in custody; **Opposite, above right:** Amber Frey, Peterson's lover, who fully cooperated with the authorities; **Opposite, bottom left:** Laci Peterson, the murder victim. She was eight months pregnant when she was murdered; **This page, top left:** Peterson, during his trial in Redwood City, flanked by attorneys Mark Geragos, left, and Pat Harris; **Right, top to bottom:** Karen Servas, the Petersons' next-door neighbor, and a key witness for the prosecution; Jurors Richelle Nice, left, and Michael Belmessieri speak to the media after Peterson's sentencing; Ron Grantski, Laci Peterson's stepfather, after the jury's sentence was announced; Sympathizer Elizabeth Escalante sits by a makeshift memorial on the site where Laci's body was discovered.

PHIL SPECTOR
THE TROUBLED MAESTRO OF ROCK 'N' ROLL

Born Harvey Phillip Spector on December 26, 1939, in the Bronx, New York, Phil Spector was destined to leave an indelible mark on the world of music. His innovations, especially the "Wall of Sound" production technique, redefined the soundscapes of rock and roll. By layering instrumental tracks, he produced a dense, echoing sound that became his signature. Working with bands like The Beatles, The Righteous Brothers, and The Ronettes, Spector turned records into sonic masterpieces.

Early Life and Trauma

Tragedy struck early in Spector's life. At just nine years old, he faced the suicide of his father. This loss would haunt Spector throughout his life, manifesting in various eccentricities and a fascination with death. His family subsequently moved to Los Angeles, where Spector began his love affair with music. By the age of 18, he'd already produced his first hit, "To Know Him Is To Love Him," a tribute to the words on his father's tombstone.

Rising Fame and Volatile Behavior

Throughout the 1960s and 1970s, Spector's star continued to rise. He became one of the most sought-after producers in the music industry. However, as his fame grew, so did tales of his erratic behavior. Stories of Spector brandishing firearms in the studio or displaying aggressive outbursts became legendary. Despite his genius, these episodes often overshadowed his contributions to music.

Personal Life and Downward Spiral

Spector's personal life was equally tumultuous. He married Ronnie Bennett, lead singer of The Ronettes, in 1968. Their marriage was marred by allegations of abuse, control, and imprisonment. They divorced in 1974, but tales of Spector's oppressive behavior persisted. By the 1980s, Spector had mostly retreated from public life, with rumors circulating about his deteriorating mental health.

The Death of Lana Clarkson

On February 3, 2003, the music world was rocked by news far removed from its usual beats. Actress Lana Clarkson was found dead in Spector's mansion from a gunshot wound. Spector was promptly arrested. Though he claimed Clarkson's death was an "accidental suicide," evidence suggested otherwise.

Trials and Conviction

Spector's first trial in 2007 ended in a mistrial due to a hung jury. However, during his retrial, in 2009 the jury found him guilty of second-degree murder. The stories shared by his ex-wives and former colleagues during the trial painted a picture of a man capable of such violence.

The Final Years

Phil Spector was sentenced to 19 years to life imprisonment. He was incarcerated in the California Health Care Facility, a prison that catered to inmates with medical issues. On January 16, 2021, Phil Spector passed away from complications related to COVID-19.

Opposite, top left: Phil Spector in 1967, in the studio with his house band and assistant Jack Nitzsche; **Opposite, top right:** Seven-inch single label for the British version of Spector's classic 1963 hit, *Be My Baby* by The Ronettes; **Opposite, bottom left:** Phil Spector photographed in London in 1997; **This page, top left:** Ronnie Spector, leader of The Ronettes, and Spector's then wife, in April 1971; **Top, center:** Spector leaves the courthouse with his wife Rachelle Short during the Lana Clarkson murder trial at Los Angeles Superior Court, June 5, 2007; **Top right:** The murder victim, actress Lana Clarkson, who was shot dead in Spector's mansion on February 3, 2003; **Above:** Spector (right), talks with Rolling Stones' manager Andrew Loog Oldham (left), and guitarist Keith Richards, circa 1965.

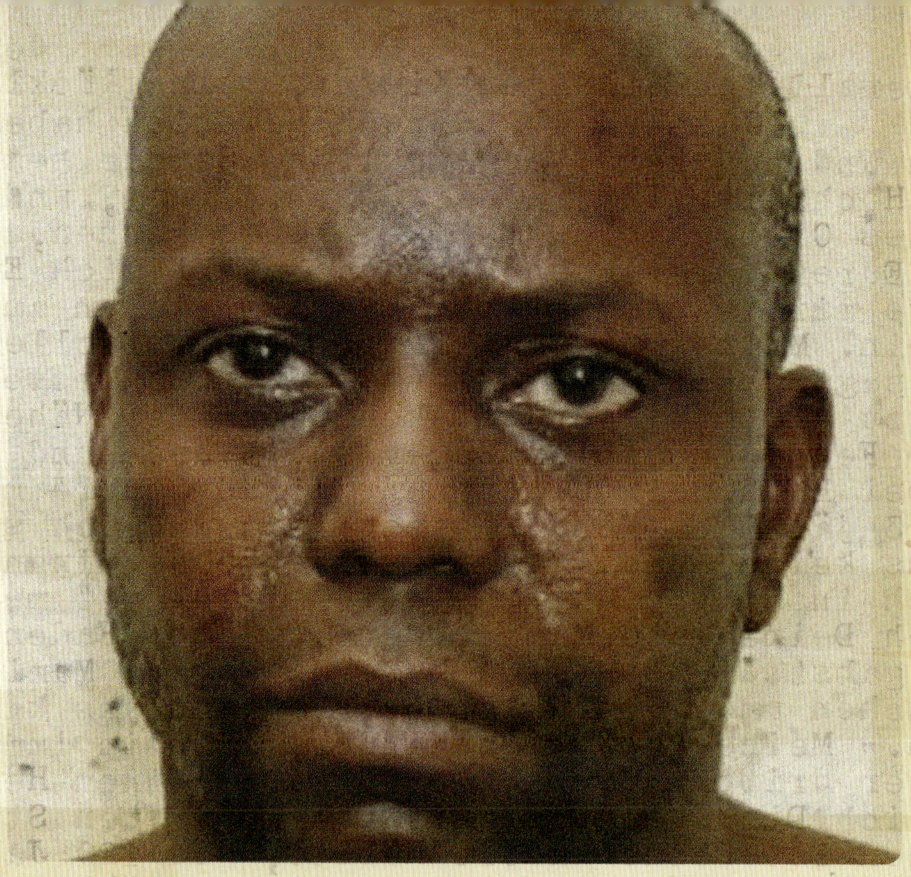

PETER BRYAN
VERY DISTURBED

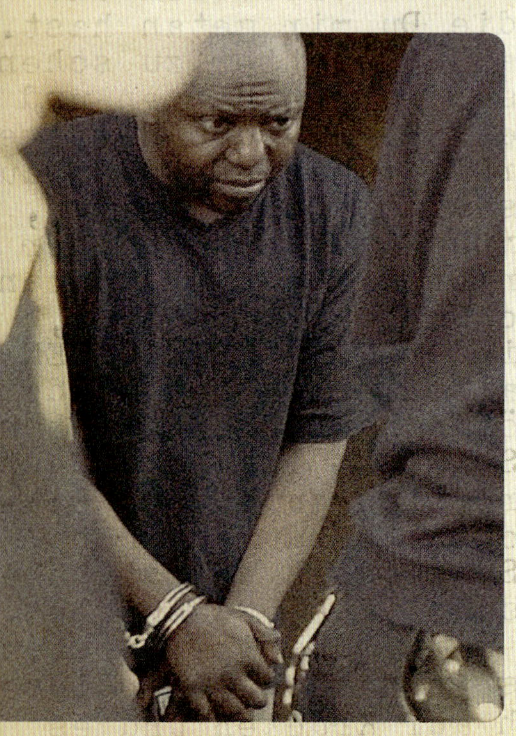

Peter Bryan, born in 1969 in London, England, represents one of the more disturbing figures in British criminal history. The particulars of Bryan's childhood and early years remain veiled, with only fragmented information available. However, what is clear from available records is a pattern of behavioral issues, particularly marked by aggressive tendencies.

First Encounter with the Criminal Justice System

The first, and very significant blip, on law enforcement's radar concerning Bryan came in 1993. That year, in a brutal and unprovoked assault, he murdered Nisha Sheth, a 20-year-old woman. The crime took place in a shop run by Sheth's family, with Bryan using a hammer as his weapon of choice. This horrific act led to his detainment in a secure psychiatric facility, given the evident mental health concerns his attack provoked.

Misguided Reintegration Efforts

By 2001, after several evaluations and assessments by psychiatric professionals, the decision was made to release Bryan back into the community. The belief was that with the right support, monitoring, and medication, he could reintegrate into society. However, this decision would prove tragically misguided. In 2004 he was taken back to a secure psychiatric facility after it was alleged he had assaulted a 16-year-old girl. Some four weeks later, and within hours of his conditional release, Bryan's violent tendencies reemerged. He targeted a friend, Brian Cherry, in an assault even more chilling than his first. After murdering Cherry, Bryan proceeded to dismember his body and, in a deeply disturbing act, consumed parts of his brain, which he had fried. This act of cannibalism sent shockwaves through the community and law enforcement agencies.

Broadmoor Hospital and Further Violence

Given the nature of his crimes and his previous psychiatric detainment, Bryan was sent to Broadmoor Hospital, a high-security psychiatric facility renowned for housing some of the UK's most dangerous individuals. The controlled environment of Broadmoor was thought to be secure enough to manage and treat individuals like Bryan. However, even within the confines of Broadmoor, Bryan's violence persisted. He attacked another patient, Richard Loudwell, resulting in injuries that subsequently led to Loudwell's death. This act reinforced the diagnosis that Bryan's violent tendencies were deeply ingrained and not easily managed or treated—even within a high-security environment.

Legal Outcomes and Confinement

Following this series of events, Bryan faced intense scrutiny in the courts. His actions, combined with comprehensive evaluations by psychiatric experts, painted the portrait of an individual with profound mental health issues, manifesting in extreme violent behavior. The court's verdict was unequivocal: Bryan was sentenced to life imprisonment, with a clear stipulation that he should not be released given the significant risk he posed to the public.

Professional Assessments

Throughout his interactions with the criminal justice system, various experts attempted to understand the motivations behind Bryan's actions. While the presence of significant mental disorders was evident, pinpointing a specific cause or trigger for his behavior proved elusive. His case remains extensively studied in criminologist and psychiatric circles, serving as a testament to the complexities inherent in such extreme criminal behaviors.

Opposite, top and below left: Peter Bryan, a profoundly disturbed man; **This page, top left:** Peter Bryan being led in handcuffs; **Above, top:** Brian Cherry, Peter Bryan's friend, killed, dismembered, and his brain tissue frying on the stove when police arrived; **Center, and above:** The crime scene: police and forensics at Bryan's residence in East London.

It felt like a huge sense of unreality. I felt betrayed, actually, by the jury. I was hoping they would see things for what they are. I felt really awful for my family and what they were thinking....

JODI ARIAS DOMESTIC VIOLENCE OR CRIME OF PASSION?

Top: Arias's mugshot in prison orange; **Above:** Arias and Alexander together as a couple.

Jodi Ann Arias was born on July 9, 1980, in Salinas, California, to William Angelo and Sandra Dee Arias. Growing up in a seemingly typical American family, Arias had a relatively unremarkable childhood, though she dropped out of high school in her junior year. She later earned a GED and pursued various professional interests, including photography, which became a significant part of her life. Arias's early life gave little indication of the tumultuous and tragic events that would later unfold.

The Death of Travis Alexander

Jodi Arias entered the national spotlight for the brutal murder of her ex-boyfriend, Travis Alexander, in his Mesa, Arizona, home on June 4, 2008. Alexander, a 30-year-old motivational speaker and insurance salesman, was found dead with multiple stab wounds, a slit throat, and a gunshot wound to the head. The relationship between Arias and Alexander had been tumultuous, marked by intense passion

and jealousy. Despite their breakup in June 2007, the pair continued an on-and-off sexual relationship. The investigation into Alexander's murder quickly focused on Arias, who initially denied any involvement. However, as evidence mounted, including a digital camera found in Alexander's washing machine containing images of Arias and Alexander from the day of the murder, as well as photos of Alexander's body, Arias's story began to unravel. She then claimed that she had killed Alexander in self-defense after he attacked her.

Arias's Capture and Trial

Jodi Arias was arrested on July 15, 2008, and charged with first-degree murder. Her trial, which began on January 2, 2013, captivated the nation, partly due to the salacious details of Arias and Alexander's relationship and the gruesome nature of the murder. Throughout the trial, Arias's defense argued that she was a victim of domestic violence and had killed Alexander in self-defense. However, the prosecution contended that Arias had premeditated the murder out of jealousy and rage after Alexander wanted to end their relationship permanently.

Verdict

On May 8, 2013, Arias was found guilty of first-degree murder. The jury found the murder to be especially cruel, making Arias eligible for the death penalty. However, after two penalty phase trials resulted in hung juries, Arias was sentenced to life in prison without the possibility of parole on April 13, 2015. She is currently serving her sentence at the Arizona State Prison Complex - Perryville.

Legacy

The Jodi Arias case remains one of the most high-profile and controversial legal battles in recent American history. It has sparked widespread media attention, debates over the nature of domestic abuse, the psychology of killers, and the impact of sensationalism in the courtroom. Arias herself has attempted to appeal her conviction, maintaining her innocence and arguing that her trial was marred by prosecutorial misconduct and a biased media.

Above left: Arias during her trial for first degree murder, sporting an image change with spectacles and away from blonde; **Above:** Travis Alexander, murder victim; **Below:** Arias spent a considerable part of her life making self-portraits.

STEPHEN PADDOCK
THE LAS VEGAS MASSACRE OF 2017

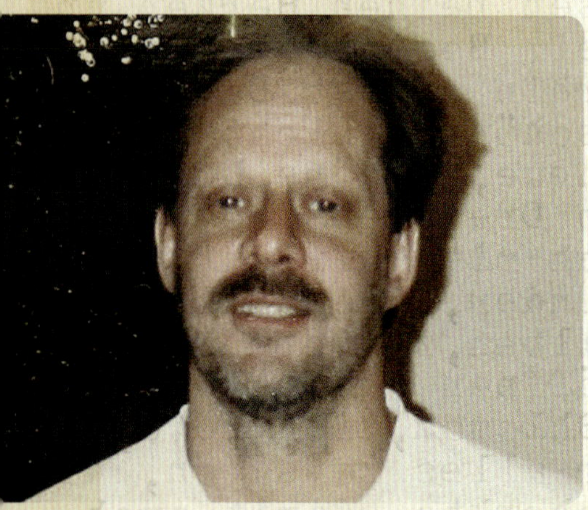

Top left: The Mandalay Bay hotel. Paddock shot down from the 32nd floor onto the crowd attending the Route 91 Harvest music festival; **Top right:** Fans scatter and flee during the shooting spree; **Above:** A rare picture of Stephen Paddock, the shooter.

Stephen Craig Paddock was born on April 9, 1953, in Clinton, Iowa. The beginning chapters of his life were marred by family complications. His father, Benjamin Hoskins Paddock, was a bank robber who was on the FBI's Ten Most Wanted Fugitives list. The younger Paddock, however, did not follow in his father's criminal footsteps early on and lived a relatively unremarkable life for many years.

Career and Personal Life

Paddock worked various jobs throughout his life. He was a postal carrier, an IRS agent, and later, an auditor for the Defense Contract Audit Agency. Eventually, he shifted into real estate and had several successful ventures, amassing considerable wealth. By the time of his retirement, he was a millionaire. In his personal life, Paddock was known as a high-stakes gambler, frequenting casinos in Las Vegas. Those who interacted with him described him as reserved and unemotive, giving away little about his internal thoughts or feelings.

The Las Vegas Shooting

On October 1, 2017, Stephen Paddock perpetrated one of the deadliest mass shootings in modern U.S. history. From his suite on the 32nd floor of the Mandalay Bay Hotel in Las Vegas, he opened fire on a crowd attending the Route 91 Harvest music festival. Using a series of modified semi-automatic weapons, Paddock killed 58 people and injured more than 800 in a matter of minutes. As police closed

in on his location, Paddock took his own life, leaving behind no immediate motive for his actions.

Investigation and Motive

The subsequent investigation into the Las Vegas shooting was extensive. Authorities discovered that Paddock had planned the attack meticulously, acquiring weapons and ammunition over a year. He had also set up surveillance cameras in and around his hotel suite to monitor the approach of law enforcement. However, despite the thorough investigation, a clear motive for Paddock's actions was never definitively determined. While authorities found evidence of his declining mental state and some financial troubles, they couldn't pinpoint a specific reason for such a large-scale attack.

Legacy and Impact

The Las Vegas shooting sparked nationwide grief and outrage. It reignited the ongoing debates about gun control in the U.S. and raised questions about hotel security measures and the monitoring of large-scale public events. Stephen Paddock's actions on that fateful October night have left a lasting scar on the city of Las Vegas and the broader American psyche. His case remains a grim testament to the unpredictability of mass violent acts and the challenges faced in preventing them.

Top left: Shocked and bemused festival visitors congregate in the immediate aftermath of the horror; **Top right, and above left:** Friends and families of the victims gather to mourn; **Above:** Bouquets and wreaths are laid beneath the well-known "Welcome to Fabulous Las Vegas, Nevada" neon signpost.

NATALIA & DMITRY BAKSHEEV EXTREME PERVERSIONS

Natalia and Dmitry Baksheev were residents of Krasnodar, a city in southern Russia. Dmitry was born in 1982, while Natalia was born in 1975. Their early lives, before they gained notoriety, are shrouded in relative obscurity, but subsequent investigations revealed snippets of a troubled past and indications of antisocial behavior.

Relationship and Marriage

The couple met in the early 2000s, and their relationship was marked by dysfunction. Neighbors and acquaintances often described them as reclusive, with episodes of erratic behavior. Natalia was an unemployed alcoholic, and Dmitry had been arrested in the past for robbery and car theft. Despite the tumultuous nature of their relationship, they lived together for several years, with their union cemented by shared dark interests.

Crimes Unearthed

The couple came under the spotlight in 2017 when a lost mobile phone belonging to Dmitry was discovered in Krasnodar. The device contained gruesome images of a dismembered woman, sparking a police investigation. This initial evidence led the authorities to their residence, where they discovered more damning evidence, including photographs of body parts, preserved human

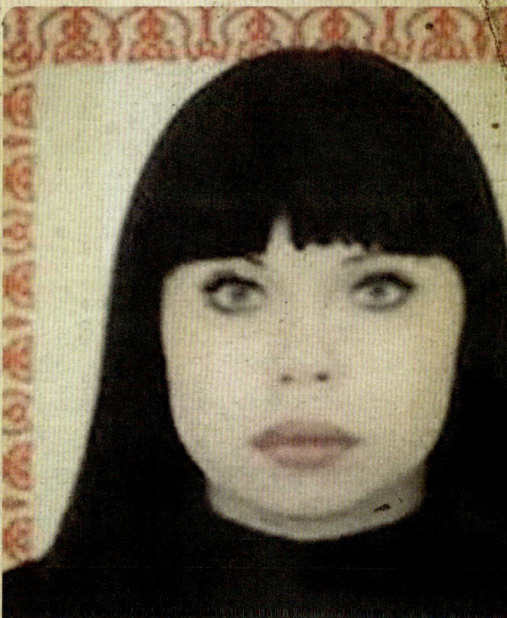

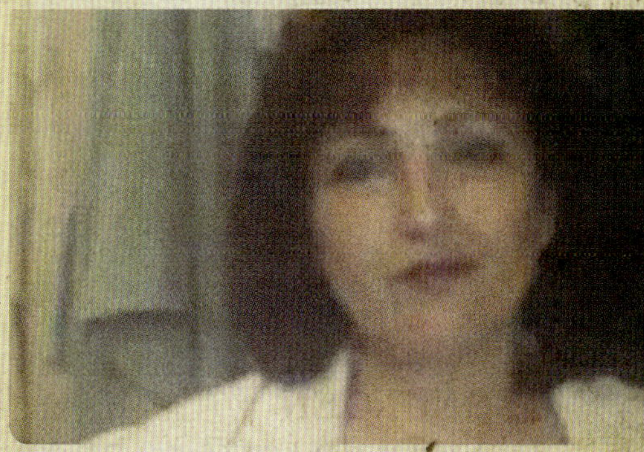

Opposite, top: Dmitry Baksheev jokingly poses with hammer and sickle—the old Soviet Communist emblem; **Opposite, below:** Natalia Baksheev turns coquettishly to camera; **Top left:** Kissing cannibals—the pair's relationship was underpinned by their shared dark secrets. (Photo courtesy Alexander Vlasenko/ AIF RU); **Above, top:** Elena Vakhrusheva—their one definite murder victim; **Center, and above:** Pictures of the two murderers.

skin, and various other body parts and physical remains. Upon interrogation, at least one murder was revealed: during a drunken argument, Natalia had encouraged Dmitry to stab their acquaintance Elena Vakhrusheva to death, then helped him dismember her body. Disturbingly, the couple admitted to acts of cannibalism, even preserving parts of their victim for later consumption.

Extent of Their Crimes

The exact number of the couple's victims remains a matter of contention. While some rumors claim that the couple confessed to as many as 30 murders, they were only ever charged with a single murder—that of Elena Vakhrusheva. The photographs recovered depicted processed, partially eaten, and dissected body parts, making the task of identification challenging. The couple's residence, located near a military academy, contained multiple containers with preserved remains, and it was rumored that written recipes for cooking human flesh were also discovered on site.

Legal Proceedings and Outcome

Given the gravity of their confessions and the evidence at hand, the Baksheev's were subjected to a thorough legal process. Psychological evaluations were commissioned to ascertain their mental state, and while there were clear indications of psychological disturbances, the court deemed them fit to stand trial. Their trial was one of the most closely-watched in recent Russian history, given the macabre nature of their crimes. The proceedings culminated with both Dmitry and Natalia receiving lengthy prison sentences. Dmitry Baksheev died of untreated type one diabetes on February 16, 2020,

A ball of fire erupts from the Branch Davidian compound in Waco, Texas, on April 19, 1993. Eighty-one Davidians, including leader David Koresh, perished as federal agents tried to drive them out of the compound. A few weeks earlier four agents from the Bureau of Alcohol, Tobacco and Firearms were slain in a shootout at the site. (Photo by Jerry W. Hoefer/Fort Worth Star-Telegram/TNS/Sipa USA)

CHAPTER FIVE

CULT LEADERS

This chapter examines the intriguing and often disturbing world of cult leaders, individuals who wield an almost supernatural influence over their followers, leading them into the depths of collective madness and, in some cases, orchestrating mass tragedies. We explore the lives of these people—almost exclusively male, the mechanisms by which they built and maintained their followings, and the devastating impacts of their actions on both individuals and society. Cult leaders often emerge from the fringes of society, presenting themselves as prophets, messiahs, or enlightened beings with access to secret knowledge or salvation. They exploit human vulnerabilities, a desire for belonging, and the search for meaning, drawing followers into their fold with promises of a better life or spiritual awakening. However, beneath the veneer of benevolence lies a core of manipulation, exploitation, and, often, violence. From Charles Manson's apocalyptic visions of race war to Jim Jones' massacre of Jonestown, these stories reveal the complex interplay of personality, power, and persuasion that defines the cult phenomenon.

CHARLES MANSON
HELTER SKELTER:
THE MIND BEHIND A CULT OF CHAOS

Charles Milles Manson, born on November 12, 1934, in Cincinnati, Ohio, is infamously known for leading the Manson Family, a quasi-commune that emerged in California in the late 1960s. Manson and his followers are responsible for a series of gruesome murders that shook America and marked the end of the idealistic era of the 1960s. From a young age, Manson's life was marked by instability and crime. His mother was a teenage runaway, and the young Manson spent much of his youth in and out of correctional institutions. Over time, he developed a manipulative persona, adept at bending people to his will.

Formation of The Manson Family

By the late 1960s, Manson had established himself as a guru in San Francisco's Haight-Ashbury district. Preying on the vulnerabilities of young people drawn to the city's burgeoning counterculture scene, Manson assembled a devoted group of followers. They soon moved to the Los Angeles area, occupying

the Spahn Ranch. Here, Manson combined a mix of pseudo-religious teachings with his interpretations of songs, particularly tracks from The Beatles' *White Album*, to establish control over his followers.

The Tate-LaBianca Murders

In August 1969, Manson ordered a group of his most loyal Family members to carry out a series of murders. Their victims included actress Sharon Tate, then eight months pregnant, and four others at Tate's residence. The following night, Leno and Rosemary LaBianca were also brutally murdered by members of the Manson Family. The crime scenes were marked by extreme violence and post-mortem mutilations, with cryptic writings left in the victims' blood. Manson hoped the murders would appear to be racially motivated, sparking an apocalyptic race war he called "Helter Skelter."

Capture and Trial

Suspicion soon fell on the Manson Family, and after a series of raids and investigations, Manson and several of his followers were arrested. The trial, which began in June 1970, was a media spectacle. Manson's erratic behavior, along with the unwavering devotion of his followers, captivated the nation. In 1971, Manson was found guilty of first-degree murder for the deaths of the Tate and LaBianca victims. He was initially sentenced to death, but after the California Supreme Court invalidated the state's death penalty statutes in 1972, his sentence was commuted to life in prison with the possibility of parole.

Imprisonment and Death

Throughout his imprisonment, Manson was denied parole twelve times. He continued to captivate public attention through interviews and his unpredictable behavior. On November 19, 2017, he died in prison at the age of 83. The legacy of Charles Manson and the Manson Family extends beyond their crimes. They represent a dark and twisted side of the counterculture era, serving as a grim reminder of the dangers of unchecked charisma and unquestioning devotion.

Opposite, top left: "The crazy killer"—Charles Manson's 1968 mugshot; **Opposite, top right:** Three members of the Manson Family, from left: Pat Krenwinkel, Susan Atkins, and Leslie Van Houten; **Opposite, bottom left:** Manson arrives in court, 1970; **This page, top left:** August 9, 1969: Sharon Tate's body is taken from her home on Cielo Drive in the Bel Air Estates area of Los Angeles; **Top right:** Jay Sebring and Sharon Tate pose for the camera before take-off; **Center right:** Leno and Rosemary LaBianca, the second night victims. Although Tex Watson killed both, Leslie Van Houten stabbed Rosemary LaBianca a further 14 times; **Right:** Manson's mugshot from 1985.

Thank you for your contribution to

PEOPLE'S TEMPLE CHRISTIAN CHURCH
P.O. Box 214
Redwood Valley, Calif. 95470

This contribution will help to aid our many missionary projects, including the children's home, the dormitories, the friendship home and many others.

Pastor Jim W. Jones

JIM JONES THE PEOPLES TEMPLE

Above left: James Warren Jones, founder and leader of the Peoples Temple; **Above right:** Donation card, and Polaroid of "Pastor Jones"; **Opposite, top right:** The Jonestown Massacre—a local boy gazes in disbelief at the sight before his eyes. There are bodies everywhere—see also overleaf; **Opposite, below right:** A survivor of the mass suicide talks to reporters.

James Warren "Jim" Jones, born on May 13, 1931, in Crete, Indiana, was the charismatic founder and leader of the Peoples Temple, a cult that gained notoriety for the mass murder-suicide of its members in Jonestown, Guyana, in 1978. Jones grew up in a deeply divided America, with the Great Depression and racial segregation shaping his early years. His interest in religion was evident from a young age. In the 1950s, Jones established the Wings of Deliverance church in Indianapolis, which would later become the Peoples Temple. The church was progressive, promoting racial integration, a rarity at the time.

The Rise of Peoples Temple

Throughout the 1960s and early 1970s, Jones expanded the reach of the Peoples Temple.

With branches in multiple cities, including San Francisco and Los Angeles, the church's membership grew exponentially. Jones combined socialist politics with apocalyptic prophecies, attracting a diverse group of followers. By the mid-1970s, amid growing scrutiny and allegations of abuse, Jones and many of his followers relocated to Guyana, South America, where they established the Peoples Temple Agricultural Project, better known as Jonestown. The settlement was promoted as a socialist utopia, but in reality, it was more akin to a prison camp, with reports of forced labor, physical punishment, and members being drugged.

The Massacre at Jonestown

In November 1978, U.S. Congressman Leo Ryan visited Jonestown to investigate allegations of human rights abuses. His visit ended in tragedy when Ryan and four others were ambushed and killed by Temple members at a nearby airstrip. Realizing that the end was near, Jones ordered his followers to participate in a "revolutionary suicide" event. On November 18, 1978, more than 900 people, including Jones, died in Jonestown, most from drinking a cyanide-laced fruit punch.

Aftermath and Legacy

The Jonestown massacre was shocking in its scale and brutality. It stands as the largest single loss of American civilian life in a non-natural disaster until the September 11 attacks in 2001. Jim Jones' legacy is a cautionary tale about the dangers of blind faith and unchecked power. The phrase "drinking the Kool-Aid," referring to the acceptance of beliefs without critical examination, originates from the Jonestown tragedy, although it is worth noting that the drink used was actually Flavor Aid. While the Peoples Temple started with seemingly good intentions, promoting racial equality and social justice, it descended into a platform for Jones' megalomania. The tragedy of Jonestown serves as a somber reminder of the need for vigilance and critical thinking in the face of charismatic leadership.

THE JONESTOWN MASSACRE

This image spread: On November 18, 1978, a total of 918 people died in the Jonestown settlement. It stands as the largest single loss of American civilian life in a non-natural disaster until the September 11 attacks in 2001. The spread image shows just some of the dead; **Inset, above:** U.S. military personnel are left with the gruesome task of readying the dead for repatriation to the United States.

The group was isolated from the outside world, and Thériault maintained control through fear, manipulation, and violence. He also took multiple "wives" from among his followers and fathered over 20 children, many of whom were abused...

ROCH THÉRIAULT
ABSOLUTE POWER CORRUPTS ABSOLUTELY

Roch "Moïse" Thériault was the founder and leader of the Ant Hill Kids, a Canadian doomsday cult that gained notoriety for its extreme abuse and violence in the 1970s and 1980s. Under the guise of religious teachings, Thériault committed an almost continuous series of heinous acts against his followers.

Early Life and Formation of the Cult

Born on May 16, 1947, in Saguenay, Quebec, Thériault dropped out of school in the seventh grade and turned to a life of petty crime. By the late 1970s, he began to portray himself as a prophet, taking the French name *Moïse*—Moses. Thériault formed the Ant Hill Kids, gathering a group of followers and establishing a commune in Burnt River, Ontario.

The Commune and Its Practices

Thériault apparently came up with the name of "the Ant Hill Kids" as he watched his followers from high on a mountainside, toiling away like ants, doing his bidding. Members of the Ant Hill Kids were required to follow strict and often arbitrary rules set by Thériault. The group was isolated from the outside world, and Thériault maintained control through fear, manipulation, and violence. He also took multiple "wives" from among his followers and fathered over 20 children, many of whom were abused. He claimed that the end of the world was imminent and that only he could lead them to salvation. Thériault's abuse of power was severe. He meted out gruesome punishments for those who defied him or were seen as unfaithful. Followers were subjected to beatings, burnings—and even amputations. When follower Solange Boilard complained of stomach pains, Thériault performed "surgery" on her. The unfortunate Solange was put naked onto a table, punched in the stomach, and a plastic tube was forced into her rectum to form a crude enema of olive oil mixed with molasses. He then slit open her abdomen and tore out some of her intestines. Follower Gabrielle Lavallée was made to sew her up. Solange died the next day. Claiming to have the power of resurrection, Thériault had his followers saw off the cap of Solange's skull and he ejaculated onto her brain. When Boilard did not return to life, her corpse was buried a short distance from the commune.

The Downfall

The horrors of the Ant Hill Kids came to light in 1989. Gabrielle Lavallée escaped and sought medical attention for her injuries—which included a missing arm. The authorities were alerted, leading to Thériault's arrest. Some four years later, he was finally brought to trial and was found guilty of two counts of second-degree murder—amongst other charges—and sentenced to life in prison.

Death and Legacy

Thériault's sadistic existence was brought to an end on February 26, 2011, when he was murdered in his cell at Dorchester Penitentiary in New Brunswick, by his cellmate. The story of the Ant Hill Kids serves as a grim reminder of the dangers and sheer lunacy of unchecked power and charismatic leadership. Thériault exploited the vulnerabilities of his followers, leading them down a dark path under the guise of religious enlightenment. His crimes remain some of the most disturbing in Canadian history, highlighting the depths of human cruelty and the vulnerability of those searching for meaning and belonging.

Opposite, top: Thériault grins, surrounded by his loving "wives"; **Opposite, below:** Roch Thériault, circa 1985; **Top main image:** Thériault and followers photographed in their log cabin compound in Burnt River, Ontario; **Above:** Thériault, the sadist guru, sits on his throne, contemplating his good fortune.

Koresh's teachings were a mix of apocalyptic prophecies and interpretations of the Bible, and he preached that the U.S. government was the the enemy of the Branch Davidians—and would play a crucial role in the end times...

DAVID KORESH THE APOCALYPTIC VISIONARY OF WACO

David Koresh, originally born Vernon Wayne Howell on August 17, 1959, in Houston, Texas, was the charismatic leader of the Branch Davidians, a religious sect that splintered from the Seventh-day Adventist Church. Under his leadership, the group became the focal point of one of the most controversial and tragic standoffs in U.S. history.

Early Life and Transformation

Koresh's upbringing was fraught with challenges. Born to a 14-year-old single mother, he never really knew his father and faced learning difficulties in school. Despite these challenges, he developed a deep passion for the Bible, displaying a remarkable ability to memorize large passages.

In his early twenties, Koresh joined the Branch Davidians in Waco, Texas. Displaying a flair for interpretation, he began to claim prophetic visions. By the mid-1980s, through a combination of charisma and claimed divine revelations, he took control of the group, changing his name to David Koresh – drawing from King David and Cyrus the Great of Persia.

Teachings and Beliefs

Koresh's teachings were a mix of apocalyptic prophecies and interpretations of the Bible, and he preached that the U.S. government was the enemy of the Branch Davidians—and would play a crucial role in the end times. Koresh claimed he was the final prophet in a line of biblical figures, tasked with decoding the Seven Seals mentioned in the Book of Revelation. Under his leadership, the community at the Mount Carmel Center near Waco became increasingly militarized. Koresh emphasized the need for armed defense against external threats, leading to an accumulation of weapons and ammunition.

The Waco Siege

In 1993, suspicions about the group's weapon stockpile and allegations of child abuse caught the attention of authorities. On February 28, the Bureau of Alcohol, Tobacco, and Firearms (ATF) attempted to execute a search warrant at the Mount Carmel Center. The attempt quickly escalated into a gunfight, resulting in

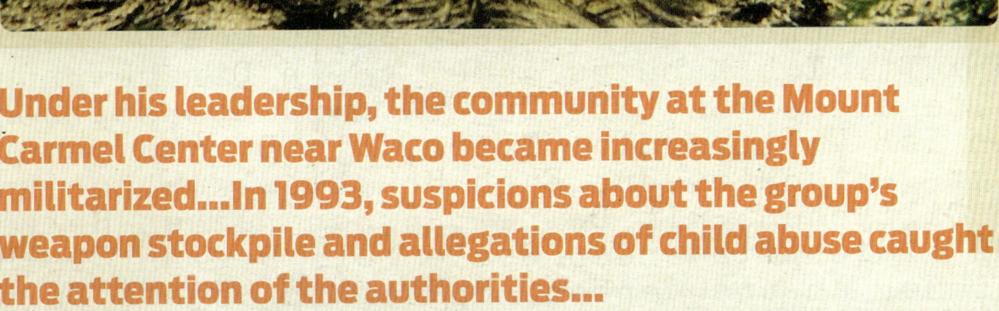

Under his leadership, the community at the Mount Carmel Center near Waco became increasingly militarized...In 1993, suspicions about the group's weapon stockpile and allegations of child abuse caught the attention of the authorities...

the deaths of four ATF agents and six Branch Davidians. This confrontation led to a 51-day standoff between the Branch Davidians and federal agents. Negotiators managed to secure the release of some individuals from the compound, but Koresh and most of his followers remained, steadfast in their belief in his prophecies. The standoff came to a catastrophic conclusion on April 19, 1993. The FBI launched a final assault, employing tear gas in an attempt to force the Davidians out. Several hours later, a massive fire engulfed the compound. The cause remains a subject of debate, but the blaze resulted in the deaths of Koresh and 76 of his followers, including children.

Legacy and Impact

The Waco siege remains a deeply controversial and studied event in American history, serving as a cautionary tale about the potential dangers of unchecked religious fervor and governmental overreach. For many, Koresh embodies the perils of absolute power and messianic delusion. His life and the tragic end of the Waco standoff are emblematic of the volatile intersection of faith, firearms, and fanaticism.

Opposite, top right: David Koresh at the Waco compound; **Opposite, center:** After the inferno, a believer leaves a makeshift altar to the perished Koresh; **Opposite, bottom:** The apocalypse begins in the Waco compound; **This page, top left:** Bagging up the bodies after the fire; **Top, center:** Surveying the wreckage; **Above left:** The tanks move in after the long standoff with ATF forces; **Above:** The survivors of Waco are led out in their County Jail jumpsuits.

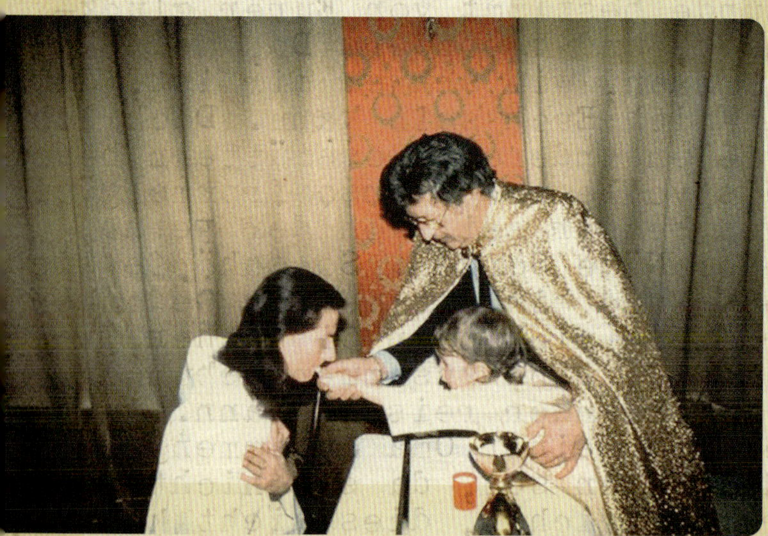

JOSEPH DI MAMBRO & LUC JOURET

WE MUST TRANSITION TO SIRIUS...

Joseph Di Mambro and Luc Jouret are infamously known as the founders of the Order of the Solar Temple (OST), a cult that combined Christian doctrine, UFO conspiracy theories, and New Age philosophy. The group came into the global spotlight after a series of mass murders and suicides in the 1990s.

Origins and Beliefs

Luc Jouret, a Belgian doctor and homeopath, began giving lectures on holistic medicine and spiritual awakening in the early 1980s. By mid-decade, he had partnered with Joseph Di Mambro, a self-styled esoteric—and (secretly) a convicted fraudster. Together, they founded the OST in 1984 in Geneva. The group blended various beliefs, with a primary focus on the second coming of Christ as a solar god-king. Di Mambro preached (or devised) the idea that life on Earth was ending, and that followers needed to transition to a solar existence on a mythical planet orbiting the star Sirius.

Expansion and Influence

The OST expanded across countries, with chapters in Switzerland, France, and Canada. Its members—many of whom were wealthy—were drawn to the group's esoteric teachings and the promise of a spiritual journey leading to another world.

The Tragedies

The group's dark side began to emerge in the early 1990s. In 1994, authorities discovered the

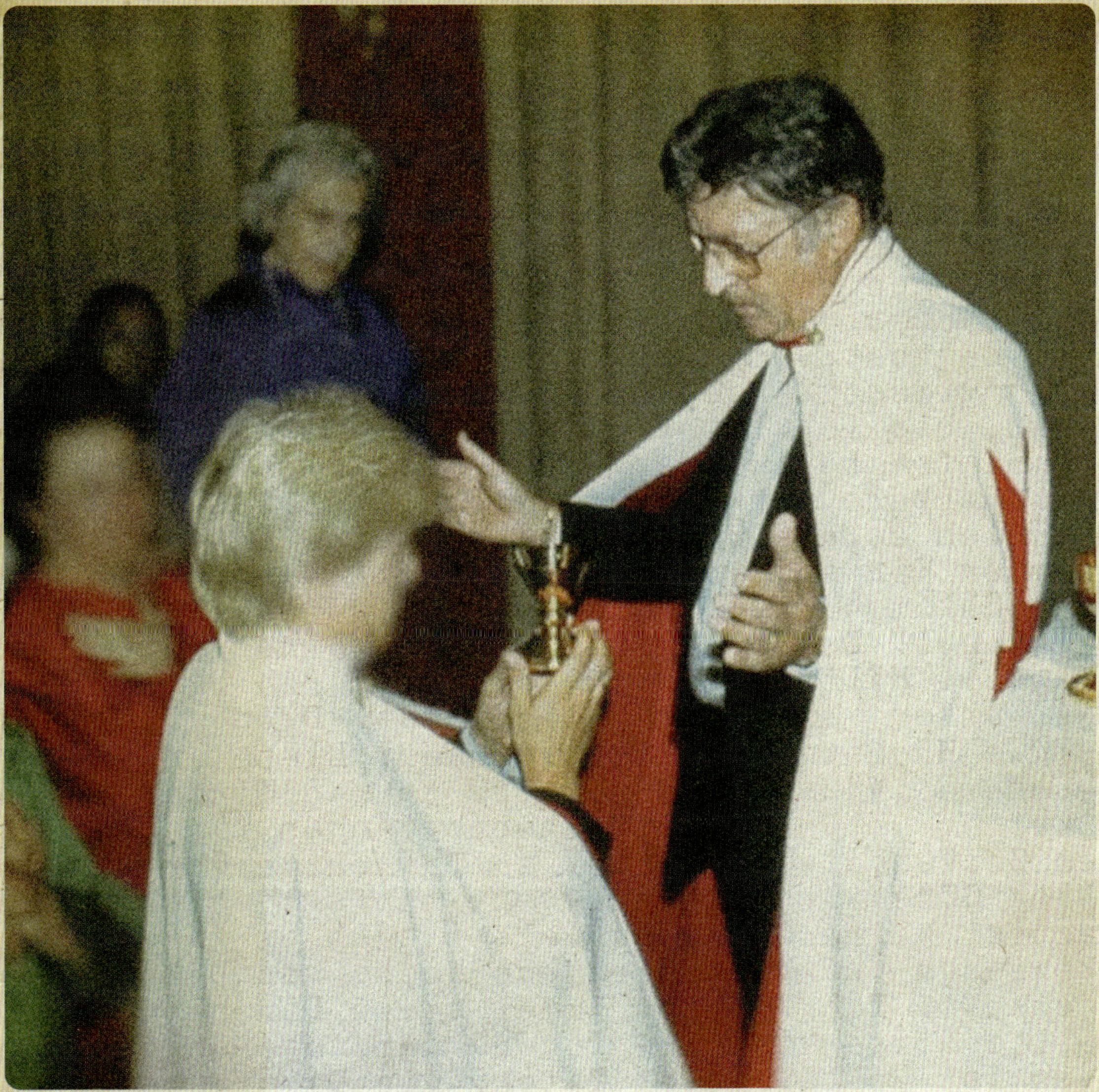

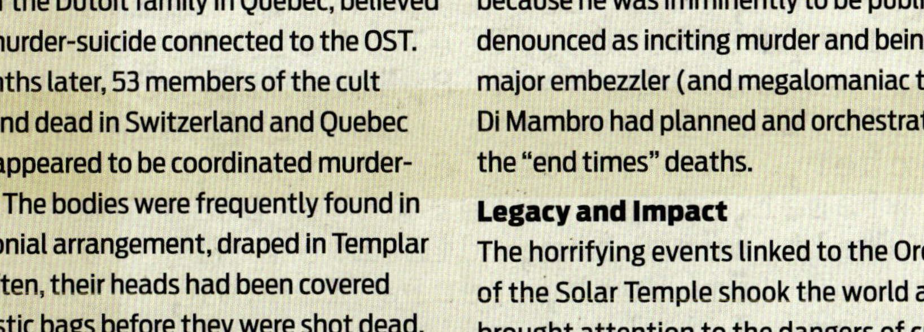

Opposite, top left: Joseph Di Mambro (right), mastermind of the OST, with wizard cape; **Opposite, top right:** Luc Jouret (left) in OST ceremonial robes. The robe emblems supposedly connected them to the 13th century Knights Templar; **Opposite, below:** Luc Jouret, most probably completely duped by the nefarious Di Mambro. (Needless to say, Di Mambro controlled all the Order's finances. The Order's Australian bank account alone was discovered to hold $93 million); **Top left:** Di Mambro plays the part of a Christian minister; **Above, top:** The Dutoit family, brutally murdered by "The Order of the Solar Temple"—under the pretext their baby was the antichrist. Dutoit had earlier criticized Di Mambro as being "a megalomaniac, deceitful, and an embezzler," and not living according to the church's teachings. The Dutoit's two-month-old baby was killed with a stake through his heart. His parents were then shot dead; **Center:** Burnt-out remains of one of the chalet residences of the OST—set ablaze by remote control—after the murders and suicides had been carried out; **Above:** Some of the bodies are brought out of the smoking ruins.

bodies of the Dutoit family in Quebec, believed to be a murder-suicide connected to the OST. Just months later, 53 members of the cult were found dead in Switzerland and Quebec in what appeared to be coordinated murder-suicides. The bodies were frequently found in a ceremonial arrangement, draped in Templar robes; often, their heads had been covered with plastic bags before they were shot dead, in apparent ritual killings. In subsequent years, more deaths linked to the cult occurred. In 1995, sixteen bodies were found in the French Alps, and in 1997, another five members died in Quebec. In total, 77 members were either ritually murdered or committed suicide.

The Leaders' End

Both Jouret and Di Mambro were among the dead in the 1994 tragedy. It's believed that because he was imminently to be publicly denounced as inciting murder and being a major embezzler (and megalomaniac to boot), Di Mambro had planned and orchestrated all the "end times" deaths.

Legacy and Impact

The horrifying events linked to the Order of the Solar Temple shook the world and brought attention to the dangers of cults. The group's ability to attract and manipulate well-educated and wealthy individuals highlighted the universal susceptibility to charismatic leaders and unorthodox beliefs. Today, the OST serves as a grim reminder of the extents to which people might go in their quest for spiritual enlightenment and the tragic outcomes that can result from unchecked devotion.

In the 1980s, Asahara began practicing yoga and soon declared himself a "holy man"...he founded Aum Shinrikyo...but the group's teachings soon took a darker turn as Asahara proclaimed himself the "Lamb of God" and predicted a catastrophic Third World War initiated by the United States...

SHOKO ASAHARA

THE DOOMSDAY CULT LEADER

Shoko Asahara, born Chizuo Matsumoto on March 2, 1955, in Yatsushiro, Japan, was the founder and spiritual leader of the cult Aum Shinrikyo. Under his guidance, the group was responsible for a series of crimes, including the deadly 1995 Tokyo subway sarin gas attack.

Early Life

Asahara was born blind in one eye and with limited vision in the other, which led him to attend a school for the blind. Despite his visual impairment, he was known to be manipulative, often bullying other students. After a failed venture in Chinese medicine and acupuncture, he shifted his focus towards spirituality.

Formation of Aum Shinrikyo

In the 1980s, Asahara began practicing yoga and soon declared himself a "holy man." By 1987, he founded Aum Shinrikyo (literally, 'Supreme Truth'), which initially started as a yoga and meditation group. The group's teachings, influenced by Buddhism, Hinduism, and Christian apocalyptic prophecies, soon took a darker turn as Asahara proclaimed himself the "Lamb of God" and predicted a catastrophic Third World War initiated by the United States.

Rise of the Cult

Throughout the late 1980s and early 1990s, Aum Shinrikyo's membership expanded rapidly, attracting thousands of followers, including scientists, engineers, and other educated professionals. The group became increasingly secretive and began amassing weapons and manufacturing drugs and chemicals.

Sarin Gas Attacks

Under Asahara's direction, Aum Shinrikyo executed a series of crimes, but their most notorious act was the Tokyo subway sarin attack on March 20, 1995. Cult members released sarin, a lethal nerve agent, in the Tokyo subway system during the morning rush hour, resulting in the deaths of 13 people and injuring over 50 others.

Capture and Execution

Following the attack, a massive manhunt was launched for Asahara and other key members of Aum Shinrikyo. Two months after the sarin attack, Asahara was found hiding in a secret compartment in one of the cult's buildings and was arrested. After an extended trial, Shoko Asahara was found guilty of multiple charges, including masterminding the Tokyo subway attack. He was sentenced to death. On July 6, 2018, Asahara was executed by hanging, ending the dark chapter of one of Japan's most infamous cult leaders. While Aum Shinrikyo was stripped of its official status as a religious organization in Japan, offshoots of the cult still exist in Japan and Russia, albeit under strict surveillance.

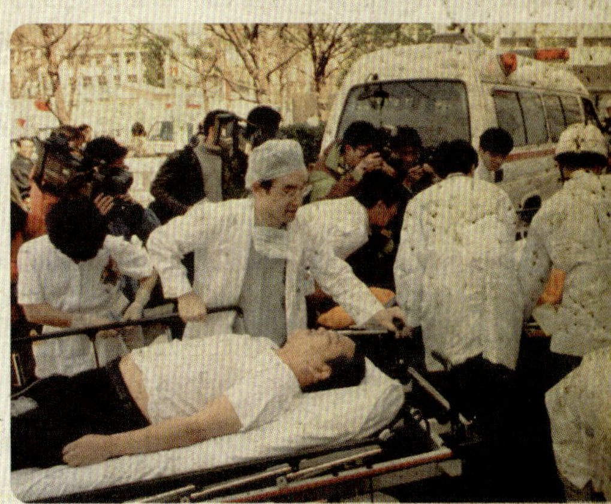

Above: Medics treat victims of the sarin nerve gas attack on the Tokyo subway, March 1995; **Top:** May 16, 1995: Army and police units enter the No. 6 Satian complex in Kamikuishiki, west of Tokyo, to arrest Shoko Asahara on suspicion of masterminding the attack; **Opposite, top:** Shoko Asahara; **Opposite, below:** In Fukuoka a passer-by watches news reports of Asahara's murder trial as the cult leader is sentenced to death at the Tokyo District Court on February 27, 1996.

MARSHALL APPLEWHITE & BONNIE NETTLES HEAVEN'S GATE

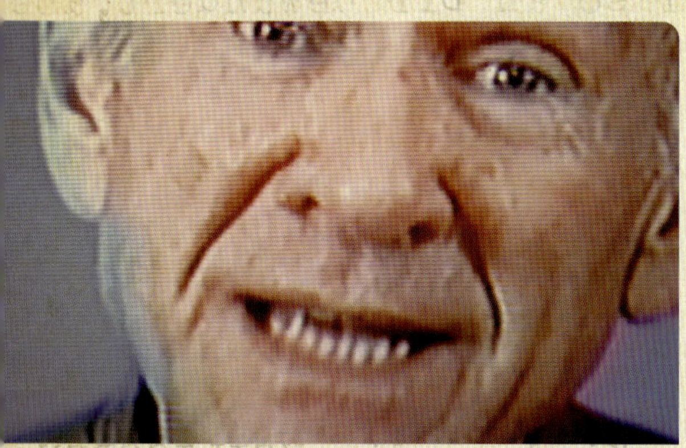

Above: Marshall Applewhite talks to camera during the filming of the "Students' Final Exit Statements," made by the Heaven's Gate followers before the ritual mass suicide—see opposite pictures. (Courtesy of ABC News #2020 Series); **Top:** "Do and Ti" talk to reporters after their lecture at the Native American Center in Minneapolis on October 28, 1975. (Courtesy Duane Braley/Star Tribune via Getty Images); **Opposite, top left:** A chilling picture of the aftermath of the suicide pact—two of the dead followers lie covered over by ritually colored death blankets; **Opposite right, top to bottom:** Stills from the ABC News #2020 Series which shows the "Students' Final Exit Statements."

Marshall Herff Applewhite and Bonnie Nettles were the co-founders of the Heaven's Gate cult. Applewhite, born May 17, 1931, in Spur, Texas, would go on to lead one of the most infamous mass suicides in U.S. history, convinced that it was the path to reach an extraterrestrial spaceship traveling behind the Hale-Bopp comet.

Applewhite's Early Life and Personal Struggles

Applewhite grew up in a religious household and, for a time, pursued a career in music, becoming a talented singer and earning a degree in music. He later served in the U.S. Army, taught music in universities, and even served as a choir director. However, personal issues, including struggles with his sexuality and a deteriorating mental state, led to him leaving his teaching position.

Meeting Bonnie Nettles and the Formation of Heaven's Gate

In the early 1970s, during a stay in a hospital, Applewhite met Bonnie Nettles, a nurse. They quickly formed a deep bond, with Applewhite believing that their meeting was foreordained. Nettles was already a devotee of astrology, and also believed in the contacting of the spirits of deceased people through seance. The pair began studying scriptures, believing in a mix of Christian doctrines and New Age philosophy, and the belief in extraterrestrials began to form a central part of their belief system. Applewhite reckoned that "Bonnie was to be the sage, whilst he was to be the speaker." By the mid-1970s, Applewhite and Nettles, referring to themselves as "Bo and Peep" or "Do and Ti," began recruiting followers. They preached that Earth was about to

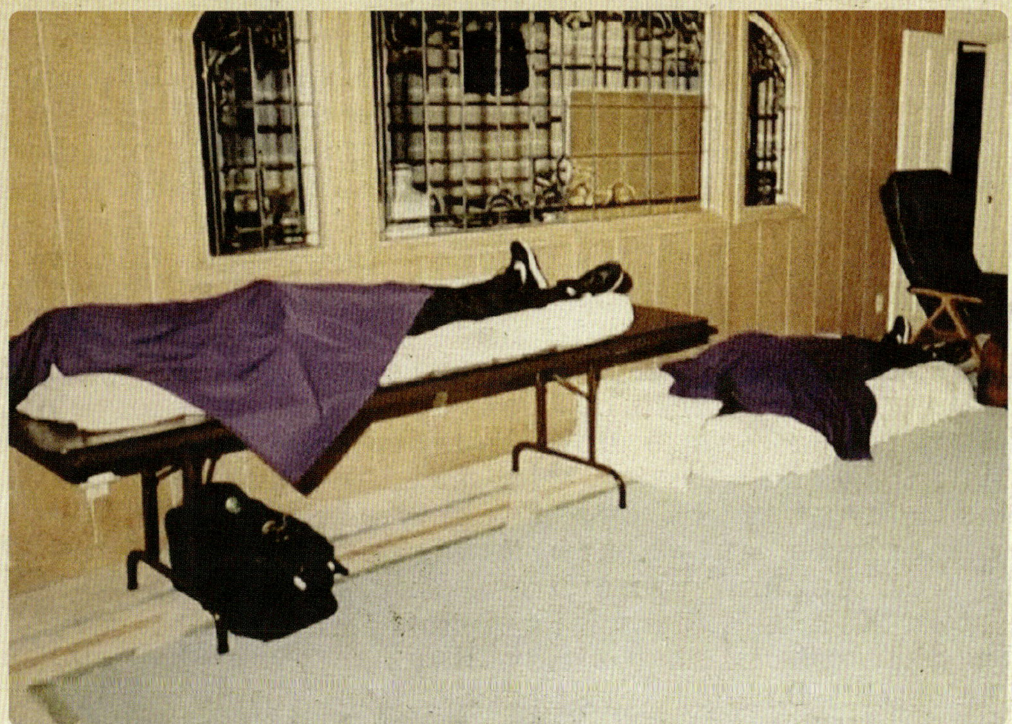

be wiped clean and that individuals needed to evolve to the "Next Level" to survive, which involved leaving behind all human desires and attachments.

Nettles' Death and Evolution of Beliefs

Over the years, the teachings of Heaven's Gate evolved. Applewhite started advocating for strict celibacy and even underwent castration to maintain this belief. The group became more secluded, relying on the internet to spread their teachings by the 1990s. Tragically, in 1985, Bonnie Nettles developed eye cancer which eventually spread to her liver. She thought the doctor was ignorant and believed, along with Applewhite, that she could not die, as they had to ascend together. However, Nettles succumbed to the disease in June 1985, at Parkland Memorial Hospital in Dallas, Texas. Applewhite convinced their followers that "Do's broken-down vehicle has been left behind." He told them that Nettles had left them because her work was done on this level...but that he himself still had more to do. Nettles would also continue to help them from the Next Level. Bonnie Nettles' death seems to have been a turning point in the development of the Heaven's Gate thinking, introducing a shift from the belief they would physically ascend to heaven whilst alive—onboard a UFO—to viewing the body as merely a "vehicle" for the soul which would be discarded upon entering heaven.

The Mass Suicide

In March 1997, as the Hale-Bopp comet approached its closest orbit to Earth, Applewhite propagated the idea that an alien spacecraft was following the comet and that it was the signal for their "ascension." He convinced 38 followers to participate in a mass suicide in order to shed their earthly "containers" and ascend to the spacecraft. Between March 22 and 26, in a mansion in Rancho Santa Fe, California, Applewhite and his followers consumed a lethal mixture of phenobarbital and vodka, lay down, and died, believing that they would be taken to a better life in outer space. They were dressed in matching black outfits with black-and-white Nike sneakers, and each had a five-dollar bill and three quarters in their pockets.

Aftermath

The event shocked the world and brought attention to the dangers of cults and extreme belief systems. The tragedy of Heaven's Gate remains a chilling reminder of the extents to which individuals might go when under the influence of charismatic leaders and isolationist beliefs.

The cult leaders claimed that the world would end on January 1, 2000. When the prophesized date came and went without incident, the leadership adjusted their prediction to March 17, 2000...

CREDONIA MWERINDE & JOSEPH KIBWETEERE

MASS MURDER IN UGANDA

Top: "Sister" Credonia Mwerinde, and **above:** Joseph Kibweteere, co-founders of the Ugandan cult. Both disappeared after the fire...

Credonia Mwerinde and Joseph Kibweteere were key figures in the Movement for the Restoration of the Ten Commandments of God, a Ugandan doomsday cult that made headlines for a series of mass suicides and murders in the year 2000.

Origins and Beliefs

Joseph Kibweteere, a former politician, and Credonia Mwerinde, a purported visionary who claimed to see visions of the Virgin Mary, co-founded the cult in the late 1980s. They preached the imminent end of the world, drawing on apocalyptic interpretations of the Bible. The cult operated with strict regulations, emphasizing the Ten Commandments and advocating for complete silence among members, arguing that speech was sinful.

Rise of the Movement

The movement attracted a significant following in Uganda. Many followers sold their belongings and turned over their proceeds to the group, driven by prophecies of an impending apocalypse. The cult leaders claimed that the world would end on January 1, 2000. When the prophesized date came and went without incident, the leadership adjusted their prediction to March 17, 2000.

The Tragic End

On March 17, 2000...a massive fire duly engulfed the cult's church in Kanungu, where members had gathered to pray and prepare for the end of the world. The blaze killed over 500 members. Initially believed to be a mass suicide, later investigations revealed it was a mass murder. The doors and windows had been boarded up from the outside, preventing anyone from escaping. Subsequent investigations led to the discovery of multiple mass graves at various properties owned by the cult, pushing the death toll to 924, making it one of the deadliest cult tragedies in history. The exact events leading up to the mass killings remain unclear, but some speculate that members had begun to question the leaders after their doomsday prophecy failed to materialize in January. This dissent could have spurred the leaders into orchestrating the murders.

Aftermath and Legacy

The whereabouts of Credonia Mwerinde and Joseph Kibweteere remain a mystery. Some believe they perished in the church fire, while others suggest they might have escaped and gone into hiding. Their fate is one of the many unanswered questions surrounding the tragedy. The horrifying events of the Movement for the Restoration of the Ten Commandments of God remain a stark reminder of the dangers of extreme religious beliefs and the degree to which leaders will manipulate their followers.

Above, main image: Ugandan police and workmen, having removed many of the charred remains, take over the ruins of the burnt-out church; **Above:** A burned corpse in the foreground gives a chilling glimpse of the horror the cult members suffered. After all the cadavers had been found, the church was bulldozed flat.

The realm of hacking isn't confined to a singular definition, it encompasses a broad array of activities that involve unauthorized intrusion into computer systems, networks, or databases. In popular culture, the term "hacker" often conjures images of rogue individuals exploiting technology for nefarious purposes, but the reality is far more nuanced. While some hackers aim to exploit vulnerabilities for financial gain or to disrupt systems, others identify as ethical hackers, who work to improve cybersecurity.

Types of Hackers

Hackers are generally categorized into different types based on their intentions and methodologies. Black hat hackers engage in unauthorized intrusions for personal or financial gain, often damaging or stealing data. White hat hackers, on the other hand, perform ethical hacking to identify vulnerabilities and strengthen security systems. Then there are grey hat hackers who operate in a morally ambiguous zone, sometimes hacking without permission but with no malicious intent.

Common Techniques

Hacking methods have evolved over time, incorporating sophisticated tactics such as spear phishing, ransomware, and distributed denial-of-service (DDoS) attacks. Techniques like social engineering, which manipulates individuals into disclosing confidential information, have added a human element to the technological exploits.

Notable Incidents

Significant hacking episodes have garnered international attention, such as the Stuxnet worm that targeted Iranian nuclear facilities, or the Sony Pictures hack in 2014, which led to a diplomatic crisis between North Korea and the United States. These incidents highlight the far-reaching consequences of hacking, affecting not just corporations but governments and international relations.

Legal Framework

Laws surrounding hacking vary by jurisdiction but are increasingly being standardized to combat the global nature of these activities. In the United States, the Computer Fraud and Abuse Act (CFAA) serves as the primary legislation for prosecuting hackers. Internationally, various agreements and collaborations, like the Budapest Convention on Cybercrime, aim to foster cooperation among nations in fighting cybercrime.

Policing and Security Measures

Combatting hacking activities requires a multi-faceted approach that involves not just legal action but also proactive security measures. Organizations invest in advanced firewalls, intrusion detection systems, and regular audits. Cybersecurity firms often hire ethical hackers to test vulnerabilities in a controlled environment.

Hacktivism

The term "hacktivism" refers to hacking activities aimed at promoting a political or social cause. This form of hacking has sparked debates over the ethical implications, blurring the lines between activism and criminal activity. While hacking poses significant risks, it also drives advancements in cybersecurity and raises important ethical and legal questions. As technology continues to advance, the world of hacking is sure to remain a significant and evolving aspect of our digital lives.

CHAPTER SIX

HACKERS

KEVIN MITNICK
CYBERCRIME: FROM SOLITARY CONFINEMENT TO PUBLIC SPEAKING

Above: Kevin Mitnick in his later years; **Top left:** Mitnick after his release from prison in 2000; **Top right:** Mitnick sitting in front of his laptop in his later years.

Kevin Mitnick was born on August 6, 1963, in Van Nuys, California. Raised by a single mother, Mitnick's interest in computers sparked during his high school years. Using ham radios, he started engaging in what would later evolve into more advanced hacking activities.

Initial Exploits

Mitnick's early exploits included unauthorized access to computer networks, phone phreaking, and breaking into systems to steal proprietary Novell software. His activities eventually attracted the attention of law enforcement agencies.

Capture and Imprisonment

Mitnick was initially arrested in 1988 for stealing software and breaking into corporate networks. He was convicted and sentenced to 12 months in prison followed by three years of supervised release. However, before completing his supervised release, he went on the run for two and a half years, engaging in various cyber-espionage activities. He was ultimately captured in 1995 in Raleigh, North Carolina. Charged with 14 counts of wire fraud, 8 counts of possession of unauthorized access devices, and other offenses, he served five years in prison, including eight months in solitary confinement.

Reformation and Legal Career

Upon his release in 2000, Mitnick faced a string of restrictions, including being banned from using computers or the internet for three years. However, he successfully pivoted his life by leveraging his expertise in cybersecurity.

After his restrictions were lifted, he founded Mitnick Security Consulting, LLC, offering penetration testing and security assessment services to clients.

Author and Public Speaker

Mitnick also carved out a niche for himself as an author and public speaker. He has penned several books on the subject of cybersecurity, including *The Art of Deception* and *Ghost in the Wires*, which detail social engineering tactics and his life story, respectively. His speaking engagements often include live hacking demonstrations to educate the public and corporations about the vulnerabilities that exist in even the most secure systems.

Consulting and Media Appearances

He has provided consulting services to Fortune 500 companies and the FBI, imparting his insights into cybersecurity. His story has been featured in various media, including documentaries and news segments, further solidifying his transformation from one of the FBI's Most Wanted to a trusted cybersecurity consultant.

Controversies and Ethical Debates

Mitnick's transformation has not been without controversies. Critics have questioned the ethics of turning a criminal hacker into a cybersecurity expert, while proponents argue that his past gives him unique insights into the mindset of potential hackers. Legal loopholes concerning "ethical hacking" have been subject to scrutiny, partly due to the profile and activities of individuals like Mitnick.

Mitnick's Untimely Death

Mitnick continued his work in cybersecurity, providing consulting services, conducting security audits, and serving as a board member for various tech companies. His journey—from committing cybercrimes to advocating for cybersecurity—offers a compelling narrative about the potentials for transformation in the digital age. Kevin Mitnick died from pancreatic cancer on July 16, 2023, at the age of 59 at a Pittsburgh, Pennsylvania hospital. He was married and his wife was pregnant with his first child at the time of his death.

Main image, top: Mitnick in 2011 at the launch of his book *Ghost in the Wires: My Adventures as the World's Most Wanted Hacker*, co-written with William L. Simon; **Above, center:** *Ghost in the Wires* packshot; **Above:** A unique photo of three of the "most wanted," at one time or another, from left to right: Adrian Lamo (*see also* pages 208-209), Kevin Mitnick, and Kevin Poulsen (pages 204-205).

KEVIN POULSEN
DARK DANTE GROWN UP AND WIRED

Above: Kevin Poulsen. After serving his time in prison (and subsequent three year computer and internet ban), the longest term which had then been handed down by a U.S. court, he moved into journalism, working initially for *SecurityFocus*, the online news portal, before moving to *Wired Magazine*, becoming a senior editor.

Kevin Poulsen was born on November 30, 1965, in Pasadena, California. He demonstrated an early interest in computers, dedicating a considerable amount of time learning about them during his teenage years.

Initial Exploits

In the 1980s, Poulsen gained notoriety as a hacker under the alias "Dark Dante." His activities ranged from hacking into databases and systems to manipulating telecommunication services. One of his most publicized stunts was commandeering all of the telephone lines for Los Angeles radio station KIIS-FM, ensuring that he would be the 102nd caller and win a brand new Porsche 944, among other prizes.

Capture and Prosecution

Poulsen's KIIS-FM stunt led to an investigation by the Federal Communications Commission (FCC) and the FBI. Recognizing the increasing scrutiny, he went into hiding but was eventually captured in 1991. In 1994, he faced trial and was subsequently convicted on several counts, including mail, wire, and computer fraud, as well as money laundering.

Incarceration

Poulsen was sentenced to 51 months in prison, which at the time was the longest sentence

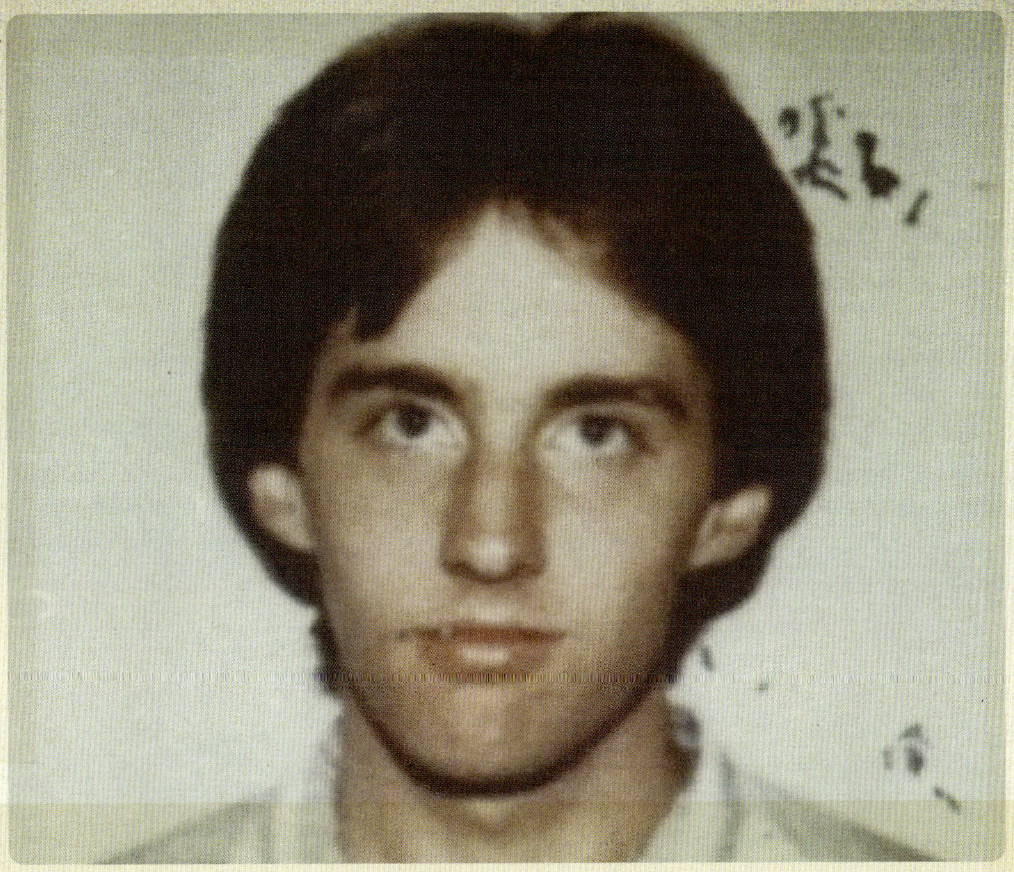

Top left: A young Poulsen, at the outset of his "Dark Dante" career in the late-1980s; **Top right:** A recent picture of Poulsen, who, as of November 2024, is 59 years old; **Above:** Poulsen's 2011-published book, *Kingpin: How One Hacker Took Over the Billion-Dollar Cybercrime Underground*; **See also page 203**, bottom right.

ever given for hacking. On his release, he was barred from using computers or the internet for a period of three years—a stipulation that he reportedly described as akin to "being released on parole with a vow of silence."

Post-Release Activities

After his period of restricted computer access ended, Poulsen transitioned into a career in journalism. He started working for *SecurityFocus* as a journalist and then moved to *Wired Magazine*, where he became a senior editor. He became involved in investigative cybersecurity journalism, leveraging his intricate knowledge of computer systems.

Notable Contributions

While working as a journalist, Poulsen conducted several investigations that led to impactful stories. Notably, he was instrumental in the identification and arrest of *MySpace* sexual predators, an investigation that he undertook in collaboration with law enforcement agencies.

Publications

Kevin Poulsen has also contributed to the world of literature, most notably by authoring the book *Kingpin: How One Hacker Took Over the Billion-Dollar Cybercrime Underground*, published in 2011. The book delves into the world of cybercrime and has been lauded for its meticulous research and storytelling.

Current Involvements

Kevin Poulsen continues to be an active contributor to the field of cybersecurity. He is a speaker at conferences and educational institutions, sharing his insights on cybersecurity issues, ethical hacking, and the evolving nature of online threats. Poulsen, with Aaron Swartz and James Dolan designed and developed *SecureDrop*, a software platform for secure communication between journalists and sources. After Swartz's death Poulsen launched the platform at *The New Yorker*, on 15 May 2013. Poulsen later gifted *SecureDrop* to the Freedom of the Press Foundation, and joined the foundation's technical advisory board. Poulsen has also been the recipient of at least seven awards for digital arts, science and journalism since the late 2000s.

MICHAEL CALCE

MAFIABOY GONE STRAIGHT

Top: Michael Calce, cybersecurity consultant; **Above:** Calce in 2008, back on the streets.

Michael Calce was born in 1984, in Montreal, Quebec, Canada. His affinity for computers became evident at an early age, and by the time he was a teenager, he was already proficient in various programming languages.

Entry into Hacking

At 15, Calce adopted the hacker alias "Mafiaboy." Initially, he was part of online hacker groups where he honed his skills. However, it was not long before he decided to venture out on his own to make a name for himself in the hacker community.

Project Rivolta

In early 2000, Calce initiated "Project Rivolta," a series of denial-of-service (DoS) attacks. These attacks targeted high-profile websites, including Yahoo!, Amazon, CNN, and eBay, among others. For several hours, these websites were rendered inaccessible, causing a significant loss of revenue and shaking the

Calce exploited the vulnerabilities of networked computers and used them as "zombies" to overload his target websites with traffic. His actions revealed significant security flaws in the architecture of major internet platforms and triggered widespread efforts to enhance cybersecurity measures...

then-nascent confidence in the security of e-commerce and online services.

Techniques and Tools

Calce exploited the vulnerabilities of networked computers and used them as "zombies" to overload his target websites with traffic. His actions revealed significant security flaws in the architecture of major internet platforms and triggered widespread efforts to enhance cybersecurity measures.

Capture

The Royal Canadian Mounted Police arrested Calce in April 2000 after an international investigation involving the FBI. His youth, combined with the Canadian legal system's limitations on juvenile offenses, led to a relatively light sentence despite the substantial damage he caused.

Legal Consequences

In 2001, Calce pleaded guilty to 55 charges of mischief to data and unauthorized access to computers. He was sentenced to eight months in a youth detention center and a year of probation. Additionally, he was prohibited from profiting from his story for a period of time.

Life After Hacking

Following his conviction and subsequent release, Michael Calce refrained from illegal activities and chose to use his skills in a constructive manner. He pursued higher education in computer science and became a cybersecurity consultant. He has been openly critical of the hacker culture he was once part of and has voiced his concerns about the potential risks associated with it.

Public Engagements

Calce participates in various speaking engagements and interviews to discuss his life journey and the evolving cybersecurity landscape. He has emphasized the importance of ethical behavior in the technology sector and has contributed to raising awareness about the risks and challenges in cybersecurity.

Above: Michael Calce; **Top, main image;** Calce presenting his Keynote Speech at CDW Canada's BTEX 2019.

Adrian Lamo was born on February 20, 1981, in Malden, Massachusetts, into a Colombian-American family. He exhibited an early affinity for technology and computers. He moved often during his youth due to his parents' missionary work, giving him an eclectic educational background, partially shaped by hacking endeavors.

Initial Activities

In the late 1990s and early 2000s, Lamo gained notoriety in the hacking community for his exploits. He was known for identifying security vulnerabilities in the computer networks of major corporations. Rather than exploiting these vulnerabilities for personal gain, Lamo would often inform the companies of their security lapses, earning him the moniker of "The Homeless Hacker" because of his nomadic lifestyle.

Major Exploits

Some of his most high-profile activities included unauthorized incursions into the computer networks of *The New York Times*, Microsoft, and Yahoo!. In the case of *The New York Times*, Lamo gained access to the newspaper's internal database, where he added his name to the list of expert sources and conducted research on high-profile public figures. His intrusion led to a criminal investigation.

Legal Consequences

In 2004, Lamo pleaded guilty to hacking into *The New York Times'* network. He was sentenced to six months of house arrest and two years of probation. Additionally, he was ordered to pay roughly $65,000 in restitution.

Chelsea Manning and Whistleblowing

Lamo came back into the spotlight in 2010 when he reported U.S. Army intelligence analyst Chelsea Manning to U.S. authorities. Manning had reached out to Lamo online and confided that she had leaked classified information, including videos and documents, to WikiLeaks. Lamo reported Manning to the FBI, leading to her arrest and eventual conviction for violating the Espionage Act.

ADRIAN LAMO
THE HOMELESS HACKER

Public Reception and Controversy
Lamo's decision to report Manning was highly controversial and polarized public opinion. Some viewed him as a patriot who had taken appropriate action, while others labeled him a traitor to whistleblowers. Lamo defended his actions by claiming he believed Manning's leaks would endanger lives.

Later Life
After the Manning incident, Lamo kept a relatively low profile. He continued to work in cybersecurity but faced criticism and ostracization from a segment of the hacking community. He took an interest in charity work, especially in programs aimed at helping young people understand the ethical implications of hacking.

A Very Untimely Death
Adrian Lamo died on March 14, 2018, in Wichita, Kansas. The cause of death was not publicly disclosed, but it was stated that there were no signs of foul play. Lamo was 37 years old at the time of his death. His life remains a subject of ethical debate in the realms of cybersecurity, whistleblowing, and national security.

Opposite, and above: Adrian Lamo, the young "Homeless Hacker"; **Top left:** A late picture of Lamo, posted online, looking very burnt-out; **Top right:** Lamo poses for the photographer in a flower garden, circa 2016; **See also page 203**, bottom right.

In 2005, Butler took control of several black-market websites and consolidated them into one, known as CardersMarket. The platform quickly became the largest and most infamous online marketplace for stolen credit card information and counterfeit identification documents...

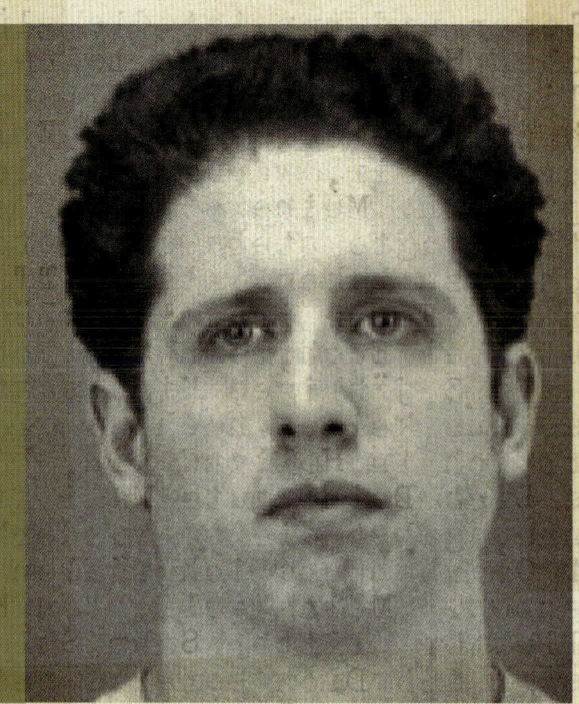

MAX RAY BUTLER
THE CREDIT CARD FRAUD MASTERMIND

Max Ray Butler was born on July 10, 1972, in Meridian, Idaho. From a young age, he showed an aptitude for computing, quickly learning the ins and outs of computer systems.

Early Encounters with Law Enforcement

Under the pseudonym "Max Vision," Butler engaged in white-hat hacking activities in the late '90s. He would penetrate systems to identify vulnerabilities and then report them to the administrators or the companies involved. However, these actions led to his first encounter with law enforcement in 1998, when he was charged with unauthorized access to federal computers. He pleaded guilty and was sentenced to 18 months in prison, which he began serving in 2001.

Turn to Cybercrime

After his release, Butler seemed to abandon his white-hat activities and delved into the world of cybercrime. Operating under a new alias, "Iceman," he infiltrated various online forums that specialized in credit card fraud, identity theft, and other forms of cybercrime.

CardersMarket

In 2005, Butler took control of several black-market websites and consolidated them into one, known as CardersMarket. The platform quickly became the largest and most infamous online marketplace for

stolen credit card information and counterfeit identification documents.

Methods and Operations

Butler's operations were sophisticated. He hacked into corporate databases to acquire credit card information and employed various techniques to maintain his anonymity. Furthermore, he implemented rigorous security protocols on CardersMarket to protect its users and himself from law enforcement agencies.

Capture and Conviction

In September 2007, Butler was arrested in San Francisco by the FBI. His capture was a result of a two-year investigation named Operation Firewall. In 2010, he was convicted on multiple counts, including wire fraud and identity theft, and was sentenced to 13 years in federal prison, one of the longest sentences for hacking-related activities at that time. It also included a five-year supervised release and a restitution amount of approximately $27.5 million.

Financial Impact

The scale of financial damage attributed to Butler is staggering. Estimates suggest that he was responsible for at least $86 million in fraudulent credit card charges. His activities affected thousands of individuals and numerous financial institutions.

Imprisonment and Rehabilitation

Butler was released from FCI Victorville Medium 2 prison on April 14, 2021. There are no reports suggesting that he is engaged in any form of rehabilitation or has shown remorse for his actions.

Above: Butler snapped, circa 2005; **Opposite, top:** Max Ray Butler, possibly a police department mugshot; **Opposite, bottom:** Butler is interviewed in prison, circa 2002.

The scale of Gonzalez's crimes escalated dramatically between 2005 and 2007. He orchestrated a series of hacks into major U.S. retail and financial organizations, including TJX Companies, Heartland Payment Systems, and Dave & Buster's. These hacks led to the theft of over 170 million card numbers, making it, at the time, the largest such fraud in history...

ALBERT GONZALEZ
CUMBAJOHNY AND THE SHADOWCREW

Albert Gonzalez was born in 1981. His father came to the United States from Cuba in the 1970s. He married a fellow Cuban. They settled in Miami, Florida, where Gonzalez developed a keen interest in computers. By the time he was in high school, he was already showing a proclivity for hacking.

Formative Hacks

In his early twenties, Gonzalez founded a hacker group called "ShadowCrew." This online forum became a marketplace for stolen credit card information, counterfeit passports, and other illicit activities. The group's activities eventually caught the attention of law enforcement agencies.

Turning Informant

Gonzalez was first arrested in 2003 for credit card fraud. Remarkably, he managed to strike a deal with the authorities, becoming an informant for the Secret Service. Working under the code name "Cumbajohny," he aided the Secret Service in bringing down various hacker groups, even while continuing his own illegal activities.

Major Cybercrimes

The scale of Gonzalez's crimes escalated dramatically between 2005 and 2007. He orchestrated a series of hacks into major U.S. retail and financial organizations, including TJX Companies, Heartland Payment Systems, and Dave & Buster's. These hacks led to the theft of over 170 million card numbers, making it the largest such fraud in history at the time. His methodology involved SQL injection techniques and sniffing software to breach security systems and access confidential data.

Capture

In May 2008, Gonzalez was arrested in Miami. By then, he had amassed a small fortune, reportedly burying over a million dollars in his parents' backyard. He was charged with multiple counts, including identity theft, wire fraud, and conspiracy. It was later revealed that he had been double-dealing while working as an informant, thus violating the terms of his agreement with the Secret Service.

Trial and Sentencing

During the trial, it came to light that Gonzalez had spent extravagantly on luxurious parties and had even contemplated chartering a yacht to escape to a country without an extradition treaty with the United States. He pleaded guilty to 19 counts of fraud and related charges and was sentenced to two concurrent 20-year terms in federal prison in 2010. It remains one of the longest sentences ever given for hacking in the United States.

Prison Life

Gonzalez served his sentence in a federal prison and was released in 2023. He has not made any public statements since his incarceration, and it remains unclear whether he has taken any steps towards rehabilitation. His activities have had a lasting impact on cybersecurity protocols in financial institutions and have been studied as case examples in the limitations of even high-level security systems.

Opposite, top: Albert Gonzalez, "Cumbajohny"; **Opposite, below:** Gonzalez, circa 2008; **Above:** Gonzalez orchestrated a series of hacks into major U.S. retail and financial organizations, including TJX Companies.

The WannaCry ransomware generated a relatively small sum for the attackers, around $130,000 in Bitcoin. However, the financial repercussions for the affected organizations ran into billions of dollars, including costs for system repairs, data recovery, and lost revenue...

THE LAZARUS GROUP WANNACRY RANSOMWARE

The Lazarus Group is widely believed to be a North Korean state-sponsored hacking group, although North Korea has denied these allegations. The group has been operational since at least 2009 and is known for its high-profile cyberattacks. One of its most infamous exploits is the WannaCry ransomware attack that unfolded in May 2017.

The WannaCry Attack

On May 12, 2017, a massive cyberattack was launched, crippling computer systems worldwide. The ransomware encrypted user data, rendering systems useless, and demanded a ransom payable in Bitcoin. Within a day, more than 200,000 computers across 150 countries were infected. Organizations affected included Britain's National Health Service (NHS), FedEx, and Telefonica in Spain.

Methodology and Exploits

The WannaCry ransomware exploited a Microsoft Windows vulnerability, known as EternalBlue, which was initially discovered by the United States National Security Agency (NSA). The exploit had been leaked by a hacking group called The Shadow Brokers a month before the attack. This allowed the Lazarus Group to rapidly spread the ransomware across networks, affecting not just individual users but entire organizations.

Response and Containment

Security researchers and organizations scrambled to contain the spread of the ransomware. A young British cybersecurity researcher, Marcus Hutchins, discovered a "kill switch" in the WannaCry code, which was essentially a domain that the ransomware tried to contact. Registering this domain effectively halted the ransomware's spread, but not before it had inflicted significant damage.

Charges and Attribution

On December 18, 2017, the United States officially attributed the WannaCry attack to North Korea. While North Korea denied responsibility, evidence such as code similarities and patterns of activity led cybersecurity experts to attribute the attack to the Lazarus Group. The United Nations Security Council held discussions regarding the implications of state-sponsored cyberattacks but did not arrive at a consensus on actions against North Korea.

Impact on Cybersecurity

The WannaCry attack led to a renewed focus on cybersecurity measures and policy. Companies started to invest more in updating their systems, and governments took a closer look at the legislation concerning cybercrime. The incident also sparked a debate on the ethical ramifications of intelligence agencies discovering vulnerabilities but not disclosing them, thereby leaving systems at risk.

Investigations and Ongoing Activities

Investigations into the activities of the Lazarus Group are ongoing. The group has been implicated in various other cyberattacks, including the 2014 Sony Pictures hack and operations against South Korean institutions. These activities show that the Lazarus Group remains a significant cyber threat with likely state-sponsored backing, capable of executing large-scale, disruptive attacks.

Financial Gains

The WannaCry ransomware generated a relatively small sum for the attackers, around 140,000 in Bitcoin. However, the financial repercussions for the affected organizations ran into billions of dollars, including costs for system repairs, data recovery, and lost revenue. The Lazarus Group and the WannaCry ransomware attack signify the evolving complexities of cyber warfare, where boundaries blur between criminal activities and state-sponsored operations.

Spread images: A photographer's visualization of an anonymous and covert hacker. (Photo by Gorodenkoff/Shutterstock)

INDEX

GOTBUSTED PENITENTIARY
Don't Miss Bernie Madoff
Slimeball Billionaire & Swin
Author
"How I Made-off With Your Money &
See You In 2159 For My

This image: The Doo Dah Parade in Columbus, Ohio, shortly after the full extent of Bernie Madoff's financial crimes had been revealed to the American nation. The float pictured states: **"Don't Miss Bernie Madoff Starring in Slimeball Billionaire & Swindlers List"**; **"How I Made-off With Your Money & 8 Billion Reasons Why I Did It"**; **"Buy My New Book America I-Con"**; And finally: **"See You In 2159 For My Comeback Tour!"** (Photo by Jim Snyders/Alamy Stock Photo)

This image: Young Colombian men take snapshots of themselves while visiting the tomb of the drug lord Pablo Escobar at the cemetery of Montesacro, in Itagüí, Colombia, December 2017. 24 years after Escobar's death, the legacy of the Medellín Cartel leader was alive and flourishing. Although many Colombians who lived through the decades of drug wars, assassinations, and kidnappings rejected Pablo Escobar's cult and his celebrity status, a significant number of his compatriots admired him, worshipping his dubious "Robin Hood" status. Moreover, in recent years, the "Narcos" TV series has inspired thousands of tourists to visit Medellín, creating a booming business for many, but causing a controversial rise of narco-tourism. (Photo by Jan Sochor/ Alamy Stock Photo); **Overleaf, left:** Whitey Bulger, his Alcatraz mugshot, November 16, 1959; **Overleaf, right:** Dennis Rader leaves the courtroom after pleading guilty on June 27, 2005 to 10 murders across a period of 30 years, in the Wichita, Kansas, area; **Final page image:** A close-up of Ted Bundy's name carved into the Defense Table of the Old Courthouse. (Orange County Regional History Center)

PICTURE CREDITS

Images are for the most part in the Public Domain but in all cases are courtesy of: **Alamy**; **Wikipedia**; **Wikimedia Commons**; **Shutterstock**; **Associated Press**; **Getty Images**; **Library of Congress**; Wall Street Journal; The Chicago Tribune; Chicago Architecture Center; The Daily Express; Dallas Sheriff's Dept.; NY Daily News; The Boston Globe; The Herald Sun; The Independent; The Whitman Family; San Francisco Chronicle; The Times of India; FBI/Bureau Of Investigation (HarrisEwing); 9News.com; History Site; FBI Fingerprint Files; Canadian Press; Lorenzo Folli; Martin Zielinski; Facebook; Rob Schumacher; The Schmale Family; Las Vegas 2017 Tributes; The Daily Mirror; The Sun; The Daily Mail; The Paris Review; Old Police Cells Museum; UK National Archives, Kew; PNAS; Alchetron; Biography; Famous Bio; Medium; Mob Museum; Pinterest; Tumgir: Tumblr; Rare Historical Photos; New York Times; IMDb; Chloe Jafe/Huck Mag; Ang Yi; Vintage Everyday; Adelstein; ABC News; Sky News; Stratfor 2011; Wikiwand; The BBC; Wales Online; Police Bulletin; Finney County Museum; People.com; OutNow.Ch; Heather Monroe Site; The BFI; Witzel; Crime Online; ETV Bharat; Quint; International Business Times; Brian Hamill; The Telegraph; Buzzfeed News; Rich Addicks/Atlanta Journal Constitution; UPI Photos/Paul Aikens; Reuters/Rick Wilking; Globe Photos; Zuma Press, Inc.; Women's Health Mag; Bio; iNews; DailyStar.co.uk; All That's Interesting; NBC News; E!Online; Scoopnest; Independent.ie; CBS News; MirrorOnline; DailyMailOnline/AssociatedPress; The Daily Record; Skeleton Key Chronicles; Corbis; The Liverpool Echo; The Japan Times; New York Daily News; The Irish Sun; Hamilton Spectator; CNN; The Telegraph; The Sun; Reel Urban News; This is an Exclusive; The King's Necktie; Criminal Minds Wiki; NYPD; ITV Productions; News Groove; La Porte County Historical Society Museum; Texas Monthly; Liaison Agency; Crime Museum; True Crime Magazine; Dick Leonhardt/Vintage Everyday; South Yorkshire Police; Bustle; Telegraph & Argus; The Guardian; Julian Blanco @ Murderpedia; History of Yesterday; Medium; Famous People; Hell Horror; Serial Killer Database Wiki; Biograph; L'Est Republicain; Get Reading; The Hanneman Archive; Wikiwand; Vocal Media; Mirrorpix; Business Insider India; Grave Reviews; ABC; Film Daily; Scooper; ViceVideo; South China Morning Post; Chicagology; History; Metropolitan Museum of Art; Dallas Morning News; New South Wales Forensic Dept; Groovy History; The Hagerman Family; The Sydney Morning Herald; RTE; Lost Girl's Blog; Birmingham Mail (UK); Adam Film Advertising; The Miami Herald; The Walsh Family; The Oregonian; Marca; Musée Picasso; Reddit; Folklife Today; Photo News Services; China Daily; Kent Online; The Daily Star; Huff Post; Business Insider; Murder Friends; Smithsonian Magazine; Scoop Whoop; Idaho Statesman; History Today; and Military Wiki. Contact Moseley Road Inc. for errors or omissions.

ED BUND